From Ought to Is

From Ought to Is

Catalysing Change and Movement in a Polarised World

Deborah Rowland

Registered Offices
John Wiley & Sons, Inc., 111 River Street, Hoboken, NJ 07030, USA
John Wiley & Sons Ltd, New Era House, 8 Oldlands Way, Bognor Regis, West Sussex, PO22 9NQ, UK

For details of our global editorial offices, customer services, and more information about Wiley products visit us at www.wiley.com.

The manufacturer's authorized representative according to the EU General Product Safety Regulation is Wiley-VCH GmbH, Boschstr. 12, 69469 Weinheim, Germany, e-mail: Product_Safety@wiley.com.

Wiley also publishes its books in a variety of electronic formats and by print-on-demand. Some content that appears in standard print versions of this book may not be available in other formats.

Library of Congress Cataloging-in-Publication Data Applied for:
Hardback ISBN: 9781394265114
ePDF: 9781394265138
ePub: 9781394265121
Obook: 9781394265145

Cover Design: Wiley
Cover Image: © Fred Johnsson
Author Photo by Walter van Dyk

Set in 9.5/12.5pt STIX Two Text by Straive, Pondicherry, India

Printed and bound by CPI Group (UK) Ltd, Croydon, CR0 4YY

C9781394265114_050825

To both my sets of parents and my Creator

Praise for *From Ought to Is: Catalysing Change and Movement in a Polarised World*

Working with Deborah has been transformative and a highlight of my career! This book is not just about catalysing change, it is so much more than that: *From Ought to Is* engages the reader on a journey on how to navigate human complexity providing you with a thorough map of how to create movement in your life and the world around you. It contains a superb mix of theory and emotional real-life stories, which you will never forget ...
Laure Roberts, ex-Chief Human Resources Officer, Syngenta Group

I await each of Deborah Rowland's books wondering if she can possibly deliver another literary change masterpiece. The answer? Of course she can. In *From Ought to Is,* Deborah uniquely combines philosophy, politics, literature, religion, biology and neuroscience with her real-world experience at some of the most influential organisations in the world. Her astute, enquiring mind and her courage to uncover and give voice to what is usually concealed have produced a book for our times with an unrivalled take on what keeps individuals, societies and organisations in deadlock. Deborah offers a personal perspective, new insights anchored in her previous work and practical guidance to bring ease and flow to accelerate change. If you dare to follow her advice, that is. Chapter after chapter set off fireworks in my brain, speaking directly to the stickiest of change challenges. I can't wait to start my own transit *from ought to is*. I'm recommending it to every change practitioner I know.
Emma Coatsworth, Global Business Implementation Manager,
Royal Dutch Shell

Deborah Rowland is an exceptionally gifted individual whose brilliant work on leadership has had a profound impact on countless individuals and organisations. In this groundbreaking new work, she brings together her huge experience in this field with profound insights from the world of spirituality and psychology. The result is a must-read: the journey of which Deborah writes, from a world of oughts to one in which we more fully experience all of reality could bring much needed ease, truth-telling, freedom and movement to all of us as individuals and, through us, to the 'stuck' places in today's world. It's a journey into life in all its fullness, which I cannot recommend highly enough.
Dr John Inge, former Bishop of Worcester

Wow! Reading this book felt like a gift from the muses, whispered straight to the heart of what matters now. Deborah masterfully blends timeless wisdom, groundbreaking research, heartfelt human compassion, compelling personal stories and a career filled with practical experience at the highest levels to deliver a message with the power to transform leadership in these challenging times. It has profoundly changed me, leaving me more hopeful and inspired in my work facilitating change with some of the world's top family enterprise leaders and within my own team. I am deeply grateful for everything that went into the creation of this treasure. It will be a blessing to us all if leaders everywhere read this book.

Don Opatrny, Managing Partner, The Lovins Group

In *From Ought to Is,* Deborah offers a deeply philosophical and profoundly practical guide to navigating our increasingly turbulent and divided world. True to her characteristic approach, she emphasises truth, compassion and curiosity as essential tools for leaders and individuals seeking meaningful change. This is not just another book about leadership – it is an urgent call to action for all of us to reconnect with what is, rather than remaining tethered to what we think ought to be. By taking a visceral, phenomenological approach, *From Ought to Is* invites us to delve deeper into the truths of our existence, encouraging us to understand the world in a more holistic, interconnected way. Far from despairing at today's social and political climes, Deborah provides a 'compass of compassion'. Her vision is both discomforting and reassuring: a reminder that growth requires humility, patience and an unwavering commitment to authenticity and truth.

Prof Dr Andrew Sharman
Chief Executive, International Institute of Leadership & Safety Culture,
and Professor of Risk & Resilience, IMD, Switzerland

This thought-provoking book is very timely for anyone who is trying to figure out how to navigate a world that is becoming more and more polarised. Whether you are a business leader, a community member or a parent - you would want to follow Deborah's advice on how to move *From Ought to Is* and resist the temptation to give in to quick judgement to things, events or ideas, and open your mind and heart to new ways of being and thinking. I cannot wait to put it into practice.

Natalia Wallenberg, Chief Human Resources Officer, Ahold Delhaize

In her new book *From Ought to Is*, Deborah builds on the concepts for successful systemic change lined out in her earlier works and widens and deepens them into a new dimension. For me, the idea of this mindset shift from Ought to Is is a foundational new step for making positive change happen in this ever more VUCA world. Like so often with great concepts, it seems so obvious and logical once you have come across it and you wonder why you haven't seen it earlier. I immediately started applying this idea to professional and private contexts – with a very positive effect.

Bernhard Günther, former CFO RWE, Innogy and Fortum

Contents

List of Figures

Foreword

I am honoured that Deborah has asked me to introduce this book, and what a huge accomplishment. *From Ought to Is* is an inspiring interweaving of ideas and practices that marks Deborah out as a true thought leader in the field of organisational development and the leadership of innovation. In this book, she gives us a fresh and comprehensive road map for those seeking genuine or lasting change.

Every thought world has its areas of wisdom, which are too useful to be kept within those boundaries. Psychotherapy, for example (my area of knowledge), is familiar with the focus on attitudes and beliefs that we carry from earlier times (our *oughts*) and on the crucial importance of learning to live in the present (the *only* place where we actually live) as the starting point from which change can begin (our ease with *is*). Such deep insights and practices are also crucial for those who work in larger systems and want to support effective change, feeding into a practical approach to the worlds of *ought* and *is* in larger systems. Deborah has now managed the subtle task of highlighting their importance to a different audience, widening their spread and relevance.

Initially, what brought Deborah and me into contact more than 20 years ago was her wish to live the very best way her story of having been adopted. That led her to discover more of the systemic approach I used with her as a constellation therapist, the principles she then creatively offered with high value in her corporate work. I was later fortunate to join her team supporting transformational leadership development in a large international energy corporation. My approach – developed from the field of systemic psychotherapy – fitted well with hers, which focused on the power of mindfulness, leadership development, and societal and systemic transformation.

Deborah's ability to cross boundaries and bring things together in a helpful way is on full display within this book. You will encounter diverse areas of learning, whether from literature and psychotherapy or anthropology and various spiritual traditions, that enhance the work of those of us involved in systemic change. As with her other books, she disarmingly offers stories from her own life and career to illustrate what she wants to convey about the power and value of the inner journey from *ought* to *is*. Her synthesis goes beyond those borrowed ideas to create a new *gestalt*, grounding it through her own careful, evidence-based research.

I appreciate such dedication and skill. Organisational consulting practices do not always display such rigour. Through her own integration and application, she has made many profound insights accessible and reliable in this book that you are now starting to read, enlivened throughout by stories, case studies and opportunities for active enquiry.

However, this book is no toolkit. You will benefit from taking time to absorb its depths. Deborah takes you on a journey of new ideas and approaches, to which she gives reliability by inviting enquiry into personal experience. The reader can experience ideas as well as name them. Her insights are the fruit of a long and thoughtful career to be savoured and not rushed. For instance, she shows us how the personal and the societal (the micro and the macro) are not discontinuous. Oughts that govern our intimate life and those that shape societies are developed and held in similar ways. You'll know this at a visceral level when you follow her suggestions for personal enquiry. You'll feel the tension between *is* and *ought* as it exists in individuals, groups and organisations.

All this adds up to a highly relevant book in a world that today greatly suffers from polarisation and splitting. In all diverse societies, discussion of 'oughts' bristles with conflict, and most of us operate as though there are some values or beliefs that really are true or better – as if they matter in an absolute way rather than contextually. Humans have always welcomed people with similar outlooks and rejected those who differ, even when the specific context that makes sense of those beliefs does not exist or is long gone. We seek and find acceptance within groups who share our values, even if their source is personal and eccentric and has harmful impacts, and thus are born religions, political parties and cultural imperatives – particular ways of speaking, eating, behaving, exchanging and understanding.

As Deborah writes, if we are born into a thieving family, it will feel right (safe or innocent) to steal and wrong (endangering or guilt-provoking) to be too honest. Like thieves, we all have the tendency to lose connection with inconvenient evidence when faced with our absolute imperative to belong, since believing tends to be inhospitable to any kind of data that contradicts it. Deborah shows us how this need to belong explains why there is so much ideological disagreement and inefficiency among those who want to support change, as we see in our institutions. Deborah poses the question of how to 'see' more reliably in a way that isn't dominated by such out-of-context *'oughtyness'*.

Her answer takes us into the world of *'is'*, that phenomenological capacity to take in reality just as it is without judgement or preference: an existential leap, with all its powerful consequences for movement and change. It is an ability dependent on our capacity for mindfulness, a place of greater reflection and lesser reactivity. In exploring the impact of *is* and *ought* as fundamental dimensions of human behaviour, Deborah has aligned herself with the philosophical approach of Bert Hellinger, founder of systemic constellations, as well as showing a deep appreciation of other older wisdom and sacred traditions and practices – from Julian of Norwich and Heidegger to Einstein and Foucault.

What she demonstrates is that by acceptance of what is, genuine change is possible. If we can befriend all that comes our way and give it a place, less tied to our familiar loyalties by a conscience held out of awareness, then we can unlock the door to a life of greater ease and flow. This is a deceptively simple task because letting go of the comfort of belonging to a conscience group always costs us something – it is the lonelier path to tread. *Oughts* are, of course, essential for evolutionary survival; they encourage continuity of social structures and give us direction and cohesion. Those of us who shift more into the world of *is* may sometimes feel like whistle-blowers, lonely and endangered.

Deborah helps the reader to understand why this is so, and she shows the components of the journey into the wiser path of including reality more fully. I hope this book takes you, the reader, into this more hopeful territory.

Judith Hemming
London, November 2024

For more than 30 years, Judith has trained generations of psychotherapists in the Gestalt model. In 1991, she trained in constellations work from its founder, Bert Hellinger, among others, and is now a leading innovative figure in this worldwide community of practitioners and teachers.

A founding member and teacher at the Centre for the Study of Intimate & Social Systems, she has played a lead role in research into the application of systemic solutions in the corporate world, as well as management and learning processes in schools. She has led the development of the constellating process for 'in-tact teams', as an executive coaching process and to support the development of learning cultures. A pioneer of innovation, Judith is dedicated to bringing systemic approaches to family, educational, organisational and wider social systems.

Acknowledgements

From Ought to Is has had many intellectual, spiritual, companion and practical guides for me, without whom you would not have the book you are about to read. I am deeply grateful for them all.

First, I wish to thank all the indispensable reviewers who painstakingly and lovingly read every word of the chapters as they were written and gave me comments and suggestions along the way. They built my confidence and belief that this book would be worth the sweat and toil.

First, Nicole Brauckmann, who arrived in my life as a client, is now a cherished colleague and leader within the Still Moving community and who provided me with the wisest of counsel, warmth of encouragement and insightful reflection throughout the writing process. Michael Thorley, my much-valued collaborator in this field of change and its leadership and who for 20 years has been a rigorous co-champion in the world for our successive rounds of research – his content challenge has enriched the book. Laure Roberts, who, from her decades of experience at the most senior levels of leadership in large organisations, would give my writing valuable strategic guidance and a reality check, and much more than that, bring out the warmth, passion and boldness of me as the author. Bishop John Inge, who, for the first time in my writing career, became my 'spiritual director' for the journey; great content advice (and split infinitive spotting) aside, our joint contemplative moments and summoning of the divine brought soul and spirit into this book's creation process.

You will encounter many teachers I brought in alongside me as 'faculty' within *From Ought to Is,* including thinkers and artists from the past long gone and those still with us in this world. I enjoy finding wisdom in many places. But I wish to single out one of those teachers who remains my professional supervisor and personal mentor, the psychotherapist and systemic teacher Judith Hemming. Judith, more than any other in my career, has taught me so much about the inner structure of our mind and how that plays out in our individual and collective action – either taking us towards destinations we wish for or those we would rather not. She has been an invaluable intellectual inspiration for this book.

Since I wrote *Still Moving: How to Lead Mindful Change*, I have been nourished by the Still Moving change practitioner community. They are both well versed in and keenly contribute to the ongoing research and development of my change leadership frameworks and their practical offerings. Whether internal leaders of change or external coaches, all have been through the Still Moving change accreditation programme and are passionate flag-wavers (I think 'influencers' is today's word ...) for this mindful and systemic approach to change. In particular, I thank the eight of you who were at our 2023 annual Masterclass gathering that is mentioned as a key spur to this book (Hilde Arns, Nicole Brauckmann, Emma Coatsworth, Phil King, Spiros Milonas, Joey-David Ovey, Edith Rian and Oscar Wiegel).

Book writing is not for the faint-hearted, and I need a ton of encouragement and cheerleading from the pavements as I run its marathon. Thank you first to my publisher, Wiley, and to Jake Opie, Commissioning Editor, who, from the first moment I described this new book to him, insightfully called it 'the spiritual successor to *Still Moving*'. That gave me all the initial impetus I needed. I would also like to thank my friends Katie Jones and Mara Buchanan-Jones (not related), who both, from the first chapter onwards, continually checked in with me and gave me the space to go bonkers when needed and held mini-celebrations along the way as milestones were passed. Thank you to Laurence Whiteley for the figures within the book and for accurately interpreting what was in my head into illustrations. And finally, a thank you to all my family members who put up with not seeing me much this year and to those of you who kept issuing me a precious holding energy – to Susan, Martin, Pauline and my incredible dad, Ron.

My Brain is a Palimpsest – A Note About the Front Cover

An old photo of my mum and me in her estate. My mother was the starting point for my being in the world today. I made the palimpsest after her death a few years ago because I still have to deal with my 'inner mother' and the desire to please her. This work explores, what made me who I am today? What were the milestones in my life that shaped and changed me? Which events and relationships had a lasting impact on me, which did not and were removed from my consciousness, pushed aside or simply overwritten? Which of these experiences still have an impact today and influence the way I think and feel and my perception of the world? But did these experiences really happen as I remember them? An old photo and so many questions, doubts and ambivalences!

It's a self-portrait on Polaroid integral film (an instant film that integrates all the layers to expose and develop the photo and fix it into the frame). After exposing the Polaroid, I carefully separated its layers with a knife. I placed the top transparent layer with the image on an old photo of me and my mum so that the scene shines through. The dried developer paste of the Polaroid, which was not completely removed, gives the whole picture a disturbance, a picture noise.

Fred Johnsson
Hamburg, December 2024

1

Introduction

Everything in Life that we really accept undergoes a change.

Katherine Mansfield

I am so glad you have chosen to read *From Ought to Is*. I wonder, what has been your motivation? Perhaps your primary reason relates to the sub-title, *Catalysing Change and Movement in a Polarised World* – you wish for guidance on how to bring change to stuck places. But what about the title? Have the words, *Ought*, and *Is,* also caught your attention? Right now, what resonance do these two words have for you, and do they have a different quality? What associations come to mind? Do the two words elicit different feelings? Or even somatic sensations (ease, or tension)? Are you curious about what this movement means, to go *from* ought, *to* is? What is this journey?

Well, I know for sure that getting alongside the meanings of both *ought* and *is,* and discerning their distinction in how we bring the world into being, is an essential task if we wish for change: change that is true movement to a different place, change in which you can release yourself from stuck patterns and be more at ease in your life.

And this key skill, of how we navigate between *ought* and *is*, ideology and reality, is an attentional one: do we default to our imprinted codes through which to see the world, or can we intentionally summon a perceptual shift in what we experience, to see what is truly there? This fundamental distinction, and the path you choose to walk between *ought* and *is*, will shape your entire capacity to bring change to the places where you dearly long for movement.

Our world and the entire cosmos are always in motion. However, for good reasons of stability and continuity, we have become rather skilled as a

From Ought to Is: Catalysing Change and Movement in a Polarised World,
First Edition. Deborah Rowland.
© 2025 John Wiley & Sons Ltd. Published 2025 by John Wiley & Sons Ltd.

human species at creating institutions and communities that go against this grain and stay in repeating patterns. Given the waves of disruptive (and increasingly, destructive) change now coming our way, be that in technology, geo-political power relation shifts, or the wider planetary biosphere, can we up our game in adaptation to match this context?

Whether you are a local community leader seeking greater societal cohesion, a Chief Executive Officer leading business and digital innovation, a team leader implementing workplace change, a family member considering how to bring greater flow and contact among people you love, or a politician wishing to effect change in your constituency, service or nation, this book will speak to you.

Change Starts by Acknowledging What Is[1]

And here's the heads up: change that we wish for across any walk of life starts by *acknowledging what is*, not by *striving for what ought to be*. When we can bravely and respectfully stand in the full truth of a situation, movement to a new place becomes possible, whatever the challenging costs and consequences of facing *what is the case* and relinquishing our loyalties to the partial lenses through which we previously viewed reality. Conversely, when we fixate on an obligated, wished-for state – the 'oughtyness' of how we, others, or the situation needs to be – we stay stuck in our story and repeating patterns.

(Ever been in a 'tiff' with a neighbour and gone round to them with all kinds of *ought to* sentences in your head about the upset? Only to find these scripts melted away when, on meeting your neighbour, you allowed the pure relational contact between the two of you about *what is here now* in the conversation to take over, and then found that the issues got resolved?)

It's a paradox: we are better able to initiate change when we give up our proclamations of and attachments to how the world needs to be (ought) and fully immerse ourselves in the lived matter of things (is).[2]

This immersion, being fully with *what is*, means making an equal, non-hierarchical, unprejudiced space for everything to exist (yes, including those elements that irritate, even repel us). Contrast this with the experience of ought, which is the pressure that drives us to retain conformity to values (be they from family, our profession, or faith) that interfere with our capacity to allow what is to exist; we bend reality to our loyalties.

What a distinction: do we dare seek out reality, or stick with our wiring? Move towards *is*, or stay within *ought*?

From Ought to Is will take you on an educational and experiential journey, and I recommend you have a real-life change case in mind to work through as you go; a situation from your life or your workplace that seems stuck, over which you have agency, and where you long to spark some movement. Along the way, I will be sharing experiences from my life and my work in the field of change to help illustrate the concepts and encourage your exploration.

Here's why I believe us all getting on this journey between *ought* and *is* is invaluable: I can easily say that it was my realisation of this paradox – that we are best able to initiate change by *really accepting* what is currently the case (thank you, Katherine Mansfield, for the opening quote) – that has had the most transformative punch for me in my life, both personally and professionally.

Transformative for sure, yet an extremely challenging insight to translate into practice; as I found that giving up my loyalties to how I wished, expected or imagined the world to be – my oughts – very, very hard (I still find that, if I am honest). How so?

While an *is* predisposition to the world might be better than an *ought* fixation when initiating change, as meeting reality *as it is* releases movement far more effortlessly than prodding it towards where we wish it to be, I will show in Chapter 2 how *the oughts that underlie this prodding come from an unrelenting source in our neurobiology,* and unless we can see and honour their source, we will be forever in their grip.*

Moving From *Ought* to *Is* Is Not Easy, But It's Worth It

So here is the upfront warning: the *ought* to *is* journey I will guide you through is no stroll in the park. I didn't realise quite how hard it was to loosen a loyalty to an ought so that I could fully meet reality as it is, until I had an anaphylactic shock in a pub garden outside Marlborough, England.

What can I attribute this episode to? Well, I was in the middle of telling my adopted mum and dad that I was tracing my birth family – an act that felt like I was threatening the very seat of my belonging to my adopted Rowlands' family.

The twin feelings of alarm and guilt at transgressing this loyalty to the parents who had so lovingly picked up my six-month-old self from the floor of a mother and babies' home, now felt like evolutionary danger (will I be abandoned by parents, again?), and within an hour, I was being pumped with adrenalin on a bed within Savernake Community Hospital.

---

* The philosopher David Hume's is-ought fallacy points out the risk of us leaping from descriptive fact to ethical prescription ('as everyone speeds in their car, I ought to too'). An is, does not make an ought. This book takes a different angle: unpacking the systemic source of our oughts and the power they have to distort reality and hold back change. While it can be dangerous to go from is to ought, I shall argue that it is extremely advantageous to go from ought to is!

Thankfully, my mum and dad's hearts were large enough to embrace a vast field of loving inclusion, and from that moment I gingerly embarked on my journey to discover and become known to my Irish birth family, my ancestral *is*, I had never felt more alive and quakingly free. I was starting to experience both the prize (greater ease in my life by discovering the truth, or 'is-ness' of my birth) and the price (fear of becoming outcast from a belonging group) of moving from *ought*, to *is*.

Looking back now, I can also see how the breathlessness and burning welts that arose across my body in the pub garden that day were the somatic price I had to pay to feel free of an obligation to always please others (a commonly held *ought* of an adoptee).

Moving from *ought* to *is* is far from being a cognitive, academic exercise. You *feel* this work in your body.

I did not know that at the time, and after my recovery from the anaphylactic shock (for which no medical, allergic reaction cause could be found), continued to tremble at the thought of how the trace for my birth family, and unconcealment of my full identity, might detrimentally impact my adopted family, to-be-met Irish relatives, loving close relationships and the work that had previously defined my life. Challenging my ought-based loyalty to please felt both liberating and frightening, in equal measure.

Yet moving beyond the safety of my imprinted codes, while bringing feelings of guilt, became utterly worth it.

From my infancy, I had trod a safe path, hard-wired as an adoptee to please others and be perfect so that I could secure belonging. Casting to one side this fiercely preserved 'oughtyness' (a word I am coining to denote a state of being trapped within one's oughts) – 'don't rock the boat', 'get on with my given life', 'for goodness' sake Deborah, don't show your inner vulnerability to the world!' – I, for one, embarked on the long truth-uncovering journey to cast aside the instinctual impulses that had kept me safe and integrate the alienated parts of me.

And it turned out that I was able to trace and meet both my birth father and, separately, my birth mother. By openly and respectfully agreeing to the reality of my cast-out birth – a 1960s child shamefully conceived to unwed parents in Catholic Ireland, and secretly born in a mother-and-babies home in Lancashire, England – I stood fully in my genealogy of truth, my own *is-ness* (a word I will use in this book, alongside *oughtyness*, to describe the essence of being with what is). I was shot through with intense joy – though it was quite scary to be separately reunited with birth families on both my mother's and father's sides while preserving the life-giving love of my adopted family.

What did this outcome teach me? Well, I had startlingly learned that my wiring to please others (my ought), and the reality of how others would receive me (what is), were not one and the same thing: I *could* initiate an unsettling experience, risking displeasure, without loss. How our oughts can deceive us!

This key to finding, experiencing and revealing the *is* of my origin story unlocked the door to a fulsome life that has brought ease, flow and astonishing outcomes. In particular, the experience of discovering and standing in my previously hidden familial truth gifted me a cellular insight for my destined work in the field of whole system change and its leadership: *deep in my bones, I know how reality disclosure releases movement* (you only need to see the superlative Mike Leigh film, *Secrets and Lies,* to understand this).

Oughts close off those parts of reality we humans don't want to see. Yet, hushing things over and denying the existence of something doesn't ever make the hidden go away. I, however, can now stand in the fullness of sight. And this 20-year personal journey, threaded through 35 years in the field of organisational change and its leadership, has given affirming insight into these central messages that I will unpack in this book.

Change flows with greater ease when we can bravely agree to the reality of the present and respect all that has led to this point (what 'is'). Whereas change takes so much more effort when we exclude or denigrate what is felt as difficult or disturbing, and force things into how we wish them to be (our 'ought'). If we wish for greater ease in enabling change, we need to learn how to discern our baked-in oughts, the chains of conscience that loyally guard our belonging to groups, and by acknowledging them, break free of their power to hold back change and living life in all its fullness.

The Price of Ought

What do we risk in not taking the *ought* to *is* journey? Well, it could help explain why breaking patterns and catalysing change towards more helpful places is so challenging, and we end up with the societies that we have.

It is not without trepidation that I write a book about the counter-intuitive power of accepting reality – acknowledging what truly is the case – to initiate change. Acceptance, and getting alongside it all in today's world of strident moral opinions, enflamed by social media, can be seen as soft and excusing: to belong to this conscience group, it is your duty to take sides! Any attempt to get alongside all positions feels weak and 'centrist'. Flexibly adjusting one's views as the nuances of a complex reality become visible is criticised as 'flip-flopping', or a disingenuous tactic to garner more votes/likes.

Moreover, the task of defining 'truth', the nature of reality, has tested the likes of philosophers, natural and social scientists, artists and theologians for millennia, and is particularly problematic in today's so-called post-truth conspiracy-theory-laden era. Can we ever arrive at a complete objective truth and know the world *as it is*, independent from the clouded eyes of the observer? Isn't what is 'true', or deemed to be the case, embedded in a set of power relations that seek to control, gain an advantage over and manipulate others?

To top it all today, with the breakdown of trust in our institutions, a growing cynicism of 'experts', the growth of populist political leaders and the rise of truth-democratising social media, whose truth, in any case, counts ('recollections may vary' being an apt statement from the UK's now-departed Queen Elizabeth)?

I value these societal trends as attempts at heart to seek a wider ground of truth to stand on. Yet they are also creating a divided, disenchanted, destabilising and polarising world – where coordinates about how to think, speak, act and live out our lives seem to have been thrown out of the window.

This is why I feel compelled to write this book now. We are caught up in a world of *ought*, a battleground of strongly held opinions that criticise (even cancel) others and stridently (and blindly) hold forth on what is good, necessary, or imperative. This at times dogmatic drive towards what is desired, or ideal, can also have a devastating impact on mental health and well-being as we agonise over our appearance, identity and status in the eyes of others.

Ought is essential. I have earlier stated its primal, evolutionary survival value. We cannot secure our belonging without this inner wiring of conscience that teaches us to stay innocent within loyalty groups. Collectively, the continuity of our social structures rests on these hidden, unwritten rules that allow a system to be the same tomorrow as it is today. Society would have no governing codes without a sense of imperative and correctness. And yet, ought can become a real liability as the desire to be faithful and loyal to a position can lead to severe distortions of what is deemed to be true.

Perhaps the most visible consequence of an *ought* world in the United Kingdom recently has been the Post Office's widespread miscarriage of justice: an instructive case in the inability and reluctance to confront truth and reality (what *is* the case). Out of a deep-seated loyalty to preserve the identity, reputation and continuity of a 400-year-old reputable institution (remember, oughts ensure survival), the Post Office leadership wrongly accused hundreds of their sub-postmasters and sub-postmistresses in communities across the land of fraud, taking money from the till. Whereas the 'money-gone-missing' in the accounts was due to a fault in the new Fujitsu Horizon accounting software programme the Post Office was introducing: a secret reality that the Post Office senior leadership knew about yet failed to pursue or openly acknowledge.

Because of this reality denial by the Post Office and Fujitsu, more than 900 sub-postmasters and mistresses were wrongly prosecuted as criminals: 236 went to prison, convicted of theft, many were financially ruined and lost their relationships, homes and livelihoods, and there have been four recorded suicides.

Oughts, our inner survival wiring (and I have no doubt that the Post Office senior leaders felt 'innocent' through this, as they viewed the institution's protection and survival as paramount), can distort reality in damaging ways. They give us a blind quality of allegiance, which can have us end up in less than comfortable places (such as prison, if we are a Rudy Giuliani turning himself in on election racketeering charges for Donald Trump).

Do we want truth and reality to matter anymore? In a world that is comfortable with alternative facts, I do. My work in the field of systems, change and leadership demands it. More broadly, I can feel lost – blindly reaching for a felt sense of how to think, speak and act, but with no clarity on what that is or if it can exist.

If we genuinely wish for the changes we seek, I invite us all to resist the onslaught on truth too.

The Founding Energy This Book Stands On

Alongside my personal ought-to-is story and today's ought-proliferation context, stands my three decades plus in the field of change, whose wisdom I also feel compelled to share in this book.

Throughout these decades I have been continually struck by the realisation that, if only we can learn to lead change *as it actually happens* (continual attention and adaptation to dynamic, emergent reality, as in the living world around us), rather than leading change based on how we believe it *ought to be managed* (unfreeze a static, resistant system, change it to where it needs to go, and then embed the new state), then we achieve sustainable change with far greater ease. I have made it my mission and ministry to stand for a change approach that works from messy, lived reality, not the illusory comfort of command and control.

This field experience is backed up by my leadership of four rounds of global, empirically based research, and I have now written three previous books about change and its leadership. *Sustaining Change*[3] set out my earliest research into the practical approaches and behaviours correlated with success in situations of high magnitude disruption and change complexity – what one needs to *do*. More recently, *Still Moving*[4] and the *Still Moving Field Guide*[5] added to these *Sustaining Change* frameworks the inner state skills required of a leader taking their organisation through change – how one needs to *be*.

This time, in this book, I will go one step further and add a final, vital ingredient into the leading successful change mix: a base note that was faintly present in my previous books, but which now needs to make its presence louder and clearer – as this element is essential for all who want to 'go past Go on the Monopoly board' of change.

In this book, I will focus on how the capacity to willingly stand alongside all of reality (and not just that towards which oughtyness propels us) catalyses change. Our belonging and survival needs need not be threatened when we dare seek and disclose wider truths that will challenge those of our team, friendship groups, community movements, political party, entire organisation and even nation.

This is a challenging statement, but do let it sit with you for a while: reality is always friendly. But believing this does seem to depend on us seeing the innate goodness and purpose of all that comes our way.

Working with *What Is* Requires a Shift in Attention

Writing this book was not on my radar screen, and yet the valuable things in life can come unbidden – if one is sufficiently alert. Having established a *Still Moving* change practitioner community over the years, I was greatly looking forward to our annual practitioner 'Masterclass' gathering. What unexpectedly unfolded in and around that gathering became the final spur for writing this book.

Fifteen of us were due to gather. Yet in the two days running up to the event, even at the airport the night before, as I was checking in, six people contacted us to pull out. I found myself oscillating between calm acceptance ('It is what it *is*, let's work with the disturbance as a resource, as it must be part of something bigger than us') and agitated projection ('They *ought* to be more committed', 'actually, I *ought* to have set this up better'). Just as our hands play across the piano keys left to right and back again, so can our minds zip between *is* and *ought*.

Nonetheless, I and my co-facilitator decided to go ahead: a decision we did not rush into, but one taken after we had explored our immediate emotions (the is-ness of disappointment, sadness, anger) and instinctive reactions (the oughtyness of 'how could they', 'we didn't do it right'). Without fully knowing what potential would unfold (working with *what is* is like walking into mystery), we decided to go ahead, stick with the messiness of the situation and *be with what was the case.*

On the plane ride to the location that evening, I paid attention to the oscillating tussle still coursing through my inner state and wrote down three large words on a piece of paper, '*IS* VS *OUGHT*'. My mind was alive through the night, processing how these words summed up the wrestle between one part of myself that was inviting me into a full immersion of *what is*, and, in the other corner, another part of myself trying to control and direct the situation by wishing reality were *something else*. Oh, the agony!

Yet given my primal instinct for full immersion in the truth of reality ('Hello birth family!'), on the opening morning the next day, I set up 15 chairs to represent in the room all who had wished to be there, not just seat the 9 who showed. My aim was to give the missing participants – and the impact that that was having on the 9 present – a powerful force in the field. Systems require to be whole: if there is unacknowledged exclusion, someone present would need to carry their energy. As we all sat down, the sense of missing colleagues was palpable, and, in the discomfort, some of the participants wished to move the empty chairs away (we *ought* to be sitting closer to each other).

I invited them not to do that, to sit with the discomforting reality of the *is*, and instead led an opening dialogue to not only name what had happened, without any judgement, but also explore how to work with loss, out-of-control change and uncertainty (we were change practitioners, after all!). The seating arrangement allowed us to fully *experience* the is-ness of the situation (working with *what is* requires accessing intelligence beyond cognition and speech, as my anaphylactic story above shows).

It was an intense, honest and moving opening that included us facing the consequences of being a smaller group. We decided – after much consideration – against setting up a virtual dial-in call with those absent colleagues who had asked if they could join online, as the cost of that to our own experience was felt to be too great (working with *what is* can require tough choices and the risk of making oneself unpopular).

We did, however, keep communications flowing through the experience with those of us who could not make it, not as an obligated chore but as a genuine acknowledgement of how the dramatic drop in group size had acted as a valuable point of learning. My impulse to turn the contrasting orientations of *ought* and *is* into a whole book became the resonating theme through our two-day retreat, and as I sit here writing I have before me the sticky notes of how we came to contrast these two quite different ways of showing up to experience.

In a nutshell, here's what the sticky notes said: to journey from *ought* to *is* calls for us to focus on the reality of the living present – what's here now, not the desired for future; it challenges us to include all that happens with a welcoming and including heart, not judgemental indignation; it assumes that all that happens is the only thing that could have happened, our task is to find meaning in experience, not wish things to be different; it requires our right-brain[6] skill to see the bigger picture, welcome novelty and incorporate our emotional and somatic intelligence, not just our left brain analytical skill to break what we find down into logical and familiar parts.

All the above asks that we relinquish our attachment and loyalty to deeply held fields of belonging and identify with something bigger than ourselves. Easy to say, harder to do, as this 'loosening of the oughteries' to discover a larger, more unified field beyond our wiring requires us to befriend feelings of guilt and loneliness (it was tough to say 'no' to the request of our no-show colleagues for an on-line connection to our gathering).

None of these attentional modes of showing up to life are the default mode of our human species, which seeks comfort over truth. And yet, I believe the prize of seeking and working with *what is* far outweighs the perceived comfort of staying gripped in an *ought*.

I wish that the messages that come through me in *From Ought to Is* will help a wider world. On behalf of the whole Still Moving change community, I look forward to bringing them alive in this book.

This Book

From Ought to Is will offer you an educational and experiential journey to feel less trapped by your loyalties and more able to be with what is the case. This move from *ought* to *is* will not always be comfortable, as our oughts arise from such treasured places, but I wish you to feel well-resourced along the way. You may wish to read this book alongside a close friend or colleague, as some of my reviewers have said how more powerful (and fun!) it was to put the insights into practice by having a partner walk the journey with them, discussing and applying each chapter in turn. Our formation journey is always better undertaken when in community.

I will be weaving together three related commentaries: my journey since the completion of Still Moving that I hope will be personally relatable and invite you to reflect on how you live your life; extensive practical insights and advice for leading systems and organisations through change from my 35 years in the field; and finally, my observations on the broader changes flooding through the broader socio-political-cultural landscape today that I hope will be stimulating and thought-provoking and influence how we can collectively show up to life.

I will be your primary guide, but I will draw on the wisdom of poets, philosophers, social and natural scientists, and theologians along the way. Be prepared to meet quite a medley of characters, all of whom, though, share a deep, compassionate drive to help humankind see the true nature of reality.

There will be reflective questions and mini-activities throughout to help you experience and apply the messages to sticky situations in your life – culminating in the penultimate chapter dedicated to application. Finally, I invite you to read the book at a second level: not only taking in the content but also *noticing your own is-ness vs oughtyness responses* as you read. Register how reading the book impacts you in the present moment and notice how you might wish for it to be a different reading experience, where you wish to jump onto your own oughtyness!

Here is what to look forward to.

Chapter 2: The Deep Power of Ought

In this chapter, I will define what is meant by the word, *ought,* and show how our loyalty to imprinted codes about how to be in the world is rooted in our need to belong, with the associated powerful workings of conscience. While of value in this context, I will set out the costs and problematic consequences of an ought stance when seeking change, showing how its fixations and excessive judgements narrow our perceptions of what is real, limit creativity, sow division and discord, and create unease in our lives. From this default grip of ought, what are the pointers to an alternate way?

Chapter 3: The Transformative Punch of Is

In this chapter, I will explore the task of how to be fully with *what is*; how can we find within ourselves that place from which we are at ease with all that comes our way, approaching life with greater awareness, compassion and choice? To fully grasp what I mean by *is,* I will set out two contrasting definitions of what is truth: the correctness of a proposition vs the disclosure of what is being, yet hidden. I will show how it is this latter, dispositional definition of truth that clears the pathway to change. While not without discomfort, it is only by noticing, naming and facing the truth and the reality of what is ordinarily concealed, that we can be free to walk a new path.

Having defined, illustrated and contrasted the world of *ought* and the world of *is*, the next four chapters offer practical resources for how to keep steering towards *what is* when seeking change.

Chapter 4: Systems and the Pursuit of Truth

In this chapter, I will look at four underlying properties of all collective human life – the systemic orders of Time, Belonging, Place and Exchange – to enable you to see a little more wisely into the undercurrents that are governing the functioning of your team, family, company and nation. Understanding and working with these deeper soul voicings of a system are not optional if you wish for change and movement. I will share Still Moving's most recent round of research into change and its leadership, which, for the first time, compellingly found a positive correlation between change success and your capacity to attend to these deep systemic realities, and I will advise on how best to approach change in a way that attends to them.

Chapter 5: Leading Change From *Is*, the Personal Skills Required

Having described and illustrated an invaluable framework for meeting a system's *collective* is-ness, or reality, what about the *personal* leadership skills you will need to pull this off? As I have said earlier, heading towards truth and reality need not risk your survival, but it sure does take some skill. In this chapter, I will share the Still Moving Change Leadership skills framework, which we have researched as being vital in change: a set of interdependent *inner* state capacities (quality of your *being*) and *outer* action practices (quality of your *doing*). Combined, these skills enable you to release your system from its loyalties and catalyse sustainable, more effortless change.

Chapter 6: The Journey of the Soul

Our soul is at the dead centre of our being, and therefore any sense of skill in change. In this chapter, I will explore the nature of soul as our essential accompaniment, guide and beckoner for our passageway from *ought* to *is*. It is nigh on impossible to have real contact with the depths of *what is* without the grounding ballast of our soul: as our essential character, calling, connector with wider fields and fate, our soul longs for us to be free of our oughts. The chapter will resource you in two sections: *living* with soul as an enabler of ease and flow in our personal lives and *leading* with soul as the ineffable quality that will take your change leadership to a level of greatness.

Chapter 7: Emotions and Movement

As voicings of the soul, our emotions are an essential resource in change. Learning to handle the emotions that arise out of awareness (reality can be confronting...) is another key skill in catalysing change and movement. In this chapter, I will explore the nature of emotions, their source, and what they are trying to tell us and fly the flag for placing emotions firmly and respectfully into the arena of change and its leadership. I will pay special attention to the nature of guilt, grief and joy, as I can guarantee this tryptic of emotions will pop up in the journey to break free from our loyalties to ought, as we head towards wider truths.

Chapter 8: The Journey Between Ought and Is – A Hothouse

In this chapter, you can take a 'rapid transit journey' from *ought* to *is*. I provide you with a sequential build of practical, immersive exercises drawing on all the previous chapters that will guide you through a lived experience of moving from a world in which you are governed by your oughts, to a world where you are open to taking in wider realities. I hope you enjoy the exercises and consider taking them out into the world to conduct within the systems for which you wish movement. Try them on for size!

Chapter 9: Conclusion

Would the world as we know it collapse if we abandoned *ought*? For sure, we would inherit a psychopathic society devoid of glue and shared values. In this final chapter, I will address the knotty philosophical and ethical question – in the face of any suffering or difficulty, be that human or ecological, should there be a template of what *ought* to be? If one abandons an ought world completely, what is left of our dreams, aspirations, sense of justice and right/wrong, research endeavours to find breakthrough solutions, and cultural templates that guide identity and give boundaries for belonging?

There will be no neat concluding answer to this conundrum, but an invitation to become *aware* of when we are in *ought,* and when we are in *is*. Based on this heightened self-awareness, can we dial down on our ought-y codes – or at least, update our 'red lines' – and in their place befriend the more spacious *is-ness* as our starting point for healing, change and movement?

The worlds of *ought* and *is* are not straightforward. As we arrive in the world, we are given their tension: do we open our eyes to all of reality, or just head towards a version valued from our early field of belonging? How we resolve this tension between *ought* and *is*, wiring and reality, will become our signature tune in life. *From Ought to Is* is an invitation to expand our contact with reality, feel less trapped by our loyalties, and, by respectfully putting our wiring to one side, make greater peace with our lives and more clear-sighted sense of our ever-increasing complex world.

I hope you can join me.

2

The Deep Power of Ought

Dogma is the besetting sin of the age.

Dr. Iain McGilchrist

Oughts are a solution to our need to belong.

Judith Hemming

This is a book that distinguishes two orientations to how we situate ourselves in life: either wishing or imagining reality to be something else, *ought*, or meeting and greeting all of experience as it *is*. The stance of *ought* strives to interpret and will situations to conform to our inner codes of correctness and instructions about how to be in the world – only partially stepping into the terrain of life, which we perceive through a belief-laminated map. The stance of *is* inclusively seeks truth and reality independently of our a priori judgements, wishes and beliefs – open-heartedly getting alongside all that comes our way, standing deep in the full messiness of matter.

Ought and *is* are at the heart of our being, and the tussle between them goes on every moment of our lives. Due to my deeply imprinted oughts to be perfect and please others, I still find it agonisingly hard to leave my bed unmade in the morning or not respond to an email within an hour – rather than just letting things be. Only just now, a friend called round to rehearse a difficult upcoming work conversation, and he found it nigh on impossible to remove the 'dumbing down' parts of his language (he could only imagine saying to his colleague, 'I am a bit upset', rather than 'I am upset'), given his ingrained script from early life that being kind to others and glossing over truth, secured belonging.

From Ought to Is: Catalysing Change and Movement in a Polarised World,
First Edition. Deborah Rowland.
© 2025 John Wiley & Sons Ltd. Published 2025 by John Wiley & Sons Ltd.

Do we dare loosen our loyalties to these inner scripts that from infancy have run us, so that we can see or step into something afresh; or do we stay innocent within their boundaries, preserving our story at the cost of our freedom to discover truths beyond our fields of belonging?

Reflect: do your political affiliations compel you to view certain media outlets, but not others (I can find myself tuning out of a news feed when it has negative stories about the party I support, or turning off the radio when the reporter is interviewing a politician whose views I find it hard to entertain)? Do your opinions about climate change allow you to accept only certain meteorological studies as true? Has any faith affiliation governed who you do, and do not listen to, when it comes to the debates on abortion, gay marriage and assisted dying?

Our loyalties to such fields of belonging that we acquire as we grow into adulthood generate oughts that govern what we can, and cannot see; dictate what we must, and cannot believe to be true; affect what and who we gladly approach and indignantly avoid.

Oughts Come from a Good Place, and Yet...

As I will show in this chapter, oughts' distortionary and divisive conse-quences are highly problematic when we wish for change and movement, which requires accurate perception and a together force; in their collective and dogmatic extreme they have become, as contemporary psychiatrist, neuroscientist and philosopher Dr. Iain McGilchrist says,[1] a nefarious agent in our society today, blinding us to our shared humanity, goodness and truth. Yet, given that oughts so run our lives, they must be helpful for something!

Therefore, congratulate and do not berate yourself if you can identify yours. I have learned from systemic coach and therapist, Judith Hemming, just how we would not have made it to adulthood without learning how to attach ourselves to codes that guaranteed our belonging to early survival groups – a capacity we carry through our adult life, as we attach ourselves beyond the personal and familial to wider groups of affiliation. Our oughts show our deep capacity for love and loyalty. How wonderful is that? It would be very troubling if we did not have them.

In this chapter, I will take you on a journey through the tugging terrain of *ought*. I will start with a more in-depth examination of what we mean by our oughts and value the place and purpose of these inner instructional codes in our lives. Within this causal context, I will then set out their trou-bling shadow; the costs and consequences of our unexamined oughts for creating greater ease in our lives, achieving peace and movement within the wider world and initiating the changes we long for.

While blind allegiance to our oughts can cut us off from the fullness of life, I hope that this chapter allows you to bring a respectful awareness to these hidden, yet ever-present codes that run yours, and by so doing, creates a perceptual shift in how you view them. While ever-present, they need not be ever potent. While our deepest oughts may have been conceived in early primal love, we can yet call on a more meta-level love to treasure, but no longer be bound, by the loyalties they demand.

There is a wider field of belonging out there, ready and awaiting you.

Welcome to the World of Ought

As I have already said, two of my instructional oughts are my instinctual impulses to please and be perfect; inner scripts that bought me a survival ticket in my adopted family. What a prize. Why would I *not* be loyal to the codes that secured me my first attachment experience of love? Without them, I thought I risked another abandonment.

Yet, my unaware loyalty to these 'must do's' can limit what I am able to see, experience and hence effect, as this early career experience shows.

I had just joined the global change unit of my new employer and was launching into my very first encounter with the leadership team of its largest business (*note:* very often, our oughts are aroused when we enter a new setting – for example, an online call with a new group of people, or meeting your in-laws for the first time – as our need to secure belonging can bring out old survival scripts). Hired due to my track record with my previous employer, I was pretty sure I knew what needed to happen here. Buoyed up by my credentials (I had made that last transformation a success!), feeling sure of my judgements already formed (crikey, do they really do things like that around here, there's a long way to go. . .), and armed with a ton of books about how to lead change (which of course, I had all read from front to back), I stood up bristling with slides at the front of the room, and began a presentation.

Outwardly, I heard myself opining about what customer-facing companies look and feel like, naming the barriers to that ideal state in this organisation, and setting out the clear pathway to change necessary for this team. Inwardly, beneath all my postulating, I felt that my most secure path to belonging in this new setting was to be the most perfect change coach they'd ever encountered and to be able to please the boss of this team, who was my key client. Early in the meeting, I got a little anxious when I noticed he had moved away from me at the front of the table, joking about the imposingly high stack of books that threatened to fall on him.

Halfway through my allotted time (which I'd carefully mapped out to the minute), a few questions started to emerge from the team that I attempted to answer intelligently, directly, and one by one; not noticing the group, as a live intact team in front of me, let alone being able to name what I felt was being experienced in the room. To be honest, I felt irritation and little compassion and fell back on my loyalty to cognitive interpretation and argument to justify why I had been hired.

I could (embarrassingly) go on. The experience did not end in a place that felt good. After days and nights of preparation, I felt crushed and fearful of early rejection. Rather than creating pull and insight, my self-validating thought and language seemed to have immobilised the team. With my mind gripped in conventional change dogma, convinced by what I thought to be helpful, I was already in danger of creating a polarising 'me vs you'. Leaping to premature solutions and judgements, I had stopped in-the-moment exploration of the team's inquiry, and so their rich, complex story became unavailable to me: I could only see partial truth.

Fortunately, this experience came early on in my change career. Not only that, but the team leader also graciously saw something of the raw talent in me, and he and I proceeded from this experience into one of the most stimulating and developmental change journeys of my career (more later in this book).

Nonetheless, 30 years on, do I still find myself: drenched in regret over (even tiny) things I have said and done, fearing I have committed an outcastable offence; saying 'yes' to something or someone when I wanted to say 'no'; sitting with excessive (often moral) judgement over others, or the situation; launching into solutions for someone, rather than leaving them with the thorny questions; feeling unfriendly towards people with different views to my own, especially on topics that are dear to me; glossing over difficulty out of fear of losing relationship.

Um, yes. All visible signs of (my) oughts. So, what is going on here? Why their relentless pulling power?

Ought Versus *Should*

When I conceived the title of this book several people asked me, 'What do you mean by "ought," and how does this differ from, "should?"' Good questions. Maybe they are on your mind, too, so let me put the second question back to you. Can you close your eyes and imagine these two words, or maybe write them down on two separate pieces of paper and sit back to register their impact. (Do not worry if English is not your native language; simply become curious as to the differing energy of these words and how their presence makes you feel.)

⇒ *Do ought* and *should* have a different quality to you? What is that? Are you more drawn to one word than the other? What differing associations, images and memories come to you as you contemplate these two words? Does your body give you any data? Breath, heartbeat, areas of tension, holding on, or ease?
⇒ What have you noticed and concluded? Has it sharpened your felt sense of what *ought,* is?

I will now take us on a little journey into the subtlety of the English language, since understanding the distinction between *ought* and *should* is important for the messages in this book. In your language, you might not have two equivalent words (as I sit writing at my home in France, they both end up as 'devoir'), and even for the native English speaker, this distinction might be unclear, as *ought* is a less used and familiar word. What is the difference, for example, between 'You *ought* to be with your parents more often' and 'You *should* be with your parents more often'?

The etymology of the English word *ought,* comes from the old English word *ahte,* the past tense of *agan,* meaning to 'owe'. Ought implies *duty, obligation, or debt*: children owe their parents (their life), and therefore they ought to spend time with them; it would be considered affronting to your ancestors not to! Whereas the word 'should', is more often deployed when one is thinking of *what is best for* the concerned person or subject, it's akin to giving advice; 'You should be with your parents more often as it makes them happy, and you come away well fed!'

Illustrated and explained as such, the two words can feel quite different. Loyalty to ought feels like it has more survival consequences; the stakes are higher if you ignore its pull. *As instructions on how to be in the world, oughts truly ask for our compliance.* Whereas should enables you to take it or leave it; you might lose out on something good for you if you ignore a should, but that's still your free choice. A related distinction, therefore, is that the *experience of ought feels like it draws its authority from the collective*; inhabiting ought is a more 'entangled' place, like a spider's web hold over you that invisibly, yet compellingly, guides you towards what has to be thought and believed, said and done.

While you might feel guilty before others when you ignore an ought, you might be just a little regretful to yourself when you ignore a should. There is nothing harmful about using a 'should' now and then to guide yourself and others towards a beneficial course of action: sometimes, 'wake-up calls' and wise exhortations are needed for necessary change ('We should be paying more attention to changing societal needs'). However, this is a book about the fixations and loyalties that the more hidden, systemic oughts bring to our lives, so we will focus there.

As oughts demand our allegiance to a collective, having us veer between feelings of guilt and innocence in what we say and do, let us find out more about how and why they have such pulling power on our lives. I am indebted in this next section to the teachings of both Judith Hemming and Bert Hellinger,[2] from whose joint wisdom I have greatly learned about oughts, systemic loyalties and the deep pulling power of conscience. This innovative field (which began within family therapy and expanded into organisational change and coaching), more than any other, has helped me see both why change is so tricky to pull off and what one can do to make it otherwise.

Ought and the Workings of Conscience

Our conscience is that inner sense of whether our acts take us towards guilt or innocence, and is the 'canary in the mine' that alerts us to the presence of oughts. When we are feeling a touch guilty about something we have said or done, we have likely transgressed an ought boundary, crossed the safe edge of our belonging field, and our conscience is tapping us on the shoulder, whispering in our ears to invite us back to innocence.

Just as an example, I have lost count of the times in my corporate life when I had to bear the feeling of guilt to make a difficult decision; far easier to have remained innocent and appeased the demands of others fearing or opposing the decision, than break free of my deep loyalty to please and uphold the changes that the entity needed to face. It could be gut-wrenching for me to see faces of anger or sadness, disappointment, and rejection.

So, what is conscience's task, from a systemic perspective? In society conscience might beneficially keep us out of prison, stop us from dropping litter in the streets, and compel us to help our neighbours when they are in trouble, but how does conscience shape the behavioural codes that govern our capacity to either be, or not be, fully with reality; to either see, or be blind to, what truly is the case?

Conscience has different sources and layers, through which we can travel to find the ultimate cause of our oughts.

Oughts That Derive from Correctness

At the most straightforward level, we have our societal conscience systems; imprinted beliefs, codes, and expectations we adopt from where we live. I still vividly recall a working lunch from my early days working at PepsiCo, when my British colleagues stood up from the table when I re-entered the restaurant after I had been to the bathroom, conforming to a quintessentially British point of etiquette about what one *ought* to do when a 'lady' re-enters a room (an act that completely mystified my American colleague who thought they were rudely leaving).

Such societal oughts can also make us feel that something is owed or obligated; 'I ought to invite my new neighbours here in France round to my new home because that's the "done thing"'. They can also lead us into regret or self-critique; 'I ought to have locked the gate as the dog got out and disturbed the neighbours', 'I ought to have studied something more useful and valuable to society like medicine, rather than archaeology and anthropology'.

When caught up in the oughtyness of wishing that what *has* happened were something different, we can be blind to any deeper creative value in the past situation: maybe the dog learned a helpful navigation lesson, or you are invited to look kindlier on archaeology and anthropology and place it as a resource in your life as part of humankind. But more on oughts' consequences later.

Oughts That Derive from Deep Values

More consequential, we have our legal and moral systems of conscience, systems designed to keep society safe and on the right path. I will not debate here the complex tensions between our laws and justice, forgiveness and mercy, yet I still feel guilty as I recall my eight-year-old self once furtively taking sweets off the floor of a Woolworths shop and not paying for them. My wobbly knees, almost immobilised with guilt at the time, knew that I *ought not* to have been doing that (my super-ego not yet mature enough to have stopped me).

Most of our oughts derived in adult life are not monolithic. What is the right path can be context-specific; and so dependent on our position, oughts can ask us to do different things. Take your experience of being either a pedestrian, cyclist or driver when navigating a busy street. I am sure that as a pedestrian on two feet, you might have quite a resolute set of oughts about what is innocent behaviour (it is quite OK to step out onto the road for a bit to avoid a busy pavement), that differ considerably from the oughts you carry if you are on two wheels as a cyclist (it is quite OK to endanger a pedestrian who stupidly steps out in front of you and to cycle in the middle of the road) or from those you carry when behind the driver's wheel (every moving thing that is not a car ought not to be in my way). We can get quite 'haughty' with our oughtyness.

Moral systems of conscience impel us to discern the difference between what we deem right or wrong thoughts, good or bad behaviour. Consequent oughtyness propels us into strong opinions about how to think, talk and act against a normative standard or ideal and is highly potent when guarding strongly held cultural ideologies. Oughts drive us to make judgements about everyday acts of lying, breaking promises or more pernicious and systemic acts of racism and sexism. Pornography, abortion, gender transition, and gambling – moral or immoral, ought to or ought not to?

Religious and spiritual conscience also plays a dominant role across our societies, providing a deep moral regulatory role for the human species, curbing evil and promoting good in the eyes of the Divine. Just take these words from the Anglican Book of Common Prayer, which calls upon worshippers to confess their sins in the knowledge of how they have offended God's holy laws:

> We have left undone those things
> which we *ought* to have done;
> and we have done those things
> which we *ought not* to have done;

Be it Christian confession, Islam's Five Pillars, the Buddha's Pali scriptures, Hindu's Bhagavad Gita, or the Talmud of Judaism, religious conscience has given us ethical and spiritual oughts to guide our lives over many centuries and millennia.

Societal, cultural, legal, ideological, and religious oughts manifestly ensure an institution or group's survival and govern our day-to-day lives, promoting codes of conduct and belief systems that we cherish, uphold and defend. And rightly so, as we need coordinates that help us know what to think, believe, say and do, and affiliation groups that we can choose to belong or not to belong to, shaping our identities and what we wish to stand for.

Beneath all these layers of conscience though sits the ultimate reason for our oughtyness, which explains why it is so hard for us to be able to entertain realities any other than those we are loyal to.

Oughts Are a Solution to Our Need to Belong

Our deep instinct to belong is the trigger for every ought. Before we are even aware of societal codes, cultural ideologies, morality or religious instruction, our oughts originate in the deep primal fields of love and loyalty to the familial and care groups without which we would not have made it to adulthood.

As infants, we are born to focus on survival strategies about how to be in the world that keep us innocent and thereby secure our belonging to those who care for us: what do I have to do to be loved by (especially) mother? We become hyper-alert to the signals of being in a safe, or unsafe place, saying (burbling) or doing what is acceptable, or not acceptable (are my parents smiling, or not smiling, at me?), as transgressing these oughts at such a young age risks exclusion (and, literally, extinction).

We therefore begin to perceive the world in ideals and absolutes from a very young age, which have nothing to do with morality. Children of thieves will think nothing of thieving: it's about staying innocent within one's field of belonging.

Rooted in our human biology, oughts have been constant, valuable, baked in pieces of our evolutionary equipment since time immemorial, when our ancestors formed into groups to survive in challenging landscapes. Needing to learn about what was safe and to be approached, and what was dangerous and to be avoided, our ancestors could not cohere and survive over time without loyalty and sign-up from their members to these vital codes of conduct.

Conscience – that inner sense of whether we are guilty or innocent – arose as a necessity to guard one's belonging to such survival groups. If our ancestors stayed within the oughts, they remained safe, protected and deemed innocent. If, on the other hand, they betrayed the oughts and strayed into forbidden unknown territory, taboos were created so that danger could be recognised and the guilty shamed, punished and exorcised.

Conscience, therefore, literally protected our ancestors from abandonment and loss; it is the electric wire fence that reminded us to stay within our survival groups. As a human species today, we owe our existence to this part of our neurobiology that has gifted us the capacity to inherit and carry forward a set of oughts that ensure group continuity, and our own belonging.

No wonder our oughts feel like a life buoy – we risk survival if we step beyond them. Yet the problematic cost of them remaining hidden, or unquestioned, is that we will forever experience the pressure that drives us to retain conformity to their values that interfere with our capacity to be with what truly is the case.

I might have had the codes of pleasing and perfection imprinted into my being to guarantee survival within my adopted family, yet, deeper in my psyche, is my loyalty to an untethered life that comes from the ancestral field of my displaced Irish biological parents. This pressure to conform to the pull of untethered-ness, or non-attachment, is an experience that feels like I am being summoned by history in some way, and it still makes it hard for me to believe that anyone truly wishes me to be in their lives, despite all the evidence to the contrary (including the adoration of my devoted dog). Oughts really do cloud our perception of what is true.

Here's how conscience guards the deep fields of my belonging. Put simply, I feel loyal (and innocent) to my birthparents if I stay non-attached in my personal and professional life, whereas I feel disloyal (and guilty) if I become attached and committed.

Fortunately, I have on occasions managed to override my conscience and 'un-belong' to my oughts, but only when I had the good fortune to find this field of systemic loyalties; then, I could see my oughts for what they were, value them, and respectfully step beyond the boundary they had set that precluded full seeing so that I could venture into wider realities. From *ought*, to *is*. (And the funny thing is, my birthparents would have loved me to be free of this untethered loyalty too, and to have left the cost of their fate with them. . .)

Pause a moment to reflect

⇒ Can you start to name some deep loyalties that secured your belonging in early life, and which now show up as instructional codes on how to be – your oughts – in your adult life?

The Cost of Ought When Initiating Change

Be they oughts of correctness, deep values, or belonging needs, these inner imprints of how to be in the world have a purpose and a place. The *prize* of ought is the guarantee of continuity; cherished institutions, belief group-ings, organisations, and family traditions continue to survive as they are through their members' loyalty and attachment to oughts. In return for loyalty, we secure our belonging to these groups, and our behavioural patterns remain familiar and faithful friends.

Oughts set us up for some beautiful ideals, values, standards, hopes, and aspirations that need safeguarding.

And yet, ought can become a real liability when one is seeking change, as the *price* of this innate wiring is that we must break a loyalty to its originat-ing group, tradition or pattern that until now has ensured our continuity and survival. This is a big price to pay as what might be felt as an act of betrayal – daring to step beyond the safe confines of that belonging field – also risks us abandonment and loss. Yet our allegiance to our oughts, our story of how we and the world need to be, will forever hold us back from meeting the fullness of reality that could release us into new paths.

Change requires us to *un-belong*.[3]

Oughts, therefore, have quite a price list (see my opening story to this chapter): they compel us to stay in our story, the fixed prisms of our own beliefs, which might be at quite a distance to reality, what is actually the case; they lead us to form fixed judgements about others or the situation that only serve to keep things as they are, as judgements stop us exploring (imagine a fierce pedestrian, cyclist and car driver trying to design a new road scheme. . .); we leap to premature hard-to-budge conclusions and solutions for what we experience, which could be dangerously off the mark when it comes to diagnosing what actually needs solving; and oughts constrain what we are able to see (there might be a bigger, more unified field out there) and have us narrowly striving towards goals in ways that can work against us, leaving us disappointed and disaffected (ever striven to become more happy, and gone on all kinds of pleasure trips, only to end up feeling back in the same place, if not a little more morose?!).

If change starts in the stillness, awareness and spaciousness it takes to *acknowledge what is* – making an equal, unprejudiced space for everything to exist – then you can see how oughts impede this process.

Only last week, I saw a gifted coach be able to honour an executive's seeming 'resistance' to step across a hierarchical boundary into a more senior leadership team position, the top team. The executive could only voice reality as seen from the place of her former peers ('The top team are not telling us enough!'), an act you could have easily labelled, 'grumbling about the tops'. The coach, however, had the skill to notice, name and honour the loyalty from where this resistance derived ('You are helpfully representing those who wish for better leadership from the top team'), and in so doing, enabled the executive to release her attachment to this field of former belonging, and step across its boundary into the top team.

A very natural ought-controlled tendency of someone coaching this executive, might have been to try and persuade the executive to step into the new position ('Come on, see the other side now, this is a step-up promotion!'). But the subtle skill of allowing the executive to be absolutely where she was, for the coach to value that place and honour what she had been invested in, was paradoxically the key to initiating change. Once her valuable loyalty had been named by the coach, the executive could let go of it.

The more able we are to be with, and not judge, a situation, the greater our capacity to change it.

All the above might make sense, and yet . . . society today still seems prepared to pay the high price tag clipped onto the cloak of ought. Un-belonging to our instructional codes appears an impossible act, and the consequences of this incapacity, I believe, are becoming very troubling.

Ought's Consequences

Here's what I see today. We live in an 'easy outrage' world of increasing division and conflict. Peace in Europe is precarious: on its eastern borders the Russia-Ukraine conflict still wages over three years on, shattering local towns and communities and sowing broader geo-political division as nations, bristling with their loyalties and ideologies, debate what's to be done. A war seeming to the death is horrifyingly continuing between Israel and Palestine, and now within the wider Middle East, causing a sickening humanitarian crisis and spill-over civil unrest on the streets and university campuses of major world cities far outside of the region.

Ought-led anger and indignant warfare are not confined to armed conflict. Civil wars and social friction are erupting through our societies as we increasingly seem no longer to be able to agree on what we mean by good national leadership, democracy, human rights, civil rights, multiculturalism, and gender identity. One person's right to protest is another person's mob rule, one person's free speech another person's act of extremism. Separate pools of oughtyness are obviating any nuanced, kind discourse.

This 'hardening of the oughteries', a delightful term coined in the middle of the last century by the psychiatrist and theologian, Dr. Frank Lake,[4] but even more relevant for today, is being spread via online narratives, that both innocent and predatory agents serve up in skewed reality on social media (where there are now 100 million servers around the globe), and exploited by a cacophony of politicians who stir the pot. The distinction between fact and fiction, true and false, no longer appears to exist, and moreover, is not even valued. Within these thickets of lies and propaganda, any pursuit to find out what truly is the case is becoming dangerously compromised.

I hope what follows is not me getting 'too oughty about oughtyness'. I am very conscious in writing this book section about moments when I am tempted into my own judgements – even despair – about what I see. Keeping a systemic stance can be a tall order. At those moments, I try to step back from my indignation, seeking the belonging-based loyalties beneath the seeming 'dysfunction' (writing this book is an instructive training ground for me in moving from *ought,* to *is).*

What *does* focus my attention, however, is my task to set out the consequences of ought that are seriously troubling and problematic in society, in the hope that this exposure will create a perceptual shift in what needs to be done to bring movement and change to a polarised world. Things will never change if all we do is keep loyally shouting and prodding from our separate pools of oughtyness. Reframing how we go about change is what I believe I *should* do. With that intention, I will highlight four salient and damaging consequences of ought: glossing over truth, polarisation, intolerance of others, and disaffection and disappointment.

Ought's Consequence 1: Glossing Over Truth

The most problematic consequence of being caught up in our oughts when it comes to initiating change is that we lose the capacity to be in full contact with reality. Initiating change from a partial picture is extremely dangerous as we could be working on the wrong thing, bringing a crude solution to a complex picture and alienating those parts of our surrounding system that have answers to what most needs attending to.

Oughts Distort Truth

Our oughts dictate what we can and cannot see, acting as the bouncers on the doors of the nightclub of truth, dictating what can and cannot enter our vision. In destroying our capacity to see things with a full, clear eye, oughts create situations where there are bits of information we do not want to know about – as they upset our field of belonging. No, this data point cannot enter the nightclub! For example, one of my friends, having voted for the Labour party in the UK's last election, is now reluctant to read about any latest whiff of scandal about politicians' undeclared personal cash donations (be that for clothes, designer spectacles, or tickets to a Taylor Swift concert. . .), as that disturbs his attachment to the story of a morally upright left-of-centre political party.

Oughts, therefore, keep us either seeking or seeing a reality different from what we encounter and can even lead us to believe lies (for a still relevant book about how we are increasingly living in a lying culture with less than desirable consequences, I highly recommend you check out Lying,[5] by Sissela Blok).

I mentioned the UK's Post Office scandal in the Introduction chapter. To recap, nearly 1,000 of this institution's frontline staff were wrongly convicted by their senior leaders for theft and false accounting, when the truth of the matter was that the new IT system was at fault. During this week of writing, I learned from the public inquiry into the scandal that a former CEO intentionally dumbed down language that would have signalled a problem with this IT system. This CEO asked her husband for a more palatable word to 'bugs', and he came up with 'anomalies and exceptions'. Senior executives felt that this language was 'less emotive' and so started to refer to known IT system defects not as 'bugs', but as 'exceptions'. How language can protect us from truth, in case it hurts us.

This less emotive, pessimism-aversion, reality distortion institutional culture damaged lives and livelihoods wreaking havoc on mental well-being. Just imagine yourself as a loyal frontline staff member running a local community Post Office. Your new accounting system at the end of the week is telling you that £5,000 is missing from the accounts. You call the IT helpline to get support, to be told, 'You are the only one having this problem'. Feeling incompetent, isolated and helpless, you struggle with the system, and it only starts showing more errors and escalating financial deficits. In this Kafkaesque nightmare, you are put under investigation and most probably criminally tried for theft. Over time, and due to the heroic campaigning efforts of a certain Mr. Bates, a local sub-postmaster who refused to accept after he was sacked that he was in the wrong, you find that there are *hundreds* of your frontline colleagues in the same situation as you – and who had equally been told when they reported the money shortfall, that 'you are the only one', the exception.

Both IT errors and human beings, twistingly put on the same footing as 'anomalies'.

But, seen through the lens of systemic belonging, this truth distortion makes sense. Remember, the side effect of conscience is the exclusion of fields of data that threaten our belonging. Loyalty to the institution kept Post Office leaders feeling 'innocent', and prevented them from seeking out, seeing and naming truth, as that act risked institutional (and personal) survival.

Oughts Keep Reality at a Distance

The Post Office's widespread miscarriage of justice is, for sure, not the only incident of how institutions and their leaders dumb down or manipulate truth – what *is* the case, in service of self and system survival – what *ought* to be. I can get bewildered at the number of venerable institutions such as the Catholic Church, the Church of England, the Metropolitan Police, the BBC, and the retail store, Harrods, all now mired in investigations into knowing cover-ups of sexual abuse. And I can think of several current and recently past world leaders who, caught up in their ought-led illusions, fixations and narratives, play a very dangerous game with the truth. Eliminating the truth-telling awkward – be they dissenters to your regime, former sexual partners, an electoral vote that went against you, reputable institutions who happen to disagree with your fiscal plan, judges who tell you that your government cannot do something – now feels the norm.

When we see or wish for reality to be something other than it is (the world of ought) we are naturally wary of discovering our perceptions and theories about reality have been wrong, and even when proven so, our language stubbornly keeps reality at a distance.

In his inspiring book, *Ecological Intelligence: Rediscovering Ourselves in Nature*,[6] the South African environmentalist and wilderness campaigner, Ian McCallum, writes eloquently about the five wake-up calls to reality mankind has had over the centuries, including the Copernican discovery that it is the Earth that rotates around the sun, and not the other way round. Yet, we still say 'sunrise' and 'sundown', as if the Earth *ought* to be at the centre of things, and that the sun rotates around us. If we were truly in contact with reality, we would be saying that the earth *rises* into the night and *dips sharply* into the day. As McCallum writes, '500 years later we still don't quite believe Copernicus'.

Left Versus Right Hemisphere Attention

We can all knowingly use language that bends reality to what we believe *ought* to be the case, turning what we experience into a *re-presentation* of truth, rather than presence our experience in what really is the matter of things. This proclivity to distort truth is also neurologically wired; a fact magically and comprehensively set out in the writings and talks of Dr. Iain McGilchrist.[7] Perhaps more than any other contemporary thinker and writer, McGilchrist has put forward the case that it is valuing our predominant left-hemisphere brain attention that is divorcing humankind from the true nature of reality, what is the case.

In his monumental latest work, *The Matter With Things*, he writes how 'the left hemisphere's job is to create a model and maintain it at all costs. It adopts a theory and then denies what does not fit that theory'. Sounds 'ought-y'? In contrast, the right hemisphere's job is to pay continuous attention to the contextualised world and update its interpretations based on new information. The right hemisphere sees 'the bigger picture, *and what is actually the case* – regardless of the theory'. Sounds 'is-y'?

How does this truth distortion manifest, day to day? My deep ought to please can still have me misinterpret situations where people choose not to sit beside me, as evidence of my having caused displeasure (rarely the actual case): argh. To more overt reality-bending habits, how many of us have tried a few filters on social media or an online meeting platform to make ourselves look a little younger? Have you ever found yourself tidying up a messy meeting room with people and flip charts all over the place so that all is neat for when the big wig senior leader visits – denying him or her the chance to contact the true lived nature of your organisation? When out for a weekend walk with your partner, have you ever become lost due to sticking to your view of where the path ought to be, ignoring all the signals the landscape is telling you to the contrary? I can say 'yes' to all three.

A Post-Truth World

This difficulty of getting close to truth is exacerbated today by a 'post-truth' world. Post-truth was Oxford Dictionary's 2016 word of the year, a phrase that came to prominence due to that year's UK Brexit vote and the US presidential election, and became defined as 'relating to or denoting circumstances in which objective facts are less influential in shaping public opinion than appeals to emotion and personal belief'. Two consequences of a post-truth world are an increased focus on subjective, lived experience ('my truth') and the prolific spread of misinformation, disinformation and fake news.

I am all for emotion and personal belief – we access our truth about the world and the nature of reality as much through our intuition and imagination as via science and reason. Our individual feelings *do* matter, and perhaps individual experience is, in some way, the ultimate truth. But to overplay 'my truth' as a defensive tactic against hearing 'another truth' is a sure-fire way of avoiding looking at how our perceiving creates partial reality, an avoidance that precludes us from finding that unified field of wisdom, healing, and release in which movement can occur (would that the pedestrian, cyclist and driver could disinvest themselves of their narrow loyalties!).

A post-truth world also gives license to ought-led dogmas infiltrating our information sources, where misinformation, disinformation and fake news are now rampant. Pew Research[8] has discovered that one in four American adults admitted to sharing misinformation on their social media platforms. Since May 2023, websites hosting AI-created false articles have increased by more than 1,000%, ballooning from 49 sites to now more than 1,100, according to NewsGuard, an organisation that tracks misinformation. Practically anyone can now use AI engines to spread false narratives.

As the number and variety of information sources have increased it has become more difficult for us to discern 'what is true' in the world. Worryingly, we now see this proliferation of unreliable information sources and false narratives having the power to shape elections, impact personal reputations and influence people's beliefs in many areas such as medicine, the environment and international espionage and skulduggery.

I am not here to stand for absolutism and the proclamation that there exists an irrefutable objective truth that we can only access through one broadcast media. We have seen through scientific, socio-political and philosophical inquiry across the millennia just how dynamic a concept, truth, is. *But I am here to stand for valuing truth pursuit*, and for us all to become aware of how our ought-led mental processes shape our beliefs' formation and reality construction.

If change and movement stand on truth, we cannot be comfortable with a world caught up in reality denial and distortion.

Pause a while to reflect

⇒ Can you take a prominent ought that you hold, and identify any realities it might be closing you off to?

⇒ Can you dare to recall a time when one of your oughts led you to bend the truth a little, out of loyalty to your position?

Ought's Consequence 2: Polarisation

Oughts sow division, as the belonging needs that propel them demand the exclusion of those who are different. The more we break down barriers between us the less differentiation we have, and then where would we belong? So, the oughts that bind us to our groups are fiercely defended, dividing and creating enemies, leading to a state of polarisation in which we hold opposite views to another person or group with (seemingly) little overlap or connection between us. We stand separate in our pools of beliefs, and the identities we assume for ourselves and those we allot to others. It can seem impossible to reach out over the partisan divide and any attempt to form a wider tent is seen as weak and compromising.

Loyalties to Our In-Groups Trump Truth and Change

In this state of splitting, coming to any agreement on how to improve the livelihoods of our communities or tackle collective challenges is problematic as *conscience removes a sense of 'we' in the world, and change is a together task*. Splitting makes it very hard to budge stuck patterns because the source of our patterns – and therefore the solution for movement – is likely to be found from within an interdependent set of relationships.

Yet this necessary joined-up-ness is unlikely to happen when our loyalty to the position of our in-group becomes more important than using one's critical and empathetic faculties to arrive at a complete picture of reality. Belonging necessities mean that what one holds to be true is fiercely declared and defended out of fear of vilification and exclusion from that in-group if one dared step out of the party line. Partial blindness is preferable to expulsion.

Just look at the political polarisation in many Western[9] democracies today, where we see the increasing affiliation of the population to either the 'hard left' or 'hard right' ideologies of the political centre. In the United States, there has been a significant decline in the number of 'swing states' over the last decade, a sign that people will decidedly vote either Republican or Democrat when it comes to an election – whatever the realities of the state of their nation and their preferred candidate's character. Again, conscience to our belonging groups dictates what we are and what we are not allowed to see. Minds are made up in the electorate, and their politicians[10] will continue to make decisions and pass legislature that conforms to their partisan position: breaking free of one's loyalties to partisan oughts could be career suicide.

In my last book, *Still Moving*, I wrote optimistically of the 2015 Paris Climate Agreement to keep the rise in global temperature to well below two degrees, an unprecedented coming together of 190 nations across geopolitical divides. Since then, a study[11] of COP discussions on the social media platform X has revealed a fourfold increase in ideological polarisation during COP26, an increase driven by growing right-wing activity as a prominent opposition group to the hitherto prominent pro-climate discourse. This polarisation is being accompanied by the growing rise in populist politicians who know that anti-climate science sentiment and local protectionism of industries that exacerbate climate change, wins votes.

In this book I am not standing for one side of the climate debate or the other. I both fear for Earth's longer-term survival *and* (as a resident of rural communities in both the United Kingdom and France) can stand alongside the concerns of farmers who, from 21 European countries this year, took to the streets, partially in protest against action needed to reduce agricultural emissions on climate.

My point is that ought-led polarisation of whatever nature (does not have to be about party politics and climate action, but also gender identity, so-called cultural 'wokery', class and faith divides) *generates deadlock*. Sticking to my viewpoint and in-group while antagonistically failing to engage with the other only hardens the opposing view keeping the whole system unable to see the deeper unitary truth that could guide healing and change. Staying stuck keeps me safe at one level, but it creates dodgy ground for the wider system of which I am a part.

How Ought-Outrage Fuels Polarisation and Impedes Change

Arguably the most polarising event in the UK's recent history was the momentous 2016 Brexit referendum vote to leave the European Union. From the moment the UK government announced the referendum, the nation divided into Remainers' or Leavers' camps, and a fiercely fought battle for the future of the UK's place in the world got played out: Remainers – we ought to stay alongside our neighbours who represent our biggest trading bloc; Leavers – we ought to take back control of our borders and laws. Animosity was such that it split families who had both Leave and Remain members. The historic vote fell slightly in favour of Leave and left the nation politically divided.

I still hold vivid memories of the morning after the momentous decision when I – a staunch Remainer – went into the local pub where the community was having breakfast to celebrate – or commiserate – the vote. I was the only Remainer who showed their face, and, as I entered the pub, the valedictory jollity of the Leavers' celebration over sausages, eggs and bacon almost had me turn around and scuttle back to my cottage. But I breathed deeply and sat down. I was keen to understand *why* the Leavers had voted as they did, as their decision to exit a social, economic, political and cultural union with our biggest neighbour (fraught as it might be at times, but hey, so is any close relationship) felt nuts. But maybe I only had a partial view.

Fortunately, one of the Leavers asked how I was – he showed curiosity about my inner state and voting rationale. Putting aside his oughts, he was willing to engage with people and realities from the other side. We were both seeking a way out of our own filter bubbles and echo chambers. But goodness, it took a lot of humility on both sides.

At the national level, the processing of difficult emotions by facing into *what is the case* did not happen; indeed, two subsequent Prime Ministers visibly ignored the Remainers' views. How the exit process was led resulted in an ought-outraged fractured society (continued protests, demonstrations and blocking tactics in parliament) that severely impacted the speed at which the change could be implemented. Far from being able to *face together what is* and from that place find a meta-stance that could have increased friendliness and acceptance all around, the nation remained divided, and it took almost four tortuous years – at great national expense (estimates range from 4% to 5% of UK Gross Domestic Product) – to 'get Brexit done'.

Is There a Way Out of Partisanship and Negotiated Compromise?
Ought-fixated ideological stances result in polarisation that isolates, divides and hardens the ground, making any attempt at initiating and following through on change nigh on impossible. But some stories of hope.

To help overcome political party partisanship, we are seeing increasing use of National, or Citizen Assemblies; representative cross-sections of a nation's population who are brought together from across divides to advise central and local governments on how to face collective challenges such as climate change and shifting social policy. I have also been recently inspired by learning about Audrey Tang, who became Taiwan's first Digital Minister. By aligning her world of technology with her belief in democracy, she has managed to put in place collaborative grass-roots tech platforms, through which civic society groups can work alongside partisan politicians to successfully tackle collective problems such as the spread of COVID-19. Now championing her cause outside of government via her Plurality[12] movement, these collaboration-enhancing technologies override polarised positions, foster empathy, allow people to step into another's shoes, and offer a real alternative to top-down and potentially biased Artificial Intelligence-derived tech solutions.

Within a single entity, I have also been working with a faith-based institution that tries its very hardest to find common ground across a sea of differing faith traditions. At times, it feels like loyalty to one's tradition and theological stance on such live issues as gay marriage and female ordination trumps the very survival of the institution – even when the institution is in visible decline in terms of number of worshippers. The price of leaving one's tradition loyalty is higher than that of failing to stem the institution's decline in popularity. Leaders I have seen who can effect movement in this institution are those who can put their oughtyness to a position to one side and hold a wider space.

Accepting the prophet Isaiah's exhortation to 'enlarge the site of your tent' (54:2), they bring together cross-sections of the whole institution to face the *is-ness* of the differing ideological stances, consider their consequences and impacts and from this bigger place, find the discernment and empathy for common resolution. But it's a struggle to budge from one's interpretation of what is 'right' and to see things differently from the way we are accustomed. Too often than not, this institution can end up in a negotiated compromise, rather than a new generative place.

Oughts create polarities as their belonging sources necessitate boundaries and exclusion. This state of division compromises change, as the need to defend one's position becomes more important than seeking wider truths that could bring innovative solutions and movement.

Pause a while to reflect

⇒ Could you imagine drawing a picture of circles to represent one or two of your primary oughts, and those that your oughts stand apart from? What does this visualisation elicit within you?

⇒ Now imagine standing in one of your own 'ought circles' and take in all the love and loyalties that bind you to it. Look across to a contrasting ought – can you imagine taking any small steps to reach out across the divide, not to 'join the other side' but, to stand alongside it?

⇒ If you did cross your belonging boundary, what did it feel like to 'betray' the loyalties to your conscience system? What felt as a loss, and what felt as a gain?

⇒ Can you now imagine yourself standing with a greater distance from the whole picture, to take it all in? What does that feel like, and enable?

Ought's Consequence 3: Intolerance of the Other

The morning after the recent UK general election, I was sitting around a table having lunch with a dear friend who was visibly distressed. When our newly elected Prime Minister, Sir Keir Starmer, came on the television to give his first speech outside the door of Number 10, my friend was on the verge of leaving the room. I stopped him to inquire why. He described how he had been brought up within his family in the Methodist tradition, with loyalties to hard work and individual responsibility for getting on in life. He told me he could therefore never vote for the Labour party, as 'they were all about socialism and creating dependency', and he could not bear to hear Starmer's voice. Any openness to Starmer's views and actions would have been felt by my friend as an act of disloyalty to the deep beliefs of the group that had brought him such loving belonging.

Affective Polarisation

This is a mild story of intolerance (and I can feel inside my intolerance to certain political leaders, too). But here's the point – *our oughts will always make part of the world wrong*. When we are caught up in our ideals and absolutes, an uncompromising mindset can trigger the stress response in our brains as we defend our position, shut down the empathetic open-minded parts of our brain and prepare to fight and defend ourselves, guarding our ideals often at any cost to ourselves and others. Any bigger, wider, loving compassion (oxytocin) drains itself from our being, and fear (adrenalin, cortisol) fills its place.

The resulting fight/flight impulse leads to *affective* polarisation – a state in which an individual's feelings and emotions toward one's group become more positive, whereas one's feelings and emotions towards members of the other group become more negative. Our ideals and absolutes can quite blind us to our role in creating the situation, we create 'goodies and baddies' and pin our own disowned nastiness onto the out-group ('axis of evil', 'my weapons are for peace, yours, destruction', 'Biden's inflammatory language led to Trump's assassination attempt'). In so doing, it becomes very hard to see any humanity in the other, leading to self-justified acts of intolerance and destruction whose trauma gets passed on down generations.

Hate Speech

Such is the proliferation of pernicious and intolerant communications towards groups who we perceive are 'other', that we now have the phrase, 'hate speech', defined by the United Nations as *'any kind of communication in speech, writing or behaviour, that attacks or uses pejorative or discriminatory language with reference to a person or a group on the basis of who they are, in other words, based on their religion, ethnicity, nationality, race, colour, descent, gender or other identity factor'*.

The online world can be a breeding ground for hate – a platform that is free, spontaneous, and where you can hide your abuse behind anonymity. A recent study by the US Government Accountability Office shows that up to a third of online users have experienced such targeted invective; in the online gaming community that figure rises to 50%. Bigotry via excessive oughtyness shows up in dark ways through these hateful and divisive narratives, and in today's social media world, intolerance can transfer quickly from one geography to another.

In the United Kingdom, we have seen inter-community violence between the Hindu and Muslim faith communities spilled out onto the streets of Leicester, a ripple from the waves of violence in India.

Following the atrocity of the Palestinian Hamas attacks on Israel on 7th October 2023, and the subsequent Israeli bombardment of Gaza, we are seeing bitter and divisive unrest on our streets and university campuses between pro-Palestinian and pro-Israeli communities. Ought lenses are leading to extreme, de-humanising personalised attacks.

Cancel Culture

Alongside the calling out of hate speech we also now see the appearance of 'cancel culture'. Cancel culture is a highly emotionally fraught situation where someone (or even a cultural artefact, such as children's literature) who has been deemed to have acted or spoken unacceptably is shunned and ostracised by an ideological grouping. They (or it) are, effectively, 'cancelled'. Such extreme 'ought to have done/ought not to have done' declarations give an important voice to marginalised communities who have been shunned over decades, if not centuries – making us all aware of how to think, talk and act without bias or causing offence, and the calling out of what is now deemed offensive can bring justice to right wrongs.

At the same time, the shadow of cancelling out someone's viewpoint is that the act of eliminating that which you disagree with (however personally affronting they might be) risks any attempt to arrive at a larger and more nuanced take on truth and reality. Excluding something does not make it go away. The likelihood is that the viewpoint you wish to shut out will defend itself and shout more strongly. *Healing and system change require a journey toward acceptance and wholeness, not alienation, exclusion and fragmentation.*

Can we learn to achieve social change by creating spaces for broader, kinder nuanced discourse, where we all strive to recognise our oughts, drain judgement from our language, and openly see and compassionately engage with realities larger than just ours? I heard of a heartening story yesterday – in the Netherlands, there is a societal attempt to create and share poetry to heal and unite a country bitterly caught up in an unstable and deeply divisive political climate. There is hope.

Change for sure requires tough talk and saying unpopular things, and so I salute courageous calling-out behaviour: as I have said, it helps right wrongs. Yet when brave candour becomes blind intolerance and incapacity to see another's view, we get problems. Change does not take kindly to excessive judgement, elimination of the awkward and hateful language. Such acts of intolerance and exclusion spawn self-protection and extremism, tarnish humanity's soul and compromise our ability to be with *what truly is the case.*

Pause a while to reflect

⇒ Look inside yourself to find those people or groups you can find yourself having negative thoughts about or find yourself intentionally closing out their voices in some way.

⇒ What strong judgements about others might be attached to your oughts and can you dare to see anything of yourself in what you are projecting onto others?

⇒ Can you now look at your own love and loyalties to certain oughts, see them for what they are, and maybe achieve a little distance from them?

Ought's Consequence 4: Disaffection and Disappointment

Ought's manifestations of partial truths, polarisation and intolerance combine to create a world in which our moral, mental and social coordinates can feel uncertain. It is hardly surprising that we are reading more about 'free-floating anxiety', or 'General Anxiety Disorder' these days, a state of anxiety we get into that cannot be attributed to any specific cause, but that leaves us feeling confused, irritable and uneasy. While we have abundant access to information and modern technology, we can simultaneously be overwhelmed by its proliferation and the pressure to conform to the codes of identity, appearance and beliefs of belonging groups promulgated across social media.

While our anxiety might not be attributed to a specific situation, the issue is that it is our very own mental state that can cause our emotions. When in this yearning ought-to-belong state, we wish to associate this anxiety with a specific object, cause, or situation, not caring if the situation is right or wrong, true or false, and then we can feel connected again. (Just witness the understandable rise in the allure of populist politicians these days and blind loyalty to extreme cultural ideologies.)

How to Think, Speak and Act Within a World of Ought Is No Longer Straightforward

With intolerance abounding, reality and truth pursuit can go underground. I can find reaching out across political, cultural, generational, and ideological divides now something of a scary matter; stating one's views can be like treading on eggshells if you say something unpalatable to an opposing viewpoint, and consequently out of fear of redress, I find myself ambivalent about social media posting on controversial topics. Attempts to bring in objective data can be cursorily dismissed as a biased power play, any effort at reasoned, nuanced discourse as an intellectual-elite self-indulgence.

I value the greater awareness this super-sensitivity to a more inclusive world has brought to our hidden and harmful mental, social and cultural biases. What I wish for is that we remain open-minded and -hearted to explore all our assumptions, views and actions, as the intolerance of harsh language, redress and cancelling only triggers the stress response that when activated, will spur us into fight, flight, freeze behaviour: hardening our oughteries, shouting louder, retreating into the comfort of our in-groups, and at times withdrawing and becoming depressed.

When I scan the news and engage with the world around me, I can act quite out of character; I notice I get very 'shouty' – 'Brrrr, Metropolitan Police force, you ought to rid yourself of misogyny and racism!', increasingly bewildered – 'How come such language and behaviour is condoned in a presidential candidate?' To keep my life more peaceful I cannot be bothered to read the reporting as much as I used to. Maybe to protect myself I become desensitised, yet that only further impedes my capacity to see and be with the world as it is. I do not wish my own oughts to get the better of me and I do not want to find myself complaining in outrageous indignation, holding my judging head in my hands, or anaesthetising myself to life as it is. They are not terribly helpful responses if we wish for change. And they do not feel like, 'me'.

Oughts Set Us Up for Disappointment

Our ought-seeking state of wishing what *is the case* to be something else – 'If only it could be like this' – sets us up for disappointment. 'If only' removes us from contacting life as it truly is, and there is unfathomable wisdom and resource in what is currently available and brought us to the present moment – even if all we see is deficit. A close companion to disappointment is complaint – 'They ought to be so, why can't they!' Complaints, however, have a habit of draining us of any agency for responsibility, as we put the onus for situational causality and consequent action elsewhere.

These states of disappointment and complaint weaken us and put a distance between us and the situation that we would like to be different (a kind of 'Oh, I can't be bothered with this anymore'). We then get locked out of available life. They also create relational distance from those around us, limiting our emotional perception (which, as I will show in Chapter 7, is a sure-fire way to cut us off from being in contact with truth).

When we are in a disrespectful relationship with reality – wishing for it to be other than it is – we do not stand on solid ground, risk alienating others (including the souls of those no longer physically present), and can miss out on the fertile richness spread out before us.

It takes quite an evolved inner state of being and spiritual sensibility to be able to befriend all that comes your way, not getting surprised or indignant by what shows up in experience, unclouded by what our oughts have wished or distorted reality to be.

Flights from Reality Do Not Make Us Happier

I am not alone in feeling disoriented. Despite awareness of mental health issues at an all-time high, workplaces making extra-special efforts to foster tolerance and inclusion, and the self-improvement market booming, symptoms of depression and anxiety are still on the rise. Is that because it is less of a stigma now to reveal our struggles with mental and emotional wellbeing, or are underlying anxiety levels rising as oughtyness spreads and we increasingly anaesthetise ourselves from life *as it really is*? 2500 years ago, the Buddha bequeathed us the lesson that our suffering arises out of wishing reality to be other than it is (classic ought), and that release from suffering only comes when we lose our attachment to such striving (able to be with what is the case). What's the advice today?

Let us look at the self-improvement industry. Many of the self-improvement apps, personal coaching and self-help books I now see tend to proselyte a *way out* of the reality of feeling lost. They perpetuate the ought-striving for a happier world. Yet similar to the Buddha, most mystics and spiritual traditions would argue that it is only by going *into* unknowing, difficulty and uncertainty that one can find the state of detachment, perspective and distance necessary to uncover truth, reconciliation and contentment (and for a non-mystic/spiritual take on this I would highly recommend *A Field Guide to Getting Lost*[13] by Rebecca Solnit, a brilliant book on how to discover the value of the unknown).

This flight from reality and the craving for an idealised state is perfectly exemplified by the online pressure to look a certain way. As we pour over our feeds on social media we can get sucked into a craving for that ought-to-have physical look, using all kinds of easily available online camera tricks and poses.

While reflecting on this modish trend, I joyfully came across the story of an online influencer, Danae Mercer, who now posts side-by-side photos of herself. In the same post, and from the same shoot, she presents both her fabricated self – smooth skin, toned thighs, nipped-in waist, *and* her real self – cellulite dimpled thighs and flabby tummy. With 2.3 million followers, I do hope that her brave *From Ought to Is* message reaches more people than this book, given the damaging impact that body dysmorphia is having on our younger generation's mental health.

Oughts Make Us Fearful

Be it physical appearance dysmorphia, the spread of hate speech, the appearance of damaging misinformation, or striving for those 'likes' on your feed, the online world is an incubator for ought-to anxiety and risks us not being able to meet life *as it is*. And what are the online platform owners doing about this? While Meta's own research found that their Instagram platform was bad for teen mental health, they suppressed the report – one could argue that this is glossing over truth at the cost of our children's well-being.

So, what about parenting and educating? You might think this a helpful countervailing influence on the online world. Yet studies are pointing to a trend to shield our children from life as it really is. In *The Coddling of the American Mind: How Good Intentions and Bad Ideas Are Setting Up a Generation for Failure*,[14] authors Greg Lukianoff and Jonathan Haidt talk of how an increasing 'safety-ism' culture (such as fearful and paranoid parenting, hypersensitivity with identity politics in education) was having detrimental consequences on the mental health of Generation Z. Fuelled by the social media addiction and ideological polarisation at large, they reported on how college campuses were becoming places where speakers were increasingly being shouted down and both professors and students walked on eggshells, afraid to speak honestly.

I am not saying that safety-ism is 'wrong', and that people are misguided in voicing their troubling feelings and personal views. That takes courage. For me though, it feels a symptom of a deeper issue in which a lot of us are struggling to find our place and identity in a world where truth coordinates are faint on life's compass.

If we could learn to befriend, and not be offended by, all reality, loosen our attachment to oughts as an anaesthetic against raw truth, and give up our striving for things to be other than they are, we would have such an at-ease, meta stance in the world. Disappointment and disaffection do not give us the necessary strength, sense-making skill, wisdom and compassion to effect change.

Pause a while to reflect

⇒ Have you ever felt that sense of disappointment when pursuing what you thought *ought* to have been the case? What might that disaffection have cost you?

⇒ From your deepest survival-rooted oughts, can you see how your loyalty towards them might be causing you anxiety and unease?

⇒ What are you longing to be free of?

Ought – A Final Note

When we are in ought we strive for the ideal, wish that the present could be other than it is and find ourselves excluding that which we find difficult or disturbing, all the while feeling compelled to be loyal to instructional codes about how to be that we learned in early life. These states can personally manifest in excessive judgement, critique, denial (of self, others, the situation), stuck patterns, and disappointment when the world fails to live up to what we wish for. Collectively, our oughts result in a glossing over truth, polarisation and intolerance.

What a power the experience of ought has. Yet, this habitual stance in life inhibits change and renders unobtainable the aspirations we most wish for. Yes, we might be compelled by our oughts due to our baked-in evolutionary biology, but their root cause cannot be the only explanation as to why they have such a relentless hold on our lives. What else is exacerbating their grip?

Is it that we are simply unaware that there is an alternate route to this needing, seeking and striving? A counterintuitive one, as to simply acknowledge and be with what is the case challenges how we have been brought up to believe that 'you get what you strive for'. A far less comfortable one, as to step beyond our deep fields of belonging to seek wider realities will bring us feelings of shame, guilt and disloyalty. However, meeting and accepting life as it is – as I will show in the next chapter – is a far more powerful strategy for achieving change.

I believe we *are* aware of this alternate route, but the reason we feel so wobbly and reluctant to undertake it is that we – certainly, within the Western world – are becoming increasingly detached from the wider forces of nature and the sacred realm, which hold the potential for such grounding energy in our lives. Rather wonderfully, the Chinese character for nature, 自然, or Ziran (a two-word compound of Zi, and Ran), also refers to a state of 'as-it-isness'.

Nature – and the forces behind her – are constantly living 'in is'. You do not see the weather system saying 'OK, it is now May 2nd, so it ought to be sunny and 22 degrees centigrade'. But for whatever reason, it is now that date as I write, and the weather is unseasonably (to my mind) raining, 12 degrees, and with 27 kmph gusts of wind. Our ancestors and still some societies today (including my farmer neighbours) live their lives very much according to the rhythm of the landscape and the seasonal cycles. We came from the earth and we will return to it, yet still, humankind (partly fuelled by both science and religious dogma) likes to put itself separate from and 'above' nature.

Perhaps this distancing from nature's is-ness is one of the reasons why we have lost out on the chance to bring a more befriending, free-flowing attention to experience. *Ziran* is a central concept of Daoism, a practice of effortless action, and to become nearer to its state, we must separate ourselves from unnatural influences (read, *oughts*) and return ourselves to a natural and spontaneous state (read, *is*).

I was fortunate to have been able to flee my London flat for the coastal landscape of Cornwall during the first COVID-19-related lockdown, but I warmly recall how my urban-situated friends and family spoke excitedly about how nature was making herself manifest: more time available to ponder and notice that changing tree outside your window, greater bird-song being heard, foxes brazenly walking down city streets during daytime. Studies[15] have shown how contact with nature during lockdown led us to have a greater sense of peace and well-being[16] and acceptance of the difficult situation. Being with what is nature's case made us more resourceful and adaptable – a helpful starting point for change. And change there certainly was because of COVID-19.

Change, to what? There were observations made during the COVID-19 experience of how it made us realise we are all, deep down, spiritual beings. The uniting, shared experience around the world brought us down to size. We came to accept that, whether we like it or not, we are not always 'in charge', and that there are forces greater than us. While religious worship in churches was curtailed, nonetheless, faith communities spoke of a surgency of online worship. I could sense on online Zoom calls with my clients how more deeply reflective they were becoming about the purpose of their lives and how they were connecting to themselves, each other, their communities and the sacred. There were so many opportunities to help and care for each other.

Many faith and spiritual traditions teach us how to put the awkward alongside the comfortable, as it is only by saying a big 'yes' to it all that we are released to find a new path. We must work with and not against difficult reality, include and not exclude wounds. I have already quoted Katherine Mansfield in this book (*everything in Life that we really accept undergoes a change*), a writer whose short stories exquisitely point to the is-ness of life. Another favourite writer of mine is the Jesuit poet, Gerard Manley Hopkins. His verses rebound with his inner struggle between capturing nature and life as it is, and his desperate wish for his life and the world around him to be elsewhere.

In God's Grandeur, he exquisitely moves beyond his oughtyness that berates the increasing industrialisation of the landscape (you can almost visualise him shaking his fist at what man is doing in the world), to move towards the wider field of belonging beneath it all – that nature never gives up on her is-ness on offer. Despite our ceaseless striving for what *ought to be* the case, what *is*, the 'dearest freshness deep down things', never leaves us. When our survival needs and loyalty to an ideal can quieten down, the rest becomes accessible.

God's Grandeur

The world is charged with the grandeur of God.
It will flame out, like shining from shook foil;
It gathers to a greatness, like the ooze of oil
Crushed. Why do men then now not reck his rod?
Generations have trod, have trod, have trod;
And all is seared with trade; bleared, smeared with toil;
And wears man's smudge and shares man's smell: the soil
Is bare now, nor can foot feel, being shod.

And for all this, nature is never spent;
There lives the dearest freshness deep down things (author's italics);
And though the last lights off the black West went
Oh, morning, at the brown brink eastward, springs —
Because the Holy Ghost over the bent
World broods with warm breast and with ah! bright wings.

3

The Transformative Punch of Is

She Let Go

by Safire Rose
She let go.
She let go. Without a thought or a word, she let go.
She let go of the fear.
She let go of the judgments.
She let go of the confluence of opinions swarming around her head.
She let go of the committee of indecision within her.
She let go of all the 'right' reasons.
Wholly and completely, without hesitation or worry, she just let go.
She did not ask anyone for advice.
She did not read a book on how to let go.
She did not search the scriptures.
She just let go.
She let go of all of the memories that held her back.
She let go of all of the anxiety that kept her from moving forward.
She let go of the planning and all of the calculations about how to do it
    just right.
She did not promise to let go.
She did not journal about it.
She did not write the projected date in her Day-Timer.
She made no public announcement and put no ad in the paper.
She did not check the weather report or read her daily horoscope.
She just let go.
She did not analyze whether she should let go.
She did not call her friends to discuss the matter.

She did not do a five-step Spiritual Mind Treatment.
She did not call the prayer line.
She did not utter one word.
She just let go.
No one was around when it happened.
There was no applause or congratulations.
No one thanked her or praised her.
No one noticed a thing.
Like a leaf falling from a tree, she just let go.
There was no effort.
There was no struggle.
It wasn't good and it wasn't bad.
It was what it was, and it is just that.
In the space of letting go, she let it all be.
A small smile came over her face.
A light breeze blew through her.
And the sun and the moon shone forevermore...
©2003

It was what it was, and *it is just that*. Welcome to the chapter about the world of *is*; a two-letter word easily passed over in discourse without much thought. Yet the simple word *is* is the tiniest nail in the house of the linguistic universe (thank you, Mary Oliver[1]) that holds the most utility when we seek change. Discovering and embracing *what truly is the case* leads to change that feels effortless, freeing and lasting.

Not that all the changes I have led and experienced felt as light and effortless as the 'leaf falling from a tree' as described in Safir Rose's poem – at least, not on the outside. In the tough turbulence of change, Safir's exquisite invitation is for us to cultivate a certain *inner* state so that we may access the truth of what comes our way. And it is *that* inner state quality of being that is the leaf falling from the tree.

Her poem exquisitely captures the journey we can all go on to become free of our *oughts* (that she lists so comprehensively) and be open to our lives exactly as they are, trusting that things are OK, that we are inherently whole, that our ancestors do not wish us to take on any unprocessed difficulty from their lives, and that we need not strive for things to be other than they are. Our task is to discover, not shy from, what 'is being'. This chapter will show how this unclouded *essentialisation of what is being* catalyses change.

In a nutshell: when we cut through our ought-led judgements, cravings, delusions and denials, and respectfully honour – yet not be beholden to – the deep governing loyalties that underpin them, we are released to be open to what truly is the case. We have the unconditional positive regard to befriend *all* of reality (yes, including the awkward bits). We can respond to life with greater awareness, ease, compassion and choice. We are patient to be in a state of not-knowing, allowing the outcome to emerge from a deeper contact with others and experience, as we come to appreciate that the cosmos is always unpacking something new. We can truly show up to experience without memory, desire or judgement.

The task of being fully with what is means making an equal, non-hierarchical, unprejudiced space for everything to exist.

The more we make space for everything, the more perfect it all is, as when things are given a place, they do not interfere so much. Furthermore, when we are in this state of is-ness, a wider truth to that of our ideals, oughts and dogma can come our way – even opposing truths can be reconciled. We recognise this more unified truth when we encounter it, as we drop into a deeper level of open awareness about us and matter, we are more open to the interaction between what is happening within us and without, and because of this experience a new realisation, call it destiny, taps us on the shoulder. Essentialising, becoming fully *what is*, replaces striving.

If we wish for change, especially in situations of high uncertainty and complex dilemmas, where narrow truths and fixed beliefs make only crude solutions, it is imperative to engage with the unfolding 'is-ness' of our lives.

Befriending this reality though can be tough, raw and unsettling, as *we need to learn how to tolerate the emotions that arise out of awareness*. It can take courage to be able to face the feelings that come with accepting and not denying full reality – maybe shame, fear, nervousness, regret, humility. Moreover, with noticing comes responsibility – do I *do* anything with what I am now aware of? Plato's[2] poor cave dweller who escaped the internal darkness and shadows to find true reality in the outside sunshine, was mocked when he returned to share his story of enlightenment with his fellow cave dwellers who had stayed in darkness. Sometimes, it is safer to stay in our illusions.

Let me start this chapter though with an illustration of the power of acknowledging what is as the starting point for change, a story in which the prize of staying with the reality of *is* (and not that of the cave) ended up far outweighing its concomitant emotional price.

She Let It All Be

I was in the audience of the opera, Madame Butterfly. To be honest, I was not at that stage a real operagoer, thought the whole scene a bit elitist (yup, I was stuck in one end of an ideological polarity), and I had no idea what the story was about. But I had received this invitation, the performance was in an enchanting venue, so I thought, why not, and had arrived dressed up in what I imagined to be opera finery. And the music began.

First off, I was entranced by the opera's haunting beauty and quickly fell into the heart-rending story of a deserted bride who stayed faithful to her husband, despite his three-year absence from her after their wedding night. But nothing had prepared me for what happened *to me* in Act III.

On the stage was the scene when Butterfly reveals to the compatriot of her unfaithful husband – who has returned with a new, second bride – that she had had a son, conceived on their wedding night. Her husband's new bride then arrives and promises to take Butterfly's son away and bring him up as her own child. In anguish at the marriage betrayal and loss of love, and on the cusp of committing suicide, Butterfly hands her clearly distressed young child over for his new life. Caressing him for the last time, she asks her child not to feel sorrow for his mother's desertion, and Butterfly's tiny, abandoned son walks away from her across the abyss.

Well, I find it hard to express in words what was going on for me through this scene, but all I can say is that the world went extremely fuzzy, and I felt I was having some kind of fit. I could hardly breathe, I had the impulse to scream and run away but chose to stay, glued to the scene before me and howling with rage and grief inside. And I remember choosing to stay not out of decorum to the august setting (please and be perfect...), but because I trusted that this unprecedented somatic experience (at one point, I recall snot from my silently crying face alighting onto my fine dress and not even bothering) had some deep signifying value for my life. I let go of my oughts, and I let it all be.

I am so glad now that in that turbulent moment, I gave up on the oughter-ies of how to feel, be, speak, and act and became fully with what was. I simply allowed what was the case to be the case, giving space to my emotions and choosing to trust in the unknown unfolding potential of present-moment experience. To be honest, I am not sure if that was even my choice, I felt as if guided. But I did choose to listen to this inner guide. This experience during Madame Butterfly Act III was a moment that ignited my realisation – the truth of the matter – that I had not yet fully faced, acknowledged and agreed to my own story of abandonment and adoption. I had a bit of work to do on that! As Proust says, 'We are healed of a suffering only by experiencing it to the full[3]'.

That raw is-ness moment 22 years ago not only set me on the deepest per-sonal development discovery of my life, but the experience also delivered up a keenly felt lesson for my chosen profession:

A truth encounter clears the pathway to change.

In this chapter, I will define the nature of *is* via an in-depth exploration of how we can access truth and encounter reality in its fullness. Based on this exploration, I will put forward some illustrated hypotheses as to why this encounter and contact with the full is-ness of experience catalyses change. I hope I do not get too *ought-y* about *is-ness* (although should-ness about is-ness is permitted!) but rather offer some resourcing provocation and questions that can guide you towards greater is-ness in your life.

In line with Safire Rose's invitation to cultivate a certain inner state for what comes our way, as you read the words tune into yourself and observe, not just be your experience. What feels present and alive? Maybe a small smile will come across your face, or a light breeze blow through you. It is not good, and it is not bad. I hope there is no struggle or effort. Simply allow what is the case, to be the case.

What Is, *Is?*

The word *is* is a present tense verb used with a third-person singular subject and refers to the *act of being*. Something is in existence. It is being. Today the sun is shining. My dog is lying on the floor beside me. Writing this book is a worthwhile challenge. Thank goodness we have *is* as without this verb we would not be here. A small word with a big meaning. How awesome is the act of being? As McGilchrist says, 'To some it is impossible to get beyond the view that "is" is just a verbal copula'.[4]

This book examines the power of *acknowledging* what is as a change catalyst. I am again in debt to Bert Hellinger (the founding father of the field of systemic constellations and change) for this expression and insight, richly passed on to me via the teaching of Judith Hemming. My pathway to this world of fully presencing what is being has also been influenced by the work of MIT professor, Otto Scharmer, who has recently written of 'Fourth Level Knowing'.[5] More broadly, there has been increased awareness of the benefits of being able to be non-judgementally with what is the case, through the last two decades explosion of popularity in *mindfulness*.

What I have learned most about how to catalyse change through working with what is, is this accompanying act of *acknowledgement*, an act which, for me, goes beyond just *being* with, *allowing,* or *accepting* what is the case. Acknowledgement is an intentional act of giving all of what is a place. Through gestures as well as words, we visibly honour, express gratitude for and respect all of what is being experienced, has been, and ever shall be. Saying 'hello' to what is now, 'thank you' to what was, and 'yes' to what is to come. That's quite a big place for what is, and a small one for us.

So here I wish to unpack what it means to be able to actively and appreciatively engage with *what is the case* as the starting point for greater ease and flow in our lives – a journey I have been on personally and professionally. Putting my professional and academic loyalties to one side, my pathway to faith and my own spiritual reckoning has enabled me to do two things at the same time: on the one hand, access greater intimacy and heart-led contact with the world and all I encounter; and on the other, find that place within me that gives me distance from the immediacy of the world and its needs and tensions. Empathy and distance combined enable me to see, as it were, a wider reality, a 'richer is'.

Perhaps it is also the embedded archaeologist in me, coupled with the reality of being an adopted child who had been a secret to her Irish family for four decades, but I am particularly drawn to being able to face into the reality of that which has been hidden, is presenting difficulties, or is out of our awareness. The 'what is the case' statements above about the sun, my dog and this book are on the more obvious and easier end of the spectrum – not all 'acknowledging what is' is so!

Is-ness I define as 'the quality of being unprejudicially, non-hierarchically and inclusively with *what is*'. Let us now get alongside this quality's two critical dimensions – *truth* and *reality*. I will attempt to unpack these two change buddies in some detail to provide foundational pointers for the rest of this book.

Pause a while to reflect

⇒ Can you tune into the *is-ness* of your experience right now, taking in all of its joys and all of its niggles, saying 'hello' to it all?

⇒ To say 'thank you' to all that stands behind you and 'yes' to all that will come your way, what or who might need acknowledging?

The Nature of Truth

'What Is Truth?'

So asked Pilate of Jesus when officiating at Jesus's trial (John 18:38), having heard the accused say that he was born and came into the world to testify to the truth. Theologians since have pondered whether Pilate's question should be taken as dismissive jest of the trial (he then walked away) or a genuine attempt at higher reflection on his part (what was Jesus getting at, exactly, to testify to the truth?). But the question Pilate posed, 'What is truth?', has certainly exercised the minds of many erudite thinkers both before and since (so it must be true that truth matters!).

'Truth is the beginning of every good to the gods, and of every good to man'. Well, Plato certainly felt truth had value for the world, and we can thank him for his most famous allegory: man as a prisoner in the cave, only able to see shadows cast on the wall in front of him as truth - when in fact these shadows are merely illusions, projected appearances of puppets dancing behind the prisoners in the firelight: a truth they cannot see. So does humankind wrestle with the eternal conflict between appearance, and reality.[6]

Yet while the concept of truth, or at least its pursuit, is generally viewed as bringing great benefit to our lives, centuries of theologians, mystics, philosophers, scientists and more recently psychologists wrestle with a central conundrum: is there a completely objective, certain, pure, universal, mind-independent truth – a Foucauldian, 'truth demonstration' out there to be scientifically discovered; or is truth subjective, dynamic, dispersed and discontinuous, what humankind *chooses to believe* is true at the time – a Foucauldian, 'truth event' to be experienced? In 1781, Kant gifted us this distinction as the difference between *noumenal* and *phenomenal* truth.[7]

Personally, I say it is a bit of both, which I know is not a neat answer. However, this book is not intended to answer this either/or question (thankfully...), yet the rich lines of inquiry into the nature and pursuit of truth over the centuries can offer us insights into its power to effect change.

Power Shapes Truth

For sure, the lenses through which we search for truth – our knowledge of what is real and certain – are never completely unvarnished and objective. As Thomas Nagel[8] says, 'the view from nowhere is impossible'; reality will always be framed by our concepts. Not only that, once we believe we have hold of the truth neither are our truth proclamations unsullied.

The French philosopher Michel Foucault,[9] perhaps more than any other, has postulated that truth-telling is inextricably caught up in ethico-political power relations, where truth becomes a tool of propaganda and manipulation. Just look at how politicians, needing to conform with their party's position, are briefed by their parties to take 'lines' to the media, even when it is clear from their discomfort under questioning that they inwardly find this truth hard to stand behind. But the goal is to either hold on to or usurp power. Power shapes knowledge and can lead to glossing over truth, as illustrated in the previous chapter.

Is truth, therefore, just a social construct designed by humankind to exercise will over others? Truth distortion by the UK's Post Office leadership and lawyers led their sub-postmasters and postmistresses to confess guilt to fraud, even when they knew they were innocent. Bending truth to serve power over the more vulnerable and preserve reputation is a common situation, and while you might be tempted to argue, a cheap shot at exercising leadership, can be perfectly understood through the lens of deep survival loyalties. Let us acknowledge this as it is and even value it as a catalyst to build our capacity to sniff out truth distortion (more complex and harder to spot these days with AI-created online fakery). Truth-bending can keep us alert and on an intentional path to discovering *what really is the case.*

Truth Is Trust

So, what else can we learn about the truth of truth? The Old English word for 'truth' is *trīewth*, *trēowth* meaning 'faithfulness, constancy', just as to a loved one we are true, and 'plight our troth' (an older form of the word, 'truth'). Truth is an act of trust in, or faithfulness towards, whatever *is*; it is hard to trust in something we do not believe to be true. Truth is indeed linguistically closely connected to the word 'trust', they share the same linguistic root: proto-Indo-European – *deru*, meaning something firm, solid, and steadfast. The word truth therefore indicates as much a disposition – an inherent quality of mind and character, as a proposition – what we believe to be the case.

But does truth exist outside of what we are faithful towards and choose to believe in? It's an important question for this book, as loyalty towards self-referential truth becomes a liability in change as it closes the field of possibility. As problematic, and slippery, as the nature of truth is, we can say that there are things that exist that are immediately evident and obvious to everyone, like, there is a full moon tonight (I do not think it can be painted onto the sky), or we are born of our parents. Is that what is meant by 'truth', what is generally admitted as known?

Drawing from my own experience of powerful truth moments, and the wisdom of truth-and-matter thinkers before me, I offer these perspectives on understanding truth as a catalyst for change.

Truth as the Correctness of Propositions

Truth defined as the correctness of propositions takes truth to mean the stating of *what we generally believe to be the case*; truth is a characteristic of knowledge, and of knowledge and matter corresponding ('Have *I* got *this* right?' 'Is it true that...?'). In this manifestation of truth, the subject, you as the truth seeker, and the object, what you are seeking the truth about, are distinct and split.

This classic framing of truth is defined by the Oxford Dictionary; 'Truth is that which is true or in accordance with fact or reality'. I know from my verified birth certificate that I was born in 1962 and therefore the statement, 'I am aged 62' is *factually* true (feels true at times too...). I can ask someone who knows me well to certify that my passport photo is a true likeness of me, meaning, the photo accords with how he or she has seen me, and it is, *really* me. It is a true photo.

Truth as correctness, therefore, invites us to discern whether a proposition is 'true' or 'false', i.e., does the statement under question *accord with* the matter about which the statement is made? When I say, 'My hot water pump is not working because there is an air leak in the valves', the machine technician, on a recent inspection, verified that to be the case. So, my statement is a true statement. At this level, truth – be that of practical experience, philosophical inquiry, technical consideration, scientific research, or economic calculation – is what is generally and indisputably regarded as known and is the predominant logico-scientific take on truth.

Truth That Arises from Inspection, Left Hemisphere Brain
As such, truth as correctness is the result of reasoning and *inspection* – scrutiny, assessment, critique, adjustment and checking up. And, as McGilchrist has so creatively and comprehensively shown us, this version of truth quest is our brain's left hemisphere's speciality,[10] the part of our minds that excels in logic and internal consistency. The impact of truth as correctness is *declaration* – a statement of explicit assertion, claim or avowal, 'this is the truth of the matter!'

At one level, truth as correctness is a helpful change initiator, classically forming what is known as the 'case for change': bringing generally known facts about reality to life as a spur. Like, how my bathroom scales assert my weight and periodically remind me to stop eating so much cake. Climate change data put forward by the meteorologists that halts my propensity to use planes for travel. Or, confronting ourselves with our performance: 'We are not doing as well as we hoped, we had better start trying a new approach!'

I will never forget serving on an Executive Team leading a company through change when we saw, for the first time, the roll-up of all the financial numbers of the different divisions into one profit and loss statement. With this clear statement of financial truth for the whole entity brought to us by outside accountants, the team finally saw that they had to lead the transformation in a more joined-up way.

Truth as correctness can therefore act as a change catalyst, with a flavour of *ought* to it ('I ought to eat celery sticks not cake'). However, I would need to have many hands to be able to count the fingers of the number of occasions when the correctness of facts and their accordance with reality has been hotly debated, leading to change indecision and holding back. We can dance around what is correct or not, holding steadfast to our own beliefs about what is true, as a defence against doing anything about the situation.

Is that therefore all there is to truth?

Truth as the Unconcealment of Things, a Disposition

In planning this book, I came upon the German philosopher Martin Heidegger's 1943 essay, 'On the Essence of Truth',[11], and yes(!) I felt I'd hit a resonating jackpot. In the essay, he distinguishes two takes on truth: the prevailing concept of truth as the *correctness* of a proposition and a less customary meaning of truth as the *unconcealing* of that which is 'being', yet hidden.

(I am conscious of the controversy surrounding Heidegger's association with Nazism. However, do not wish his egregious politics to cancel out his intellectual contribution to the field of how we know truth and reality. In a sense, I am *acknowledging what is* here and getting alongside it all...)

In his essay, Heidegger questions the more common-sense definition of truth – the correctness of a proposition – as he felt there was a richer, in a sense, precursory essence to truth's nature beyond palpable validity. What makes a true thing true? If it is true that a false statement is false, what is behind all the different meanings of truth? What makes correctness possible? Going back to my above example, when all of us on the Executive Team 'acknowledged what is the case' of the performance data, the experience felt much bigger than simply agreeing to the correctness of a financial statement.

Retreating in time from how the Romans defined truth, *veritas*, connoting 'rightness' (viz, correctness), Heidegger found a deeper nature to truth in the Greek word, *alētheia*. The word *alētheia* is the negation of the word *lethe,* to cover over or forget. *Alētheia,* therefore, as truth means the uncovering, the unconcealment of that which is hidden, or the summoning into awareness of that which has been forgotten or put into the recesses of memory. Truth is un-forgetting, allowing something to emerge from oblivion. (As Hopkins reminded us, concealed beneath the toil of man's foot on soil, '*There lives the dearest freshness deep down things...*')

Coining the expression *Da-sein* from his native German, literally meaning 'there-being', the concealed essential ground of humankind, Heidegger claimed that *alētheia* as truth is revealed to us *if we are able to let be.* This relinquishment of striving for truth does not mean neglect and casual indifference to life, but the active engagement of oneself with being, *letting beings be* and opening oneself to the *as-it-is-ness* of experience. For those of you who know my work on the importance of a leader's quality of *being* in change, you can imagine how joyful I was to learn that Heidegger believed this to be an active pathway to truth.

Truth That Arises from Engaging with What Is Being, Right Hemisphere Brain

In contrast, therefore, to truth as correctness – something that is verifiably determined, into which nothing of us enters, and which exhorts an 'it is thus, so therefore' response, truth as unconcealment is *a process through which we engage ourselves with the nature of 'what is being'* – inviting an acknowledgement response, 'aha, now I see you/it, with deep respect'. Subject and object are intimately engaged since what is hidden is hidden *from* someone.

McGilchrist (as previously referenced) has shown how it is our right hemisphere brain function that excels at this patient, attentive, and open response – far better at discerning reality than the left hemisphere which can be peremptory and shrouded in dogma. Bert Hellinger has said how it is our *whole body* that can discern what is true – we phenomenologically feel a sense of ease and lightness in the presence of truth; our body responds with aliveness (and a contraction if not). While what is true, what is being, might still be just out of our rational awareness and unable to be verbalised, we get a distinct feeling of 'that's right'. While it may be difficult to define truth, Hellinger says it is not difficult to feel it – as my Madame Butterfly experience showed.

The Still Moving Masterclass story from the Introduction is another illustration of how to engage with what is being, yet hidden. I could have opened the circle by saying, 'We are now nine participants, not fifteen, these are the reasons, so let's remove the empty chairs' – truth as correctness, us in certainty. Instead, I said, 'Let's now sit in the circle of fifteen chairs, we need not know all the explanations as to why the six people dropped out, let's just tune in to ourselves and notice what the experience of missing our six colleagues brings up for us somatically and signifies for our task here together' – truth as unconcealing, us in mystery.

Truth as an Experience from Within

Far from Heidegger, though, turning the nature of truth into a feature of contingent self, human caprice, and subjective whim, he asks for us to make a transformation in our thinking. In a sense, choosing to believe that the *phenomenology* of truth as an experience from within, letting be to engage oneself with being, is as valid a concept as the *scientific-logical* take on truth as something studied and determined from without.

The great theoretical physicist, Einstein himself, showed us how there are no longer any absolutes, that there are hidden variables in the universe, and that space, time and man are interdependent. How can there be an independent objective truth when every measurement depends on one's frame of reference? Certainly, my Madame Butterfly experience was a startling moment of *alētheia*, an opening up of awareness into the core of what was my being, the un-hiding and un-forgetting of the is-ness of me. Akin to Heidegger's *anwesen*, something disclosed itself, came into being for me, vital, fresh, pre-conceptual.

And I have found time and time again how it is that *this* essence of truth as unconcealment catalyses change.

On that executive team, when we were shown the one profit and loss statement, we now knew that our overall financial performance was not on track (truth as proposition). However, it was not the correctness of the financial statement that moved us to take different action. It was when I invited each team member to stand up and relate to themselves and each other in ways they had never done before (truth as disposition).

I asked them to form a semi-circle line along a spectrum according to who made or earned the most money, and who was losing or spending the most money. What was hidden from each other – not maliciously but out of a culture of independence – now got un-hidden. My colleagues needed to disclose their numbers with each other to be able to form the 'true' line. It took a little while and was messy and uncertain in places, but that did not matter.

The room went very quiet as people stopped jostling for position and the line was concluded, the profit and loss unconcealed in a living human map.

In this moment of *alethurgy*, or truth manifestation, I first invited each team member to silently check in with their quality of being, what was going on for them inside (recall Hellinger's somatic take on truth), and then invited each person from their point on the line to speak about how it felt to be standing where they were, and in relation to their colleagues. There was no debate, no questioning, no trying to make people feel different to how they were feeling ('I think you ought to be standing here, not there, as despite your numbers, you are trying so hard!').

Far from this being a shaming activity, the disclosures of truth from us all brought a deep unfolding openness and sense of collegiality – 'we are in this together', 'now I get why some people *need* to be spending and not earning as their products are in development for the future, I am happy to be able to fund that'. The line stood and burned brightly and became a circle as the leaders at its two ends of 'earners and spenders' joined up. Truth disclosure allowed for integration and holism. And this 'letting beings be as they are' line of truth (we could have just gone straight from the correctness of the financial data into 'how do we get out of this hole' action planning) brought freedom and choice to a team that had been previously stuck, divided, and closed to any new ways to operating together.

Truth as Unconcealing Takes a Very Special Form of Attention

Whereas truth as correctness is the result of inspection, truth as unconcealing is the result of *attention*. Attention is how we bring the world into being, and the quality it takes to unconceal that which is hidden takes on a different nature to the customary 'pay attention!' It means dropping into intentional, non-judgemental, present-moment awareness.

Heidegger asks us to become 'privileged listeners and responders to experience'. The poet Mary Oliver has suggested that 'attention is the beginning of devotion'[12] – we need to bring an open, affectionate intention to truth pursuit. Saint Augustine went further to say, 'One may not enter into truth *except* by means of love'.[13] Love is the ground *from which* the unflinching attention that is required to access full truth takes sustenance. When we are properly and open-heartedly attentive, what we experience, and give out, is the real deal.

In today's social media world of commandeered attention, can we regain control of the quality of our gaze? When we wake up in the morning, what do we first reach for to look at? The news feed on our smartphone or an opening of the curtain to look at the weather? If it is our news feed or favourite social media site, how long do we take in and fully absorb each story, post, or video? And with what predisposition and intention – to cleverly comment or critique, unquestionably follow and like, or to compassionately discern and get alongside all a story, help uncover what is being, yet hidden?

The impact of truth as correctness may be *declaration* and subsequent action; 'This is so and therefore we must...'. But the impact of truth as unconcealment is *resonance* – we get movement; 'We now see what is being, is being so, what does that make newly possible?'

Truth as the unconcealing of that which is being, yet hidden, is itself a powerful truth in change. And you do not need to have a Madame Butterfly-type experience to witness its power. Sometimes, even bringing awareness into a conversation of 'the missing element', like the customer or beneficiary of your task, the source of funding for your endeavour, or the spirit and blessings of those who came before us, has a revelatory impact on a team's presence and perception. Summoning the deeper wider reality to your aid.

Pause a while to reflect

⇒ How have you taken in this distinction between truth as correctness and truth as unconcealing?

⇒ Take an area in your life that is causing unsettlement – can you tune into your own somatic experience of this unsettlement, how it makes you feel, the impulses it evokes, where and how it shows up in your body, your breath?

⇒ By using this data, is anything opening up to you about what might be being, yet hidden, within the situation? What truth(s) might be coming into your awareness?

⇒ To access, or unconceal these truths, are there any oughts you hold that might prevent you from being able to be with such disclosure?

⇒ What resources might you need to take with you on this unconcealment journey? (I insisted, against familial advice, to take my dog Indi with me to Ireland when I met all my blood relations for the first time this year.)

There are two further aspects to truth-disclosure that can help us see truth's role in catalysing change and movement: *confessional* – the unconcealment of self; and *parrhesia* – the unconcealment of other.

Truth as Confessional: The Unconcealment of Self

The act of confession has been a long-standing feature of Western Christianity, a sacrament in which believers admit (to themselves and God, via an officiating priest) that they have sinned, that they are sorry for their sins, and that they will do penance for these sins: they dutifully un-hide where they have strayed. In Daniele Lorenzini's book, *The Force of Truth*,[14] in which he quite brilliantly interprets the philosopher Foucault's take on truth (as *not* questioning truth itself but rather how truth has been hi-jacked by power to govern others), he sets out *truth as confession* as one of Foucault's 'truth regimes'. People pursue truth under certain obligations, and in confession, it is to liberate, cure or save oneself. This confessional regime is not restricted to Christian ritual and has been taken into areas such as criminology and judicial avowal ('I am guilty, milord') and psychoanalytic discourse ('Yes alright, I do wish to murder my father and sleep with my mother').

Now, I am not inviting us here to confess any sin, crime, or dark thought. But what Foucault raised is relevant to how we can bring about movement and change – especially in a polarised world. Foucault alerted us to power relations, a dynamic in which the confessor, or subject, is duty-bound or forced to confess. Despite there being great value to the individual in keeping things concealed (innocence), and, conversely, a cost of unconcealing (shame, punishment), there is a societal force offering salvation (entry into heaven), freedom (a shorter jail sentence) and cure (release from depression and destructive patterns) if one does. In polarised situations, one would not dare to 'fess up' to the other for fear that such vulnerability would be taken advantage of by the other party (whereas in less polarised situations, confession can be a releasing move to the individual).

Self-Disclosure Releases Movement

However, imagine the force of truth if it is those 'in power' who do the confessing? What kind of release might that have on the stuck situation? I was once working in a merger change process. Two companies, previously competitors in the market, were joining forces. Now, one of the companies was going to have a slight formal power advantage over the other (taking 51% of the new company ownership) yet it was when the two CEOs of the merging companies admitted to their organisations that they had not led the merger process as well as they might have done, that cultural resistance to the merger melted away and co-operation began. The self-disclosure on public display was an unprecedented moment of awareness that it was not the technical aspects of the merger that were getting in the way, but *how leaders were being with each other.*

Truth acts that expose one's vulnerability build trust and understanding (a foundation for any movement and change). For those of you who like models, I have always found the Johari Window framework illuminating and straightforward. Here, we are dealing with the power of disclosing your 'hidden area', that which is known to self but unknown to others. In the merger example above, when the top two leaders unconcealed their leadership truth, the act became an invitation to all their leaders to look inside themselves to see how they, in some way too, had been consciously or unconsciously undermining the merger process ('If they can do that, so can we'). Sometimes, it is not so much the *content* of the truth statement that causes the movement as the *act* of truth-telling that has resonating power. The reality punch is in the relational contact – you trust me enough to tell me the truth.

More in Chapter 7 regarding the power of emotional truth to catalyse change, but I am also reminded of a leader once who was taking their organisation into a big change of strategy. I was helping them run a big implementation meeting of the top 100 leaders in the firm. After a morning of struggle as to where to go, one leader took the microphone in front of all his colleagues to say, 'I am scared s-----s about this new strategy and have no idea how we are going to execute it!' This powerful truth-event was another example of how self-disclosure of *what is* releases movement (an *ought* statement might have been along the lines of, 'Come on, we really ought to figure this out as we are the senior leaders!'). Others took the microphones too after this disclosure of what so easily might have remained hidden, and from this collective revelation of what is, the way forward was found.

By seeing and naming truth, we can be released from the scary clutches of its implications.

Truth as the unconcealing of self is a change catalyst. However, it requires a surrounding cultural context of psychological safety (something I will explore in the next chapter on whether systems *can* become truth-tellers). I recall my time at Royal Dutch Shell company, where we invested greatly in building leadership skills for open, courageous dialogue. For example, we introduced the Chris Argyris and Donald Schon[15] Left Hand Column tool, a powerful invitation to people to notice and track what they are thinking and feeling in a situation, yet not saying. The next step is to reflect on *why* they are keeping these thoughts and feelings hidden, and then to choose what *would* be helpful to disclose in the interests of the relationships and task at hand. What one is concealing is not always disturbing (the so-called 'elephants in the room', the big hairy things we can all see and smell but not talk of) but also beautiful images, feelings, and impulses one might simply be too embarrassed to unconceal ('I am feeling for the first-time deep affection for my colleagues in the other department').

Foucault argues, and I have certainly experienced, that truth as confession not only brings what has been hidden in someone to light to others, but it also changes the someone confessing. It modifies your relationship to yourself – typically, feeling bolder, kindlier, and more at ease ('Well, glad I got that off my chest and now I am fully seen').

Pause a while to reflect

⇒ Take the unsettling situation you brought to awareness in the previous section, can you sense an opportunity to 'confess' something hidden from view with the intention to catalyse greater awareness in others, and release movement?

Truth as Parrhesia: The Unconcealment of Other

In ancient Greek society, *parrhesia*, or candid speech, meant the invitation, indeed obligation, to freely speak the truth about someone or the situation for the common good, even at personal risk. Foucault unpicks this public space truth act as characterising: there is freedom to speak; the act is an unpredictable, unplanned moment (not a rehearsed speech); there are consequences for those speaking the truth, as it risks a shared life with others; criticism of the other(s) or the situation is inherent; a greatness of soul is needed; transparency is at its heart ('If it were possible, I would like to let you see my thoughts rather than translate them into language', Seneca's letter to his pupil, Lucilius[16]); use of bare, simple, direct, and open language; the other is free to respond; both the statement, and the act of enunciation, affects the truth teller's being – you become what you utter.

Critically, the goal of parrhesia is not persuasion, or producing an effect on the other (ought-y land...), *but the possibilising of new action* via *the opening of an awareness of what is.* In Lorenzini's Force of Truth he says, 'Although parrhesiastic utterance *may* contribute to changing the opinions and ethos of the interlocutor(s), its main objective is not to persuade, but to courageously voice a critical truth regardless of the consequences: the point of parrhesia is not persuasion or moralisation, but the violent "irruption" of the truth' (p. 87).

A Story of How Parrhesia Unsticks Stuck Situations

I recall my most vivid moment of parrhesia while working with a client. It was day three morning of an online conference, in the days of COVID-19 lockdown where we were just getting used to these forms of technology to run meetings. One hundred and forty leaders were assembled on a Zoom call across three days to create a draft vision and strategy for their institution. I was billed as the lead moderator, change expert, and leadership coach for the event. This was already scare-inducing enough. But technology, and group size and ambitious goals aside (it was an institution most unused to [I could say resistant to] co-creating governing frameworks for the whole system), all these were nothing compared to the intervention I felt compelled to make at the opening of the final day.

My intervention was born out of love for and my faith in this institution's mission. I had not slept well the previous night, as what I had been tuning into about their system in the first two days was churning over in my mind and stirring deep in my heart (attention is the beginning of devotion). Yet I spent those waking hours fruitfully; checking in with my inner state, what was the case, the truth of the experience from within and befriending this unsettlement rather than wishing it away ('I really ought to be sleeping, let's try an antihistamine tablet to knock me out!').

When I rose from my bed at 6 a.m. I wrote down four big messages that I felt I needed to convey to these leaders, and I sent an email to my lead sponsor client asking for a pre-meeting to test out the intervention. He agreed to that meeting, and, while he went a bit quiet when I tested out my messages, said, 'This needs to be said to us all'. A pact of frankness had been established.

At 9 a.m. I welcomed all leaders back to the online gathering, and, with a tiny scrap of paper in my hand with the four messages written out (which I now have in front of me, four years later), I said something along the lines of: 'I have four messages with which to open today. Number one, you invited me to take on this role to help you cross a new threshold – to join up as one institution behind a vision and strategy that will take you into a future within a very changing and challenging world. To fulfil that intention – and with little sleep due to the import of what I have been picking up in the last two days – I am now going to be the bearer of three big questions. Can you please listen to me while I talk, and do not use the chat function, as I wish you to really hear these questions. Question one – you already have all the right answers for your vision and strategy, my question is, do you have the collective courage as leaders to do it? Question two – where is the destruction needed for you to pull off this vision and strategy, what is the price to change your structures (designed for a different age), and are you prepared to pay that price? Question three – who and what is this vision and strategy for? You seem more intent on talking about the words than talking about the beneficiaries of this vision, who, quite frankly, do not worry about whether you use this word or that word'.

At that point, and on the edge of controllable emotions, I stopped talking. I thought I had lost my Wi-Fi signal as all the faces on the screen had frozen, but then I realised there was simply stunned silence. The agreed next step in the process had been to move the 140 leaders into smaller break-out groups to process my messages and then reconvene as a large group to share responses. Yet for some reason, and despite a super whizz technical support, for the first time at the conference, Zoom did not allow us to break up the group. So, I suggested that a higher power had intervened, and how about we now open the floor and share our responses within the large group? That was an eeek-y moment, as while my co-moderator had sent me a thumbs-up emoji on my phone, I had no idea how the client system was going to respond.

The chat function lit up with comments about the 'prophetic moment', and how this act of truth-telling was powerfully resonating. It seemed to have brought a different quality of attention and presence or is-ness to the group, which allowed them to be more fully with their being. Long story short, but from that moment on the meeting flowed in a far more 'real' way – disagreements about the draft vision and strategy came out more clearly and powerfully (honesty is always a good sign of change and move-ment), voices spoke in plenary that to that point in the meeting had remained hidden. The pathway to the next steps for the process moved from feeling sticky and intractable to obvious and flowing.

In looking back at Foucault's criteria for a parrhesia moment, I think this truth-telling act pretty much ticks all the boxes. Back to the Johari Window, we are now in the pane of the 'blind area', someone is sharing to the other what is known about them but which they cannot see. I hope this story does not come across as vain, but it does stand out as a moment in my decades-long career in change when I managed to override my 'inner oughteries'. I let go of being careful, put aside my instinct to please and maintain relationship at any cost, I did not let past memories or future anxieties hold me back, I did not plan, I did not ask for advice and 'in the space of letting go, she let it all be'.

Pause a while to reflect

⇒ Can you recall moments when you have been able to voice something that felt hidden and out of awareness to others? Out of genuine love and respect? What was the impact?

⇒ Within your unsettling situation today, what are you noticing about the situation, its dynamics and your place within it that you feel needs to be publicly voiced? How would it feel to do so? (This act need not be as big a deal as taking on a whole institution, viz., Mr. Bates and the Post Office, it could be as simple as saying to a colleague or friend or partner, 'I am missing you in our conversations'.)

The Value of Truth: The Discovery of Reality

> Beauty – be not caused – It Is-
> Chase it, and it ceases –
> Chase it not, and it abides

Emily Dickinson[17]

Truth, or should I say truth-as-pursuit, is our gateway to reality; that which is perceived in the world around us and within us, the natural order of things. Through truth-seeking, we explore and get to understand this reality better (as I have tried to do over the decades with my research into and experience in the natural order of change). We seek truth, and in so doing, we encounter reality – what exists. Based on our understanding of what exists we take away work-in-progress truths. We then apply these truths back into wider realities, whose contact reveals further understanding of reality and perhaps us needing to adjust our truths.

This experience, of pursuing truth, is itself a form of knowing, a knowing about how the world unfolds its order from seeming randomness, a knowing about how we encounter reality (the French, *connaitre*, I know the experience, rather than *savoir*, I know the facts). A beautiful, virtuous reinforcing loop exists between truth pursuit and reality contacting. What gets in the way of this process are our oughts, neuroses and dogma that are threatened by this loop as it might require us to accept that the codes that have run our lives – our wiring, and reality – what is the case, are not the same thing. Rather than loosen our loyalties to these codes, the more likely outcome is that we choose not to believe the reality in front of us – truth-bending and reality-distorting.

So, I hope I am showing in this chapter that *how* we access truth matters as it shapes what reality comes our way. Unlike the Irrealists, I do not believe that reality only exists through our discourse or social construction (and even if it does, that is still real), but I am with them in highlighting how our own processes shape what we come to believe as true. All human reality is an act of co-creation and social constructionism, so our understanding of reality is undeniably an inward matter. We are the creators of our universe.

Resonating with Heisenberg's Uncertainty Principle, Emily Dickinson's verse simply and purely reminds us how reality tends to elude us the more we try to pinpoint it. Through Heidegger's contrast between truth as correctness (chasing logical accuracy) and truth as unconcealment (disclosing what is being, yet hidden), we can see how much greater an awareness of reality we achieve when we let go and simply be with being. McGilchrist would call this process a letting go of our predominant left hemisphere brain's route to reality – abstract and decontextualised reasoning, fixated on prominent parts, conclusive – and welcoming in more of our right hemisphere's route to understanding reality – taking in affective states, inferring complex and implicit meaning, constantly updating interpretations, taking in the world as a whole.

Back to my moment of parrhesia above, I could have conducted an online survey with the leadership group to diagnose how they were feeling and relating to their task, and then presented their responses back to them as their reality. Head-based, subject and object distinct – which would no doubt have led to a polite yet warily defensive intellectual discussion. Instead, I chose a different path to access truth and the nature of what was being. I tuned into my troubled inner state, connected that to their struggle with and deep longing to bring their mission out differently into the world, and offered them up some big questions. Affective-based, subject and object interconnected – which, through its deep experience from within, had a vibrational quality that unlocked honest, moving exchange.

This weekend, if I wish to put my writing to one side and enjoy capturing the reality of the Dordogne landscape by painting its colours, I could go out to analyse the precise chemical constitution of its soil and leaves or simply stand, absorb, breathe in the view, stare for a while, register how it all impacts me and with a beginner's mind paint what then comes to my awareness. As Einstein says, 'Nature hides her secrets'. To unconceal the reality of our natural world, our task is not to intellectualise and break things down into parts but to be attuned, aware, and coalesce a picture of the whole.

That's the kind of open, patient, and attentive truth pursuit that unveils the reality that drives change.

Pause a while to reflect

⇒ What methods have you deployed in your life to access reality? With what impact on catalysing change?

⇒ If you were to consider switching from more left- to right-hemisphere modes, what might that look like in the situation that is currently unsettling you?

How Truth and Reality Combine to Activate Change

> *One word of truth outweighs the world.*
> Alexandr Solzhenitsyn, Nobel Lecture in Literature 1970

Quoting from a Russian proverb, the author and dissident, Solzhenitsyn, certainly felt that truth was a weighty and vital matter.[18] Having set out how truth-pursuit and its contact with reality frees up movement, what follows is my take on *why* it is that the act of starting with acknowledging what is – perhaps even one small word of truth – catalyses change more powerfully and effortlessly than *striving for today's reality to be other than it is.* And I emphasise the word, 'catalyse' here. We need to do many things through a change process, what interests me in this book is how we can initiate and accelerate change, as that always feels like the trickiest thing to do (we are always full of good intentions yet can drag our feet and put the big change off to tomorrow!).

My reasons are as follows: we can only move from solid ground; the brain can relax with truth; systems need to be whole; and working with what is, builds a 'we'.

We Can Only Move from Solid Ground

When we become fully *what we are* rather than *what we are not,* we stand on the ground of reality with a firm footing. That ground might be a temporary state, such as sadness, or a more permanent trait, such as a predisposition towards melancholia. Be it state or trait, fully accepting something or openly agreeing *to* something, however unwelcome or out-of-character, renders us more fluid, balanced and fearless. Such is the power of acknowledgement and inclusion versus resistance and denial.

It sounds like another paradox, but we get a healthy distance to things that we can welcome more fully (ever experienced being kinder to that 'awkward' neighbour and in so doing be psychologically less caught up with your inner complaints?). From a firm footing of being able to get alongside it all, we can move into a new future more resourcefully as our path through life feels authentic and secure, a bit like having an inner gyroscope as a guide rather than trying to move from a trampoline.

The moment I learned how to embrace my adoption story and pattern of preferring not-quite-committed edges to I'm-all-in centres, I gave up my striving to belong to a family, relationship, or work system in the more conventional sense. I embraced my liminality – including its primary cost of loneliness – and integrated it as my signifier strength. It's helpful to work in my field with distance to the system going through change, and more empowering to that system than me wishing to get too 'in' and involved.

From that place of acknowledgement of who I was, I could grow with more ease. Returning to Katherine Mansfield, who says so simply, 'Everything in Life that we really accept undergoes a change', by becoming 'more me' and integrating the 'niggly' bits, I turned a previously perceived deficit into a resource and became relaxed, changing my entire stance and presence. And that inner state shift brought new, wiser and more confident behaviours in how I showed up to my life, which of course, then positively impacted what came my way.

For example, in my work life, this personal realisation made me far better understand the classic change mantra, 'start with where the system *is*' (i.e., do not begin change with a template of where you think the system *ought* to be). I came across a recent perfect example. One of our Still Moving community members mentioned a case in which her company, swamped with initiatives, had been trying in vain to eliminate non-essential work. Their latest attempt was via a 'kill the darlings' initiative in which groups of leaders got together to list all their pet projects and then agreed to get rid of them. This profound disavowal of *what is* did not work and the projects' proliferation continued.

I recalled an alternative way of tackling this. A colleague and I led a 'Room 101' intervention with a client's leadership team with the same goal, prioritising the essentials. Room 101 is a TV show in which celebrities are invited to bring items that they truly love yet now wish to leave behind, and after respectfully saying how much they have taken from these items, wish now to place them in an honoured yet out-of-the-way place. So, we ran this format with this group of leaders who spoke deeply *to* (note, not *about*) each of their change projects, or ways of working, that they had fully identified with and had served them well, yet which now needed to be bid farewell to (they literally created 'boxes' of these items and placed them in a room).

This acknowledgement exercise (respecting what is and what has been), in contrast to a killing activity (I ought to get rid of you), gave the client full assuredness that things could now be left behind and new projects and behaviours pursued. Somehow, the soul of the system knew that the work that had been done to date was valued and had not been done in vain.

Acknowledgement releases attachment.

Drawing from Frederick Perls' Gestalt therapy, Arnold Beisser explains in his classic article, The Paradoxical Theory of Change,[19] that 'change does not take place through a coercive attempt by the individual or another person to change him, but it does take place if one takes the time and effort to be what he is – to be fully invested in his current positions' (written in 1970 so excuse the gender identity). *Change occurs when you become fully invested in your current position.* What a phrase. Only when we are at ease with *what is,* can we adjust what is.

The Brain Can Relax with Truth

This phenomenon – of becoming more innovative when we can respect what already is – can be neurochemically explained by brain science. As I have stated in the previous chapter, when we live in the world of *ought* we set ourselves up for disaffection and disappointment. We get unsettled when we contemplate the difference between *what is* and how we wish things *could be* ('Argh, why do we find it impossible to reduce so many projects!'). An ought stance also leads to rigid and fixed interpretations about others and the situation at hand, which we then seek to defend against at seemingly any cost ('The only way to reduce initiatives is to cut the number of corporate staff who keep launching things!').

So, when we are in oughtyness and not is-ness, we are likely to be anxious and defending, a state in which the amygdalae (threat detectors) in our limbic brain trigger the stress response – to fight, flee from, or freeze in the situation. All these adrenalised responses, while keeping our ancestors safe from predators, weaken the connection to our more reasoned, reality-interpreting pre-frontal cortex – particularly the right hemisphere. The left hemisphere is, therefore, at risk of maintaining unhelpful fantasies and fixed impulses – keeping us hard-wired to see only what we believe to be true, and so we repeat past coping behaviour. This is perfectly OK in known stable situations requiring a fast habitual response. It is not helpful in dynamic, uncertain contexts requiring movement and change.

On the other hand, when we are open to and at ease with reality and whatever comes our way, our brain relaxes, and its natural propensity to choose certainty[20] over truth[21] is overridden. The parasympathetic part of our nervous system, the relaxation response, is activated, dopamine is released, and we become curious, creative and resourceful. We hit the pause button on our autopilot reactivity and can consciously choose a fresh response. By accepting things *as they are,*[22] our brains switch from rigid anxiety to fluid creativity. And given how mood states are contagious as the mirror neurons in our brains literally transmit inner states from one person to another, the more your mind is at ease with what is, so will others settle around you, and change can flow.

I will never forget the story of a Chief Financial Officer (CFO) coming to a meeting of his senior leaders and calmly saying that their company was facing bankruptcy. Everybody had been sensing for weeks that this was a real scenario, but no one had yet heard the 'b-word' spoken. When the CFO named it in the room, you could almost hear the collective out-breath of the leadership group, expelling all the fear that was holding them back from finding fresh ways out of the situation. Likewise, earlier in my career, while at Shell, there was a curious phenomenon in the retail business. When we brought greater transparency about each retail site's profit performance to the attention of everyone, and the lowest performing countries were 'red flagged' (i.e., turn around your business within a year or you will be sold), the lowest performers miraculously sprang into creativity and achieved better performance - so much so that they then taught lessons to the higher performing sites!

However awkward, embarrassing, shaming and scary it may feel to acknowledge, rather than deny, *what is the case*, our brains will welcome the greater ease that comes with truth and with this anxiety release, creativity can flow.

Systems Need to Be Whole Before They Can Move

> God 'determines the number of the stars; he gives to all of them their names.'
>
> *Psalm 147*

Acknowledging *what is* means acknowledging *all* of what is – including facing the reality of any alienated or hidden parts of us or the systems we live and work in. Why so? This may sound a little mysterious (more in the next chapter), but systems have their own recognisable qualities and conscience that exist *through* us. One thing is for sure: systems do not like incompleteness. This brings restlessness and disquiet and can lead to individuals within the system not being able to be their true selves – they need to 'carry' the excluded element's burden.

This phenomenon often shows up in our family systems. For example, do you have a family member – living or now passed – who, for whatever reason, is estranged, kept a secret, not talked about, or if talked of, is talked about in a derogatory way, or has been struck out of the family history or photo album? How does that exclusion impact your family system? Awkwardness, sadness, guilt? Maybe there is one member now who, in some way, is trying to re-include that person and live out their fate within your family today, as an unconscious protest? No system can tolerate exclusions without someone needing to follow.

Systems, whether we like it or not, demand to be whole. Things get gummed up otherwise and any difficulty associated with the exclusion gets passed on. In Chapter 5, I will illustrate in some detail a core skill we have found that correlates with system ease and flow – *Acknowledging the Whole*, the capacity to give all that happens a place and a purpose. Here, I am concerned with exploring why change can flow when we integrate and include all, which means keeping in our sights even that which has necessarily left or departed the system.

To answer that question, just consider nature on our planet Earth, the living system that supports our life. In every ecosystem, each element – be that a leaf, stone, weather pattern, mouse, soil chemical or nutrient – has a place, and a mutually reinforcing one. Nature is not wasteful. The world is designed and created to be a whole. Just zooming out to that vast, largely unfathomable system of the entire universe, most of this is not matter but void, emptiness. Aha, so you might say, that system has redundant parts. Not so, what we think is nothing is not something inert. Scientists[23] say that nothing contains all things and is pregnant with energy that helps the universe evolve. Coming from stardust ourselves,[24] take the composition of a human being, where each cell in our body counts. Whether we are attracted to it or not, every tiny piece of us matters (even the appendix, which far from having no purpose, contributes to health as a safe house for good bacteria).

And so, our families and teams and communities and workplaces and nations – all themselves living human systems – likewise function healthily when they are whole. Who are we to believe that we are any different to that from which we came? We deep down know that, as many of our spiritual traditions emphasise oneness and unity within ourselves, and between ourselves and others, the universe and the divine. The Mandala, a geometric pattern present throughout our universe – from the concentric crystals of a snowflake to the patterned grid of a tortoiseshell to the interlocking ellipses and ovals of the cosmos – is a symbol of wholeness that found its way into the imagery of primarily Hinduism and Buddhism, but also Christianity, Native American tradition and religious architecture. Soul is the mechanism by which completeness is held.

Accessing this deep spiritual truth in our day-to-day lives can be quite practical and accessible. I recall once sitting with a leadership team who were struggling to move their institution into a new future. I could sense, via one of the unsettled team members, that we needed to map out the whole history of the key events, players and communities that had led to this moment in time (often, the most disturbed system member is a sign that something or someone needs to be re-included, there is a 'missing element' at play). Far from pushing ahead with where this institution *ought* to be, we took time to simply name and include all that *has been*.

We did this by leaders standing up and forming a line to represent the various events and key players in their genealogy from foundation to the present day (a history that included some troubling events and leaders that, to this point, they had been reluctant to talk about). This invitation to form and stand in this line of truth became a cathartic, moving moment. As the psalmist says God did with the stars, each element of their story was fully registered, named, and took up its rightful place within the deep history that had made all of today's reality possible. Finally, I set up for them someone to represent the future line of beneficiaries, those who would inherit their leadership acts of today. This was the last piece of the jigsaw the system needed to become whole.

After two hours, this hitherto disjointed team sat down and integrated the depth of the experience. From that moment onwards, they could join up to determine what was needed next. Truth as unconcealment brings a longed-for wholeness to systems, freeing up its members to choose a new path.

Working with What Is Builds a We

A friendly and unflinching attention to what's here builds togetherness, especially when we can all see how we have each, in our way, created the very situation we wish to change. Can you own that part of you that is caught up in the story of what is? What is it, *in you*, that is making the reality you wish to change troubling (I would anticipate that it could be one of your oughts that is running the show of your unsettlement)? In the above story when each leader was able to identify and share with their colleagues what was going on for them that was making the situation difficult, the disclosure built a wave of mutual understanding and empathy ('I thought you were all sorted, and I was the only one disturbed!').

Similarly, I once worked with a newly forming leadership team who, despite nine months of being together, were still not firing on all cylinders. In my 1:1 conversations with the team members, I noticed two things: that the story of their formation and all that this had cost them individually (some moved countries, some took on what might be considered a smaller role) had not yet been named; and that they were all pinning the responsibility for the team not being at optimum onto someone else. At the next team meeting, I invited each member to bravely share their 'losts and founds' from the last year: to be part of this team, what had they each had to give up, and what had they each gained? The process of both speaking to their own *is-ness* of the situation and hearing that of each colleague helped them see that they had all in some way 'suffered'. This heightened respect for each other's reality and the relational power of their shared contact with truth, provided a powerful, needed spurt to their team development.

There is a second aspect to why working with *what is* builds togetherness. Consider the distinction between the *descriptive* value of is-ness and the *normative* force of oughtyness. A descriptive stance simply names, non-judgementally, what is the case; providing an account of the world as it is. A normative stance evaluates reality against a standard of how things need to be; highlighting the gap, a deficit. In all my work in change, I find that the latter judgingly prodding approach, far from building ambition, only creates defensiveness and anxiety. Whereas being able to hold a space to notice and name what is, invites curiosity and collaboration.

And here's the rub: it is in so doing, by bringing people together to build the story of what is, *that a normative force is inherently created* – the group starts to collectively wish for a different state, yet without being cajoled and belittled. That's how you build change commitment.

In the above team example, mutual empathy was created by members sharing their 'losts and founds'. But the activity did much more than that to spark change. Each individual's story somehow evaporated into a collective, generative field in which boundaries and polarities dissipated, and the team came jointly to the realisation, 'This state is not good enough, we cannot go on as we have'.

In this chapter, I have put forward the case for how it is that the act of *acknowledging what is*, compared to striving for or wishing for reality to be different, is the more powerful catalyst for change. By unpicking the distinction between truth as correctness and truth as unconcealment, I offered guidance about what type of truth holds such power. Next, I showed how truth as unconcealment gets us in contact with the necessary depths and wholeness of reality that we need to encounter for change to flow. Finally, by providing some answers as to *why* such truth-telling and reality encounters spark change, I invite you to consider doing the same.

And this invitation is so important today. Staying flexibly in contact with reality is more important than being right in a world of flux and uncertainty, where what was right one day flies out the window the next. Can we enlarge our understanding of reality to match the scope of what exists? For sure, we need the continuity and stability of moral compasses and societal ideals. But let us notice when these turn into dogma that divides, exhortations that stultify, and loyalties that blind us to what is true. Let us be courageous enough to loosen our grip on rights and wrongs, find the humility and attentional skills to access reality-as-it-is, and, in so doing, provide a space for larger truths to emerge. This might require confessing to the hidden parts of us we wish others do not know or calling out to others that which they cannot see about themselves.

But remember, everything *we* do not face gets passed on. Let's not kick the can of truth down the road and have others need to face what we could so easily do today.

From Ought to Is: Initiating Change and Movement in a Polarised World

Intermezzo

I hope that by now you are engaged with this exploration journey to contrast a life lived through *ought* with a life lived through *is*, and can see how, by accepting life more as it is, we are paradoxically better at effecting change.

Here's a recap so far.

When we are in ought-land, we wish for or imagine reality to be different from what it is – more conforming to a certain sense of correctness, belief, or ideology. While the imprinted codes of ought can fuel our ideals and values, guide how we are to be in the world and ensure a system's continuity, they can also lead to unquestioned doctrines, intolerance of alternative truths, effortful striving, partial vision and findings ourselves in disaffection and disappointment (when the world 'doesn't go our way').

In excess, ought's fixed loyalties and strident opinions alienate and exclude others, separating and hardening the ground through intractable tensions and polarisation. Oughts not only limit the lives of us and others, but they also do a disservice to the availability of life itself – which gives so much. We somehow shrink our experience and thinly skate across life.

As our oughts fundamentally originate in our need to belong, they are difficult to budge as any peek into wider truths will be felt as an act of disloyalty to their originating affiliation groups and cherished belief systems, risking us feelings of guilt, shame and loss.

While this sounds like a high price to pay, there is so much more gain to be had in moving from our unquestioned (and often indignant) oughts into wider fields of belonging and truth. If we can accept the fullness of reality and actively 'be' with what is being (however awkward, offensive and upsetting), aiming to unconceal Heidegger's truth of what is being, yet hidden,

From Ought to Is: Catalysing Change and Movement in a Polarised World,
First Edition. Deborah Rowland.
© 2025 John Wiley & Sons Ltd. Published 2025 by John Wiley & Sons Ltd.

we might find beneath all our toil and disaffection that *dearest freshness deep down things* of which Hopkins so exquisitely writes.

However challenging it might be to open-heartedly acknowledge all of reality beyond our belonging fields, from this more perspicacious and wider place, we have greater awareness, wisdom, ease and choice in our lives. By including all, we are not only more at peace, but we are also more flexible in changing landscapes, as the emphasis is on our quality of attention, not on being right. Through ongoing truth pursuit, we fully contact and enrich our lives, enabling release in ourselves, a more creative response to experience and movement in our surrounding systems. We can radiate small pools of open-hearted inclusion and wisdom within the places where we can be heard and make a difference.

Having taken time in the last two chapters to get to know both these worlds of *ought* and *is*, and established the case for how the latter stance far more effectively propels change, in the rest of the book, I offer a series of chapters on *how* to take the power of acknowledging what is as a change catalyst into practical application: overriding the societal trends and personal neurobiology I set out in Chapter 2, the world of ought, will take some dedicated attention and skill.

Navigating between ought and is and knowing what to let go of, and what to make a fuss about, is a real skill in discernment. If we wish for change, we certainly need to make a fuss about the following.

⇒ The absolute necessity of seeing and working with the hidden (yet being) orders of human systems that can bring ease, truth, and movement to stuck and entangled places in our lives, our communities and our workplaces.

⇒ To learn how to do this, mastering a set of interdependent skills that our Still Moving research has shown are fundamental in being able to lead systems to new places in ways that are more effortless, sustainable and humanising.

⇒ To deepen these skills, summoning the depths of our soul at both the personal and system level as the wings that will beckon, propel and stabilise our movement in journeying *from ought to is*.

⇒ To be able to tolerate the feelings that will arise as we come into clearer contact with reality (truth can stir up so much), putting the positive and intentional role of our emotions centre stage when we seek change.

4

Systems and the Pursuit of Truth

The dizziness in the face of les espaces infinis – only overcome if we dare to gaze into them without any protection. And accept them as the reality before which we must justify our existence. For this is the truth we must reach to live, that everything is and we just in it.

Dag Hammarskjöld, Markings

This chapter begins our application journey at the system level: how can we best read the reality of the world around us and take up our place within it, reconciling ourselves to the big truth that a large part of our experience will forever remain mysterious, perplexing and unknowable? Within the perplexity and perturbation of a changing world, how can we still find coordinates to guide our attention, navigate our lives and lead ourselves and our systems towards places of ease and movement?

(As I am editing this chapter, we have just had the seismic and historic result of the US presidential election, with the Republican Donald Trump re-elected to office after a bitterly fought and polarising election campaign that has left a nation, and a world, divided and reeling. Just as COVID-19 gave us a global change management lesson in handling unprecedented disruption, today's shifting geopolitical tectonics away from a prevailing global liberal world order towards protective, nationalistic conservatism, of which the US election is the most vivid example, is gifting many of us an education in how to override our oughts and systemically be with *what is* within the world around us.)

From Ought to Is: Catalysing Change and Movement in a Polarised World,
First Edition. Deborah Rowland.
© 2025 John Wiley & Sons Ltd. Published 2025 by John Wiley & Sons Ltd.

Taking Our Place Within Systems Requires Courage and Humility

The opening quote holds a clue. A kindly neighbour in my Cornish village handed me the remarkable book, *Markings*,[1] by Dag Hammarskjöld. My neighbour got to know me after I moved there to write *Still Moving and* said that she thought I'd like it. *Markings* is a unique document, a compilation of journal entries exposing the inner life of a man who became the Secretary General of the United Nations during a period of extreme world tension – the late 1950s. You would not know from reading his journals that Hammarskjöld was such a senior public servant in a position of exceptional world power, as he used his diary not to record big or even day-to-day events, but to analyse his states of mind via reflections, poems and prayers.

Hammarskjöld made paying attention to how he paid attention a worthy and necessary task, the starting point for truth pursuit. How we make sense of the world and bring it into being governs the quality and direction of what we will see, experience and effect. This journal entry, in particular, gifts us an invitation to a vital truth pursuit: *how can we see the broader systems of which we are a part and take up our place within them?* What is Hammarskjöld getting at with this journal entry? How did you take in his words? When I first encountered them, I felt my whole *being* was arrested (a sign of a truth being unconcealed into my awareness). Here's my take...

First, Hammarskjöld invites us to stand *unguardedly* (without any protection) within our universe, les espaces infinis, and daringly let be, taking in all its realities. When we make ourselves more porous and less defended by our oughts, we can take more in, meeting things on their terms, not our preconceived ones. We can bow to the world we experience and take up our right place within it, rather than fight its incomprehensibility and impose our own needs, ideologies and projections. Despite Hammarskjöld's significant position of leadership of a system that, at the time, comprised around 100 nations, he humbly made himself the 'right size' and offered us a powerful reality acceptance statement:

> *Everything is, and we just in it.*

But his invitation to be just *in* the *is*-ness of life does not mean that we passively surrender to whatever comes our way, as he asks two further things of us relating to our attention and intention. Just as Heidegger believed that the act of *being* had attentional agency, the quality of our presence and perceiving can move things, Hammarskjöld asks that we *gaze into* the realities of our world. What a system we stand before, this life, this universe. How *do* we look into the systems of which we are a part (a team, an organisation, a family, a community, a nation, a belief group)? Hammarskjöld recognises this takes courage as he also asks us to *dare* to gaze. So much of our own life and experience remains conveniently and comfortably unexamined (while we make all kinds of attributions and judgements about the lives of others), so the inclusive and unclouded quality of our gazing is diminished.

Let us take the historic US election result. No doubt the Democrat party will need to look deeply at itself to find the reasons why the controversial character that is Trump won in both expected and unexpected places. But the fact of the matter is this: his messages of improving the economy, tackling immigration and putting America first spoke to the nation far more powerfully than that of the Democrat contender Kamala Harris – whose party you could say was blinded by its cultural evangelism, Trump denialism, moral rectitude and a failure to tap into the belonging needs of voters from across all classes, races and generational divides. Did partisan ideology cloud the Democrats' capacity to fully meet and see reality?

Back to Hammarskjöld, once we can gaze bravely into reality in unprotected ways, he then asks us to use our courageous attention to *justify our existence* before our systems, to hone our intention. Can we be a good reason for our families, communities, organisations, teams, nations and movements? And he lands the point fully – it is *only* by bringing an attention in which we let go of our protections (read, oughts) that the vastness of life becomes less dizzy, and we can find our right size and right place, our true intention. By letting things be, and not muddling up reality with our defences, fixations and smaller stories, we can become a consequence for our lives and those of others around us.

That is a truth worth pursuing. It enabled me this year to stand before 40 new family members at my birth father's funeral – a vast array of strangers in space and time – take up my place in the front pew of the church, and, unprompted at the after-service gathering, say some words of thanks to my Irish family for their welcome and funeral arrangements for my birth father. This could have been an extraordinarily emotionally dizzying system encounter (any wobbliness had nothing to do with the half pint of Guinness I covertly imbibed at a pub before entering the service). But by my having put my protective oughts on how to be (displaced, not-quite-belonging) to one side, I unguardedly and naturally asserted my place in their (and my) line of family time. *Everything was, and I just in it.*

Yet, how can we diminish the systems in our lives, and our own flourishing, by holding on to our stories.

This chapter will dive deeply into the relationship between truth pursuit and system attention – how *should* we gaze into *les espaces infinis*? I will begin with a story of change that shows how, if we wish to unconceal system realities, we must stop and gaze into what is being experienced wisely, letting what is being, be – and not react impulsively from our beliefs of what is desirable or expected. I will then explore the challenge that our human systems are not natural truth-tellers – our families, workplaces and communities all adopt understandable defence routines to conceal what truly is the case; just as we have personal oughts, so do systems have a conscience that guards how it is to be.

So, what is system truth and truth in systems, and how can both be attained to effect change? In the rest of the chapter, I will offer guidance in two areas. First, we need to spot and work with four underlying truths of human systems that, if left unattended, will always hold back change: *what* to direct our attention towards when seeking the *is-ness* of a system. Second, how to approach change and movement in ways that enhance a system's capacity to see and shift such realities: *how* to direct a system's attention. Both these factors – systemic orders and change approaches – have been validated by our research at Still Moving to be significantly associated with successful change.

A System Story of How *Everything Is and We Just In It*

This story illustrates how important it is when we gaze into systems – the messy, ever-shifting and interdependent dynamics of the human communities we belong to – that we see them as they truly are (is-based attention), and not conformed to how we would like them to be (ought-based attention). We must dare to meet things on their terms. I had been asked to facilitate an Open Space Technology event for a European learning community. Open Space is a large group intervention format in which, within an overarching guiding intention, the community co-creates its agenda based on the topics its members feel are the 'ripest issues' needing their current attention. Volunteers nominate and then host conversations on these hot topics, with the remaining participants free to choose the topics they wish to contribute to.

Within the loose intention and a set of firm ground rules (including, 'Whatever happens is the only thing that could have happened'), Open Space is, therefore, an emergent and free-flowing format; you never know where you are going to end up, and as a facilitator, you need to be very attuned to the group's process *as it happens*, sensing what the collective is most troubled and energised by. You see the reality of the *system in the room* as, unconstrained by any hierarchical control, the true culture of the group is made manifest.

Therefore, Open Space is quite different to the more conventional carefully pre-prepared event with a fixed list of desired outcomes, pre-selected topics and speakers, timed talks, Q&A and set break-out groups. In such events, you see only an orchestrated fragment of the system's reality as people will behave according to pre-existing cultural rules and expectations – truth as correctness. These more traditional meeting formats are less messy, but only a re-presentation and not the essential lived nature of the group and all the issues it is carrying.

The event in this story was far from that, and became an illustrative example of the power of Heidegger's *truth as unconcealing* to catalyse system change.

There was an author present at this Open Space event who had just published his latest book about systems and organisational change. He was introduced as a 'big-wig guru': getting him along had been a coup. Yet in the Open Space format, when the topics had been nominated and people dispersed to join their issues of choice, no one went to join him (he had volunteered his book's core messages as a topic). This reality became highly visible in the large room where the various topic holders had set up their dialogue stations. The conference organisers were most alarmed at what they thought was an embarrassing situation and anxiously asked me, as the overall facilitator, to 'do something' about it, as people 'ought to be going to hear what he has to say'.

I remember now, after panicking a little at the sight of six troubled people standing before me, that I paused, stood quiet and firm and asked the organisers to accept the is-ness of what was happening. I said I would not intervene in the reality of where people had moved. I invited them to see the experience as a helpful truth about the group dynamics to process when we re-gathered: a chance, as Hammarskjöld asks of us, to *gaze into* this system's realities with acceptance and without protection; an opportunity, as Heidegger encourages us, to disclose what is being, yet hidden.

As the group re-assembled to debrief – and I had gone before to check in with the guru on his sense of the dynamics in the room – I invited everyone to face and make sense of the seemingly awkward situation that nobody had joined the guru's topic: he was no nutter and he had an inviting temperament, so what was going on? Could the group dare to unguardedly explore what was being manifested? If they were to act as if reality were always friendly, what would they see here? I asked them to gaze into the system they were part of without critique of any individuals and what had happened, just with open curiosity – *at the system level* – about what had caused the moment.

The invitation led to a rich conversation about the dynamics of this group in relation to choice, the nature of power (the word 'guru' had made them kick back against hierarchy), and how they were excluding that which they most feared. The community had gathered to explore how more visible leadership could be taken up within their self-organising system, and the visiting guru's book was a deep call to personal responsibility in change – the very thing that was absent within this community – yet it had felt scary to go to that which they most needed. The guru acknowledged that he was just a visitor in this experience and had passed a delightful time in solitude. This undefendedness on his part also helped the group to truthfully own up to what they were finding too difficult to acknowledge – that all they wanted to do was to take from, and not contribute leadership to, the community.

All in all, by letting *what was being be* and desisting from forcing participants to go to the visitor's Open Space topic, my stance had enabled the group to see deeply into its collective reality and unhelpful defensive patterns far more effectively than if I had problem-solved and pushed the situation into oughtyness ('Sort things out Deborah and get people to go to the guru!'). *Everything was, and they just in it.*

The systemic truth disclosure that this stance revealed, created a collective alethurgy moment in this community, which catalysed awareness, choice and change. Participants now found the courage *to* take up leadership responsibilities in the system ('Let's not punish any of us who do step up; hierarchy is OK!'). By facing into realities, they each found their place that justified their existence within the community, and it felt like a truth ripple was blowing through the group, releasing movement. There was no need for any ought-led action planning to conclude the event. By accepting reality, we moved reality.

Pause for a moment here
Take a group in which you might feel a little unsteady or dizzy right now due to its seeming stuckness, unhelpful patterns or complexity – a team, a community, a friendship.

⇒ Can you dare gaze into this system without any of your oughts clouding the picture? What do you see that might be being (in existence), yet hidden from conscious view?

⇒ Can you accept these deeper realities that you see and acknowledge how you, too, are just 'in' them (not necessarily their cause or hero to adjust, but, in some way, caught up in their collective forces)?

⇒ With such holistic acceptance, how do you settle into yourself and your place? What release and movement might be possible if you invited others to gaze unguardedly into the system's deeper realities too?

Can Human Systems Ever Be Truth-Tellers?

The Open Space story shows how easily we humans are tempted to conspire to bend reality to a conformed ideal or sense of correctness (our oughts), rather than being able to sit with a system to let it fully be and, by seeing it in an unclouded way, invite movement *from that place of reality* (not by prodding it towards our wished-for state).

Fellow creatures in the living world are hard-wired to seek out truth and reality. Just look at how packs of antelopes constantly scan for lions, knowing that they are prey, and lions wake up, knowing that they are predators. If these animals were not effective at knowing this truth, accurately reading their environment, and sharing that information with others, then it would be game over. Truth adds to the survival chances of the species. So, how come our human systems have such a casual relationship with it?

Telling lies is part of human nature. A study[2] has shown that the average person tells one to two lies a day, an act that begins early in life – adolescents lie to their parents around 50% of the time. This truth distortion occurs in our workplaces, where approximately 75% of us have false information on our résumés, and in our relationships, where approximately 92% of people report having lied to their partner. What are our particularly human defensive routines that foster such truth concealment and reality distortion?

Fear of being exiled for one. Millennia ago, Socrates's frank speech made him very unpopular in Athenian society, leading to his trial and execution on the spurious charge of dishonouring the Gods and corrupting the young. Fast forward to the story of the nineteenth-century Hungarian-born physician Semmelweiss, who was deemed insane by his German medical colleagues when his empirical research pointed out that the high mortality rates of postpartum mothers in the obstetric wards were due to the doctors failing to wash their hands. His peers batted away this reality disclosure by saying he had no scientifically grounded basis for his hypothesis. Still, it was the personal offence that the doctors had felt at their fault exposure that led them to mock him and lock him up in an asylum, where he died 14 days later of wounds most likely incurred from a beating on entry.

After his death, Semmelweiss's findings eventually found their way into the hands of Louis Pasteur and then Joseph Lister – who validated the truth of his insights via germ theory. Thank you, Semmelweiss, for helping us found hygienic medicine – but you paid a high price for naming truth. Still today, we hear about the costs and consequences for whistleblowers who expose realities, organisational failings, regime corruption and corporate coverups: they can be vilified, mocked and done away with. It takes a courageous and morally resolute person to tell the truth in these contexts, so it is hardly surprising that systems compel us to look away. I can recall many times when I have realised an important truth or witnessed a disturbing reality and had swirling emotions within me of fear to voice or shame not to.

I have also worked in many excessively polite cultures where harmony is valued over honesty. In one, an ostensible fear of embarrassing 'important people' about their performance meant that valuable data about the organisation from across their different regions remained hidden; only the centre could see the privileged information. When I continued to ask people in the centre why this was the case, their initial explanation of fear of embarrassing their colleagues eventually led to a response that the leaders in the regions were not 'mature enough' to handle the transparent truth of performance data; how we can infantilise others and be selective with truth disclosure, to hold on to power.

Aside from self-protection, valuing harmony and preserving status and place, other strong and collectively held forces that support truth concealment include fear of shame and excessive positivism. Perhaps you have been in systems in which shameful memories from the past have led to truth concealment? I once worked with a team where the memory of the awkward exit of two recently hired leaders had become buried and blocked, to such an extent that present-day team members could not talk about their fear and anxiety about their place. I have also found in change that we tend to go first (and, at times, only) to the desired vision, where we need to head to, and avoid looking intently and realistically at the current state of reality – the only arena where change can occur. It can be much easier to dream about the ideal than to examine what we have right now.

So, with the natural tendency for human systems to glide over truth – preferring harmony to honesty, safety to risk, concealment to disclosure, innocence to shame, dreams to reality – how can we acknowledge these tendencies for what they are and, in disclosing their power and hold on truth concealment, value and actively pursue *what is the case*? If one truth about our human systems is that they find truth troubling, what lenses can we use to explain and shift this? Let us not judge but understand. What *is* being, existing beneath all human systems, yet hidden from our sight?

The Ordering Forces

Beneath all collective life exists four deep vectors that, together, exert a magnetic pull on system thought, feeling and action, mysteriously leading us away from our conscious desires. Just as we can see, feel and experience the effects of the north, south, east and west winds blowing through our landscapes, so will we keenly feel and experience the impacts of these four invisible systemic forces sweeping through our families, teams, communities, institutions and nations. Just as sailors know how to trim sails to the winds to create the optimal movement of their boat, so can we learn how to recognise and harness these Ordering Forces to achieve greater ease and flow in our lives and communities.

In summary, the Ordering Forces are: *Belonging* – the need to feel safe and secure within groups necessary for identity and survival; *Time* – the need to honour the past and the impact of the anticipated future in the present moment so that a system can be grounded and free to move; *Place* – the system strength that arises when appropriate hierarchies are acknowledged and each element of the system is in the right place viz a viz each other and the system's purpose; *Exchange* – a system's need through time to acknowledge what is owed and what is owing, and to attend to the dynamics that arise when there are imbalances between what is being given and received.

I am deeply grateful that my eyes were opened to these Ordering Forces, which, as I have come to know and work with them, represent the deep soul voicings of a system – calling out to us to be recognised and attended to. So often we attribute surface causes to explain what we see and fail to notice what lies beneath. Bert Hellinger originally called these four forces 'orders' as 'When something is in order, there's a feeling of relief, peace and of things working smoothly together'.[3] The soul of our systems is at ease when we can work with the truth, or is-ness of these orders; but this task takes a keen attentional capacity on our part as Hellinger goes on to say that the orders need to be 'observed and uncovered, not invented'.

Because the orders are invisible (we just see their effects), we need to up our perceptive powers to see them.

As system truths to be unconcealed, the orders are invariant qualities – not 'things or tools for us to bring'. They are the 'dearest freshness deep down things' beneath all our striving and toiling in the conscious realm. I therefore find that these orders bring us to a humbler stance within systems as they exist despite our intentions and efforts, and, with so much power to join up the dots across all my experience in work and non-work realms, it is now impossible for me to 'unsee' them. Not only have I applied them; via the Still Moving change practitioner community, we have demonstrated through an empirical research study that when leaders attend to these underlying system realities, change and movement can flow – even in the trickiest and seemingly most stuck circumstances. They help us counteract any 'dizziness in the face of les espaces infinis'; they are the systemic laws that allow love, not fear, to unfold.

The orders might exert impacts like the power of a gale-force wind or just a tiny slight breeze across your cheek, which nonetheless makes you stop and feel intently. And, just as my dog drops his ball when winds (and scents) pick up, his whole attention moving from more surface matters to the deeper, primal tug of the hunt, so do these forces arrest us. Can we pick up their scent?

Ordering Forces – Mini-Audit

Now, bring to your mind and heart a system you belong to that seems to be avoiding reality and getting stuck, even if you and its members are encouraging well-meaning attempts at positive relational contact and change. The system could be a work team, a volunteer community, an entire institution, a professional association, or a family. Do you ever encounter (or delicately whiff) any of these visible signs? (Table 4.1).

Table 4.1   Ordering Forces Mini-Audit

Belonging	Some people feel more 'in' than others creating insecurity; there are split loyalties between this system and another, causing tension and feelings of guilt; something or someone seems to have been or is being excluded; strong identities are fiercely guarded; competing beliefs and ideologies are creating division and polarisation.
Time	A reluctance to face into future realities; major events or people or upsets from the past are being ignored or disrespected; unclear or troubling founding energy; who came before and who came after (like length of service in a company, or sibling order in a family) is not made visible, recognised and appropriately 'weighted'; no one mentions present tensions.
Place	Unclear sense of role and place within the system and in relation to each other; sense of competence is draining away; people are taking up tasks that are not theirs to do; leadership feels faint and unstable; some people feel 'bigger' than they should be; little attendance to how this system fits within wider contexts.
Exchange	People feel they are putting in more than they are taking out; strong feelings of guilt and innocence, owing something or being owed; little gratitude and acknowledgement of contribution; over-giving creating weakness, dependency and even kick back among the receivers; benefits of this system's life are mentioned but never the costs, what it asks of you.

Do you notice any of these symptoms in the system you have in mind?

- Did the audit help you unconceal some truths about what is being, yet hidden?
- How was it to have pondered on these symptoms and registered some system truths?
- Contemplate the list again. What are the two to three realities that ring out as most true?
- How are these uppermost realities showing up in the life of the system you wish change for?
- And what are their impacts – both troubling and what are they preserving? (All these orders are in some way born out of love and loyalty.)

The *Still Moving Field Guide: Change Vitality at Your Fingertips* describes these four Ordering Forces in detail.[4] My task is not to repeat those descriptions here but, within the context of this book - catalysing change in a polarised world - show how each order contains a *tricky system truth*, an awkward reality that needs facing if we wish to unlock change and movement in the communities dear to us.

As I describe these system truths, note what you recognise and where you feel moved – these responses might be the soul of your system asking for your attention and courageous action.

Belonging: Tricky System Truth 1 – Change Requires Disloyalty

The need to feel a sense of belonging – being safe and secure – is crucial for people in any system. However, belonging can be an impediment when movement is required as change requires you to both attend to its needs and the requirement to un-belong to loyalties that no longer serve. The top 12% of effective stories within our change research featured leaders who could do both superbly well – with conscious, constant attention.

Let us start with *be*-longing. Be the system you feel closely identified with a team, company, profession, family, community, your surrounding landscape or the divine realm, we have a primal need to feel safe and secure within these fields of conscience we give our loyalty to, and where we feel we matter. We can relax, find home and in return for this joyful sense of being held, readily sign up to the obligations of what is deemed good or blameworthy within the system's boundaries – its oughts. Systems are advantaged when belonging needs are met as they can count on the cooperation of those with a secure place.

Does Your System Support Belonging?

Be you an institutional leader, parent or community lead, it is essential to tune into these dynamics and pay attention to whether and how your system supports or threatens belonging. You can do this by ensuring that all voices are heard and recognised, giving attention to including more people in matters where they can contribute, making connections to colleagues and members across your system, and seeing that nothing or no one is excluded. Whereas belonging is guaranteed within family systems (even with forced adoptions or estrangements, one never truly, psychically leaves one's birth family), the right to belong is conditional in organisational systems, dependent on one's performance and contribution. If departures are necessary from these settings, they must be handled carefully. Acknowledgement of past contributions needs to be given so that people can genuinely leave and people staying are free to move ahead.

Within complex systems of any nature, we have multiple allegiances that start to bring a sense of disloyalty when we spend too much time within one system of belonging at the expense of others. Ever felt guilty when you went to your in-laws for Christmas, and not to your own family? Have you ever felt torn between spending time at work, and being with friends? How about when you felt more loyal to your profession, such as engineering, than to the company that employs you, and you felt uncomfortable when you had to call out a major technical fault that negatively impacted your employer's share price? What field of conscience took top place then? What and to whom were you most loyal?

Having divided loyalties can make us feel unstable as we veer between feelings of guilt towards one conscience group and innocence towards another – I can feel unsettled about my adopted family when I am with my birth family, and vice versa. Maybe faith-led loyalties rub up with your attachments in the day-to-day secular world; while I do cherish all of God's kingdom, my deeply buried loyalty to England where I grew up still finds me determinedly, yet guiltily, eradicating weeds from my lawn as I seek that perfect green grass. However, what is most important to enable ease (and hence movement capacity) within systems is that the reality of these multiple and competing belonging needs are named, so that any hidden tensions or truths can become unconcealed and the uncomfortable feelings associated with disloyalty lessened. Effective system leaders make these competing loyalties clear and discussable so that multiple belonging needs are not compromised.

Change Requires Un-belonging

In significant change, though, we will need to go further as *excessive belonging impedes new futures* – strong loyalties to identities, beliefs and ways of being may no longer suit changing landscapes. In these contexts, we cannot balance between divided loyalties; we will most likely need to either detach from loyalties that no longer serve us or demote a loyalty to a subservient place within a wider system's loyalties. And these loyalties' shifts will feel extraordinarily hard as all change, systemically, is an act of betrayal to what came before. Successful change leaders, therefore, pay significant attention to not only *belonging* and helping people feel secure, but also to the counter-intuitive move to help people *un*-belong to previous conscience group identities. This means, in practice, two things:

- *Building others' capacity to detach from past loyalties,* such as to a team you now need to reconfigure, to assumptions or projects that no longer have relevance in a changing landscape, to a cherished dream that is no longer possible, to firmly held belief systems, and ways of working.
- *You being able to stand with distance from any strong belief group* in order to allow novel solutions to emerge. Can you find that larger space beyond conscience, right and wrong, and not take sides?

In today's oughty world of polarisation, securing un-belonging to a hotly defended loyalty group to create a bigger unitary field for collaborative change, becomes a significant challenge. The great risk I now see of strong belonging attachments, especially to political and other ideological groups, is that of *othering*. We attack and denigrate those (stupid enough) to belong to groups we do not identify with. However, courageous leadership means helping people see their oughts and partial stories for what they are – laminated realities, and to face the costs and consequences of standing fixedly within one's conscience field. Be it political partisanship, religious divides, or wars of cultural ideology, rigid loyalties and excessive *truth-as-correctness* stances are creating deadlock in our efforts to build the societies we wish for.

Learning to Un-belong Is Not About Being Neutral

So, what is the leadership capacity required? In our research, we saw outstanding change leaders able to guide their teams to new futures by sensitively yet firmly unhooking them from their attachments to existing structures, beliefs, charismatic leaders, social identities, and ways of working, *while resisting any temptation to side with points of view they used to hold dear themselves* – which at times felt as strong as betrayal to their colleagues or friends.

Just in this week's US presidential election, I surprised myself. Through writing this book and immersing myself more deeply in what it takes to be truly with *what is* rather than how we imagine things *ought* to be, I found myself at ease with the Republican Donald Trump's winning election result – despite my inherent allegiance to a liberal, global world order and to a form of leadership that does not intentionally falsify the truth, hold 'strong man' authoritarian tendencies, disrespect institutions and denigrate fellow human beings.

In a team meeting, this stance enabled me to step outside of a polarity my two colleagues were caught up in, one fiercely for Trump and one against. I could stand in a place that helped them see that their gripped beliefs – either that Trump has no shadow or that Trump is a neo-Nazo – were not allowing them to remain in contact with each other. Could they understand both why he won, and why his win was leaving a large part of the world in sadness and fear? Both truths exist and must be held in our sights to move forward with ease.

This meta stance is not an easy path to take; I also found myself trembling when I did not get caught up in some of my friends' despairing WhatsApp messages, as, internally, I felt guilty that I was betraying my political beliefs (and risking my relationship with them). But to attend to un-belonging requirements and allow all to exist, we need to get acquainted with guilt and standing alone. This is no lazy cop-out of failing to stand for what we believe in, *if we believe that what we must stand for is not about being right, but about creating spaces for all to see their oughts, the costs and consequences these carry, and through this truth as unconcealing, create greater ease and relational contact to find new, together paths.*

When I feel the pressure to 'take sides', *this* is the belief that keeps me from tipping into my oughts: it's not about being wishy-washy neutral, but the far more challenging stance to hold everything in my heart.

From our research,[5] we found four leadership strategies deployed for attending to this tricky system truth of the need to create un-belonging (quotes are extracts from our research transcripts):

- *Be mindful of our own emotions.* When making tough, disruptive decisions, successful leaders take the time to look inside themselves and notice any bitterness or sadness they feel when their sense of belonging is threatened. This enables them to move from reactive impulse ('I'm betraying my people's trust!') to an intentional and creative response ('This is what I know is needed to ensure our future').
- *With insight and respect, identify what people are trying to preserve, and why.* Go to the pain and cost of what giving up current belonging needs will bring to people ('You guys have been doing fantastic work, but is this current team construct right for what we need to do in the future and rather than saying, don't break us up, why don't we have a conversation about why you feel uncomfortable about being broken up?').
- *Lead difficult conversations.* Explore discomfort through truth-telling ('And I spent an awful lot of time just listening and avoiding any urge to be defensive at all. It was just about information-collecting, which helped a lot, because people started to realise, at least somebody's listening').
- *Consider the price and prize of change.* What's to be lost with this *un*-belonging move, but what's the more significant reward? Both need to be named and aired. (Recall the Room 101 story in the last chapter about giving up pet projects to focus on new future priorities? A good example of how we need to pay as much respectful attention to un-belongings and endings as we do to forging new futures.)

Our research found that Belonging was the order most significantly correlated with change success. That did not surprise me: movement in stuck systems will be impossible without attending to this primal need we have to be loyal to our belonging fields (and their accompanying oughts).

If you ticked any of Belonging's visible signs in the audit above, pause now and reflect on the system in mind where you long for greater ease and movement.

⇒ What fresh insights into its realities have you discovered? How might you name this noticing and invite others into the exploration?

While our research showed that Belonging was the order most correlated with change success, the other three were also significantly so. They are four interlocking tributaries running deep through the landscapes of our systems.

Time: Tricky System Truth 2 – No New Futures Are Possible Unless the Past Has Been Fully and Respectfully Dealt with

We tend to focus in change on the future vision, the desired state, and can spend a lot of time imagining and seeking this. However, as this book shows, change starts with acknowledging present reality, and, in particular, including and honouring all the past history that has made today possible, whatever its cost and shadow.

All life is governed by time – the impact of unalterable past events, the bequeathing legacy of a system's founding energy and the joyous anticipation or fear of what is coming our way, the future imperatives. All these impacts exert a gravitational pull on the present moment in subtle and often invisible ways. (I can sit writing this book both resourced by my career and still questioning as an adoptee if any of this is worthy; I can both tremble – and find joy, at the thought of this manuscript's deadline and book publication.)

The present moment is where the past arrives and the future begins; it is an incredibly potent and pivotal place. We stand embodied within the vivid and infinite life of the universe, deriving our lives from the societies we both belong to and come from. The social philosopher Norbert Elias wrote, 'The individual actually grows out of a network of people existing before him into a network he helps to form. The individual person is not a beginning and his relations to other people have no beginnings'.[6] So wrote Schrödinger, 'No self is of itself alone... The "I" is chained to ancestry by many factors... .This is not mere allegory but an eternal memory'.[7]

Flow Is Arrested When the Past Is Denied

Everything is through time, and we just in it. Yet, while we can be a quietly powerful node in this ongoing flowing network of life, a pivotal bead in the long necklace of eternal memory, we stunt this trajectory and arrest the ease of future movement if the past is denied. How do we stand within our line of time? What does it mean to have a responsibility to those who existed before us? Are our ancestral chains a blessing, or a curse? The more we diminish and disrespect what comes before, the more likely we are to carry forward its troubling energy. The more we can give it an acknowledged place, the freer we are to create a new story.

In times of change, we can find ourselves denigrating the past. How often have you seen new leaders come into a system with a bright, shiny vision and a judgemental attitude towards what has gone before? Let us wipe the slate clean!

I was once coaching an executive team who felt that they, and only they, could now bring the necessary change to their company, and in their conversations, were speaking quite disrespectfully of two of their predecessors. Past peers of these two individuals were still on the team, and you could sense how this disrespect unsettled them, while they still nervously wished to join their new colleagues' bravado. Can you imagine what it might have felt like to be in their shoes, oscillating between the need to both belong and un-belong, to be loyal and disloyal?

By my calling out the systemic requirement to have total respect for *all* that came before this team – including how it *was*, not how it *ought* to have been – I invited them to look on these two individuals with gratitude, and, even if they had made some missteps, genuinely see how, in their shoes, they could not have done anything better at the time. Could they become fortunate for the learning gift bequeathed, and imagine saying to these two leaders, 'You were exactly my "right" predecessors'? Including and valuing all that came before now made the new leaders the 'right size' (a little smaller in the eternal memory of time), and you could sense how the broader system around this team also started to relax and be up for change, once their past leaders were no longer spoken so mockingly of.

Exclusion Only Passes Things on

In today's oughty 'cancel culture' world, giving a respectful place to the past is particularly challenging. Consider the troubling role of past empires from countries such as the United Kingdom, Spain and the Netherlands. As I have said, troubling elements that do not get seen or included from the past get silently passed on, acting as a handbrake on new futures (often someone, or a group in the present, unconsciously needs to follow their story and stay entangled in the difficulty). The past contains hard-won wisdom that should not be disregarded. What stands behind us – *all* that stands behind us, including the events or people we would rather not bring to mind or talk about – has made today possible. This is just a simple, system truth. Fact. Reality. Acknowledging this truth can sometimes be extraordinarily painful and create feelings of anger, guilt, or shame (be that at the family, organisation or national level). Still, the reality of time must be acknowledged.

From Trash to Compost

Acknowledging the is-ness of the past does not mean sugar-coating history but bringing a different quality of attention to that which we can so easily rubbish or exclude – a quality that re-frames difficulty, what is troubling us, as a resource. I once worked with a leadership team that was going through a period of significant industry turmoil. They had had many shots at creating a new vision and strategy for their organisation, but no attempts to define and wish for a different future state seemed to 'grip' them in any new behaviour. Consequentially, the system around them remained anxious and unsure – until a moment when the leadership team spent two days together examining the impact of their difficult past in the present moment.

On day one of this retreat, I invited the team members to create a large wall of what I called 'trash'. It was a huge piece of brown paper tacked onto the wall, upon which we stuck up post-it notes of all their past legacy's unsettlements, deficits, fears, and elements they wished to be rid of. On day two, they settled into the meeting room and saw another large piece of brown paper on an adjacent wall. Fully expecting me to write up the 'desired state' on this wall (in other words, to complete a classic 'from -> to' change technique), they were mystified when I wrote up, 'compost', instead. I took them back to the trash they had identified the day before and asked them to take its major themes and explore the question, 'In what way is our inherited legacy a helpful resource for our future?' (Just as I can recycle my garden waste into rich compost.)

This day was a turning point for the team as they learned to look kindlier on the past in the present moment, to tune in more deeply to its role as an enabler, not a disabler and to be able to see emerging from within this past story glimpses of the emerging future (a financial misstep became a newly respectful regulatory connection, a troubling team a prophetic alert to what their customers needed differently from their company). The past can be released once it has been fully seen and integrated. The leadership team left the experience stronger, resolved and clearer about the next step for their organisation. Embracing and honouring the reality of what was now, rather than striving for it to be something else, also created more confidence and ease within the teams in the system around them, who felt less lambasted.

I am not saying here that vision has no place. Imagining new futures is essential in change as it gives direction. However, the past in the present moment first needs to be looked at, honoured and given an appropriate place. Otherwise, systems will not be at ease. This acknowledgement of what *already is and has been before* can be a more significant catalyst for effecting change for all the reasons set out in the last chapter: we can only move from solid ground; the brain relaxes (and becomes more creative) with truth; systems need to be whole and will kick back at you if any part of it, including its past, is disparaged and split off; joining together to acknowledge what is truly the case builds a 'we' – and we need this collective pull energy for change to flow with greater ease and sustainability.

If you checked any of the symptoms of Time in the audit above, pause now and reflect on the system you have in mind and deep in your heart.

⇒ Have you had fresh insight on some realities about the order of Time that are most troubling this system, yet are not being acknowledged? How might you approach an activity to disclose, unconceal this truth – one that invites you and others to *fully feel* time's impact? What might that ask of you, and others?

Place: Tricky System Truth 3 – When We Are Not in the Right Place, Change Cannot Flow

Systems are unstable when elements within them do not establish an appropriate hierarchy of place and function. Only when the various competing hierarchies in any group or system are acknowledged, can everyone find their right place to do their jobs properly, enabling flow and movement.

In the living world, we see how all systems are structured into hierarchies: cells, tissues, organs; proteins, atoms, molecules; worker bees, drones and queen bees; populations, communities, ecosystems, and biospheres. The multiple interdependent elements within these complex systems each have their rightful place. As I have said earlier, nature is never wasteful. Within our human systems, even when we know that we have a valid and secure right to belong in a system, where do we take up our place in relation to others, and the system's purpose? Social harmony, like in the living world, requires fair and just hierarchies. When these are established, movement becomes possible.

Hierarchy Can Be Both Formal and Informal

Typical human hierarchies include dominance – physical strength, wealth and inherited class structures; prestige – who is most learned, feted and published; ideology – belief systems claiming differentiated social strata. Within institutional structures such as governments, organised religions and the military, there are visible formal hierarchies of roles and rank – chains of command that bind us to each other. In corporate workplaces and professional associations, we see how role hierarchies are driven by length of service, reputation and professional competence attainment (and some might say, 'who knows who'). Our families have generations, age and sibling order of birth (and, in some societies and cultural traditions, gender). We often exist within a set of nested and competing hierarchies. I might be the youngest and have the shortest length of time in an organisation, yet given professional competence attainment, I am the most senior in 'rank' and role.

Outside of these formal and visible hierarchies, systems can also have more subtle yet no less influential differentiating orders of place. Just take who is helping whom in a situation. Has anyone done any coaching and discovered how power imbalances might start seeping into the relationship? Who are the spenders and the earners on your team – are there any subtle distinctions and orders of place based on who has won the most or least client business within a consulting firm? I once invited a leadership team to play with their various hierarchical places, creating multiple 'lines' of who was 'most important/bigger' in the team to who was 'least important/smaller', and they identified all kinds of wonderful dimensions to order their places (including, who brought the best coffee into the work canteen).

Here's the point. Systems are strengthened and able to move into different futures when place and hierarchy are attended to. Recall my Open Space story at the start of this chapter. This was an example of a group with a beautiful ideal to have a self-organising community, yet ignoring the underlying (being, yet hidden) system requirement for lines of leadership to be established – however subtle and fluid. In this case, the learning community did not establish one formal hierarchy. Instead, it mapped out all the community role requirements for leadership (communications, research, new membership growth). People chose to take their place and give of their time within these expertise areas (and they did this somatically by literally standing in the room in various locations to make the hierarchy visibly authorised and fully embodied and felt).

System Entanglement

Sometimes, hierarchies are misplaced and inappropriate, leading to 'system entanglement'. This often happens in change processes where line leaders ask a 'change team' to oversee a transformation and, at times, appoint a 'Head of Transformation'. This team then gets 'too big' in system terms and starts to front all the key decisions and communications with the organisation, just when it should be the line leaders owning the difficulty of the change for their people and stepping into the fray themselves. Within family systems, it can often be the case that elder children take on the role of parenting and protecting their siblings when either parents are unable or unwilling to step fully into their adult place. Maybe you have had experience being a stepparent or stepchild and felt the awkwardness of finding and naming one's place relative to each other, and the family member(s) that came before.

Likewise, in the world of work, mergers and restructuring can bring people together into awkward new groupings where the original hierarchies are (necessarily) overridden, but with often disruptive results until everyone's earlier and current roles are acknowledged and adjusted. Truth is frequently obscured in these situations, as what is in reality an acquisition or takeover is called a 'merger', and business benefits cannot fully flow until these hierarchical realities are named.

When the reality of place is not attended to, be it more formal and visible or informal and subtle, systems are not at ease. It's intriguing how the field of systems operates – these hidden Ordering Forces are there whether we like them or not. The task is to make them visible and agree *to* them, even if we do not agree *with* them. Who is in charge, and who is in support? Who has more weight, and who has less?

Can We Agree to, If Not with, Our Place?

I once asked an executive team to stand and order themselves around their CEO according to how the team felt like it was currently operating – who was closest, who was furthest from the CEO, who was looking at whom and what was the distance between them. The exercise revealed that the head of Strategy (who pressed himself closely to the right of the CEO) had become 'too big' in the team and was creating tension with the Vice Presidents of the Divisions. In organisational systems, role size carries more weight than the individual, and it was not until the head of Strategy could stand more humbly in the place for a support role that everyone else on the team could relax and take up their strength.

Sometimes, place can make itself visible in the most natural of ways. Just invite a team to come into the room, sit in a circle of chairs, and notice who sits where. When I was facilitating a leadership programme with a group from one institution, they all arrived with their cups of coffee and sat down. Circles are meant to convey equality. Well, it turned out that the four most senior leaders in the room in rank had sat to my left, in their order of role size. Systems naturally find their hierarchy. The group chuckled when this was seen and named. It was hard for one of these leaders to say that he was 'number four' in this institution, but, modesty aside, once he could say that he was number four, clearly and boldly, the group all got strengthened by his acknowledging his system place.

Let us step into the reality of place bravely and wisely. Understand the relative sizes you are in the systems you belong to and how that might either bring ease or tension (my birth role gives me sibling number one place in that family system, yet in my adopted family I am number three, and getting these natural and created hierarchies muddled is not healthy for anyone). Make the topic of place discussable in your teams. Check in with it regularly, as roles and places can be fluid in dynamic contexts. And try to do so less via cognitive discussions as by *felt* experience (these orders are felt far more exquisitely in our bodies than in our brains) – inquire how people are affected emotionally by where they are placed within the system, how their sense of place is showing up for them somatically. More on the role of emotions and body wisdom to uncover truth and enable movement in Chapter 7, but I vividly recall one executive I once worked with initiating a restructuring in his company based primarily on him registering his shifting back pain.

But do pay attention to the order of Place if you wish your system to feel secure and accountable and the right size in relation to the wider systems in which it is placed. If you are a leader of a powerful institution, consider your role within it and its place in society in a way that fully acknowledges the stakeholders and communities you serve. I believe we see such a lack of trust in our fabled institutions today (governmental, medical, media, or religious) because they have become 'too big' and out of touch with society.

Reflect on Hammarskjöld's observation, 'everything is and we just in it'.

If you ticked any of the Place symptoms in the audit above, do you have any fresh insights about this deep force that orders so much of our reality?

⇒ Maybe you have been experiencing feeling 'out of place' somewhere? What clues might this feeling give about the forces at play in your system that require registering, and not solving? (So much of systems work is about simply acknowledging the truth of what is, enabling at-easeness, rather than 'fixing' things that are sometimes too complex or bigger-than-us to resolve.)

⇒ Do you have any ideas about an activity you'd like to try out, or a conversation that is needed within the system you most dearly wish change for?

Exchange: Tricky System Truth 4 – All Change Comes with a Price Tag

The whole universe reverberates in exchange, a dynamic equilibrium between what is given and what is taken, owed and owing. Exchange sustains life and keeps it in balance. An imbalance in exchange is, therefore, essential for change and movement, which means there are always those who gain and those who pay the price. It is, therefore, a truth, not yet universally acknowledged, that change does not come for free.

I can marvel at how chemical reactions and the laws of thermodynamics show how energy is always in exchange between a system and its surroundings, and in the living world, we see all organisms exchanging oxygen and carbon dioxide between themselves and their environments. As a faith believer, I rejoice in the simplicity of offering God the gift of my life and my worship in return for His love and grace. Exchange holds our life and the universe together, as a whole.

In human systems, maintaining a dynamic balance between what is given and what is received or returned builds belonging, trust, community, and creativity. The disciplines of anthropology and archaeology have uncovered vast bartering systems among our ancestors in prehistoric society, where trade was conducted across cultures without any need for currency. Interestingly, there were always some mechanisms for lines of credit. People were inherently bound to each other when goods were owed.

And so today. The gentle breeze of exchange across your cheek can be as simple as knowing that you owe somebody an email reply, or a return invitation to a social get-together. Until that 'debt' is paid back, you are still bound to that person. And so, these delicate ping-pong exchanges keep us bound to each other. Change can disrupt these oscillating balances of exchange, and when there is imbalance and felt advantage of one group or person over another, *and this is not named*, people will feel out of sorts and not give of their best.

Naming Any Imbalance of Exchange Creates Ease and Releases Movement

I once was invited into an organisation embarking on a significant change that had become full of unease and disgruntlement. The leaders' default response to this situation had been to ask the communications department to 'up their game' in issuing 'more positive' messaging about the impending change, as people *ought* by now to have bought into the case for change.

I invited them to desist from that for the time being, and instead ran a day's session with the leadership team in which they completed a 'Return on Change' (RoChg) exercise. Again, a large piece of paper was tacked onto the wall, this time with a horizontal line across the middle. Above the line, the team listed all the *benefits* of the change – for their shareholders, customers and staff. This was easy to do, and the team got very enthusiastic. In the afternoon, I asked them, beneath the line, to identify all the *costs* that the change would incur. Initially, this became an exercise of listing the direct costs such as consultancy fees, a new IT platform and training programmes. So far, so good. I then invited them to identify all the indirect costs - the impact on the workplace, energy levels, status and autonomy – all the costs to people's lives and livelihoods that to this point had not been named.

The room became quiet, and an awkward atmosphere descended. I took them further and asked about the costs already being played out *within this team* concerning the change. How was it feeling, *for them?* What was being gained, and what was being lost, received and given? What truths about the cost of this change were being, yet hidden between them? (When you can detect and disclose the orders within your team, you can tune into the system around you with greater accuracy and compassion.)

Slowly but surely, the team opened up to each other about how one function had now become 'more important' than another, receiving more significant capital investment at the expense of others. They gain, and others lose. (At this point, I asked them to stand up in two lines facing each other, those who were to receive more and those who were to receive less investment, inviting them to, in silence, fully take in how this reality was being experienced.) Next, the head of Human Resources gingerly stated his view that his teams were taking on a disproportionate burden in the change effort; they had to deal with the human dynamics and employee relations demands of a big restructuring exercise while at the same time handling their own role changes. The demands on their time and energy were felt to be greater than those carried by the business units. (At this point, I invited the HR Director to stand in front of all his colleagues, who, also standing, looked at their colleague, and I gave them the sentence, 'Thank you, dear colleague, for carrying the load that is currently greater than mine'.)

The afternoon continued in this fashion, identifying and naming all the felt imbalances. At its conclusion, this leadership team was in a far more honest (and full-hearted) place with each other and with their organisation about the costs that their planned change was creating. After this meeting, they went into their system and held conversations with their people, and the price and the prize of change were openly put on the table. At a subsequent date, when I checked back in with this team, they reported on how profoundly settling this reality-naming and acknowledgement had been both to them and their organisation. The distress the system was feeling was not going without recognition or value. From these truth encounter moments, they felt that their teams were more able to get on with the change. The exchange imbalance did not disappear, but naming *what is* had released movement.

What Leaders Can Do to Address the Truth of Exchange Imbalance

All change comes with a price tag. And yet, while this fundamental system truth stands, I often see leaders overestimating the benefits at the expense (if not denial) of the cost. This emphasis on the gain rather than the pain of change is understandable if you are trying to take people with you – you do not want to freak people out (or lose votes if you are a politician campaigning for election). However, there is a fine line between garnering motivation and commitment, and the disingenuous avoidance of disturbance or unpopularity. While our instinct is to squirm and shy away from this tricky system truth, trained as we can be in concealing the sting in the tail, the deep soul of our teams, communities, families and institutions yearns for us to be otherwise.

Can we learn how not to shy away from naming exchange reality, and do two things: make the imbalance visible and recognised (what will be gained and given, by whom), and take action to rebalance it to ease the sense of loss – which, even if we cannot materially right the imbalance, might be as simple as saying, 'You are paying the price for the institution/team/ community to gain, thank you'. Once the truth of exchange imbalance is disclosed and the price of change is named, change will flow with far greater ease.

If you ticked any of the visible signs of Exchange in the audit above, what are you now taking away about truth pursuit in systems?

⇒ Can you bring to mind the system you care about, and, intuitively, sense the slight breeze on your cheek, or tremor in your heart, about what is being owed by you to another, or from another to you?

⇒ Can you imagine how you might dare to name the Exchange dynamics underlying any unsettlement? What might be both the prize (ease with truth) and price (your anxiety, some relational upset) of doing this, and can you bear that price?

Change Approaches That Reveal and Shift System Realities

I have now described and illustrated four profound system truths that require our keen attention if we wish for greater ease and flow in our lives and movement in our communities and workplaces: addressing both belonging and un-belonging needs; honouring the past as a deep resource; ensuring we are all in the right place to give of our best; and attending to any felt imbalance between what is given and what is taken.

These truths are *what* are to be gazed into as you contemplate a system's *les espaces infinis*. Given that the orders per se are invisible, being yet hidden, we need to up our perceptive power to recognise them. One thing is for sure: if our oughts are clouding our lenses, this task will be made more challenging – we have to be phenomenologically impeccable to discern their presence and impacts (staying in description and not judgement, putting aside personal reactivity and interpretation, staying in a witness not a 'prodding' position).

I will describe in depth in the next chapter the personal skills required. Before leaving this one, I wish to highlight *at the system level* how to go about change in a way that can surface and attend to these deep realities and lubricate the whole system to be at ease with truth. By now, you might already have picked up clues from my stories – such as using approaches that summon the emotional and somatic, as much, if not more than, the cognitive knowing realm. Pause a while. Can you jot down a few defining features that seem to be present – how were the interventions in these stories approached?

We Call Forth the System by Our Approach

How we approach change fundamentally determines where we end up – our means of intervention are vital as they affect and create the field in which we work. If we prod and cajole, we are likely to get dependent compliance. If we launch many initiatives, we will likely get a busy and weary team or organisation. If we more loosely set a direction then sit and wait, we will likely get initiative. If we implement rich feedback loops across the system, we activate curiosity and pace. Do you (and your colleagues) consciously and intentionally choose a change approach that will summon what you most wish for?

In the Introduction chapter, I talked about my early-career realisation that so much of what we do in 'change management' is doing change *to* a system. We implement change in an imposed way according to how we believe it *ought* to be done (unfreeze, change, refreeze). On the other hand, if we can approach change in the more messy and dynamic ways in which movement naturally occurs, the *is-ness* of change in all living complex systems (freeze, adjust, unfreeze), we will encounter less stickiness and achieve more lasting, sustainable outcomes. *The critical task is to help a system be able to see itself, such that it can do its 'own changing'.*

With over three decades of this realisation under my belt, bolstered by applied application and our Still Moving research, here is a summation of what enables us to design and implement a change approach that allows people to see deeply into the dynamics of the system they belong to, and from that place of acknowledgement, release movement to a new place.

Build Attentional Capacity

Just as our minds select certain factors from reality we wish to see, so do whole systems create representations, not manifestations of truth. You only need to have sat in endless PowerPoint presentations to know at some level that what you see on the slides is just a partial abstraction of the matter being presented, not *actually* its case (classic left hemisphere attention, as McGilchrist would say).

If contacting reality is the starting point for change, and that reality is fundamentally shaped by how we choose to see it – our very own activity – then we need to design a change approach that helps a system pay attention to how it pays attention. Recall that Heidegger stated how an open, patient, and loving receptivity is an essential attentional skill for truth as unconcealing. McGilchrist's call to action would be whole picture, open-minded, complexity-embracing, right hemisphere brain attention. My own anthropological stance when seeking system awareness is rooted in context valuing, ground-truth seeking and detached curiosity. Do our change approaches encourage people to value these ways of taking in the world?

In all my experience in the change field, here are the elements I have seen that best enable players in a system to 'see' their system realities and hence offer the possibility for change:

- *Encourage people to go 'out into the field'* and witness first-hand the living reality of your system, and those that your system interfaces with (such as customers, suppliers, partners, etc.). To get the accurate, lived picture, nothing beats venturing out of your location's walls and going to the places in your organisation or community and its wider context where the key tensions and opportunities for movement lie. Moreover, you then carry these stories and embodied knowing more fully into all your communications, building authentic change advocacy and narrative.
  Examples: running 'foraging' activities for people within your system to go out of their organisation and visit other institutions and places which they feel hold clues to their future; having senior leaders regularly take their teams out for customer immersion experiences with their frontline staff.
- *Require individuals and the whole system to look inside themselves,* become curious about their inner state (their thoughts, feelings, sensations, impulses at the individual level, or factors such as organisational climate

at the system level), value this data and give one's *quality of being* a place in all interaction. Change approaches rarely give this inner attention a rightful place – too much irrelevant navel gazing! Yet, at the personal level, one's inner state is valuable data about the rest of the system (see more in Chapter 7 on emotions), especially at leadership levels where you will be carrying the projections of the system internally (your frustrations, joys, sadnesses, irritations are not just about you but valuable cultural signs). At the system level, if your team/organisation/community has a certain 'mood' right now, it is as likely to be due to what it is picking up about the broader context as a consequence of the individual players within it. Listening inward helps you see the true nature of what is around you more clearly.

Examples: building in dedicated time at the start and end of team encounters for each individual to 'check in' and 'check out' with each other as to how they are feeling/being right now; incorporating mindfulness training into leadership development programmes; conducting regular 'pulse checks' within your organisation about the internal system climate and mood.

- *Incorporate the right hemisphere and phenomenological modes of attention.* Suppose we believe McGilchrist's core proposition that the right hemisphere of our brain is in closest contact with reality (and I, for one, do). In that case, for systems to encounter truth, we must build in learning, development and communication processes that draw out our imagination, feelings and intuition as much as our logic and reason. Truth is mediated and sustainably held in story, music, drama, metaphor and imagery in which both the content *and* the process carry an affective, transformational[8] charge. Can change processes value, if not prioritise, this way of encountering *what is*?

Examples: using visual capture and/or poetry as a means to record meetings and important conversations; using experiential approaches such as simulations and systemic constellations to explore reality and try out new modes of being and operating (so different from behavioural oughts 'new ways of working' statements).

- *Build people's capacity to see the parts and the whole of the system,* and how they are interconnected. Julian of Norwich, the fourteenth-century mystic and theologian (of whom more in the next chapter), famously saw God in a single small hazelnut shell[9] – a single, powerful moment of gestalt. We can encounter the truth of a whole system within one of its parts; each part contains a clue to the whole (see snowflakes as fractals of the snowstorm, one tree's inner rings as a smaller version of the whole forest). Therefore, change processes in our human communities need both big-picture and ground-level thinking; I should correct myself... .it is not 'both...and...', but an attentional capacity that sees the ground level *in* the big picture and vice versa. To see systems, you need to go up and down.

- What processes can you put in place that helps the parts see the whole, and the whole, the parts?

  Examples: interactive, big-picture maps that visualise the essence of an entire change process are created, communicated and explored in each part of an organisation undergoing change; setting up a team that is a cross-section of your system to act as a 'visible signs group' who tune into day to day events, examine them as a symptom of the wider change process, and regularly feedback their stories to the senior leadership team or whoever is steering the change at the level of the whole; creating 'learning histories' of a change journey in which groups representing various parts of the system contribute their stories and perspectives on reality as it unfolds into one 'document' that is then sent out to everyone allowing fulsome reality to be seen (such truth-compiling can be challenging to take in...).

Take a moment to reflect

⇒ How do your attempts at approaching movement in your system give primary attention to how its members pay attention and to the mechanisms through which reality is sought? How are you helping your whole system to see itself? Through both reaching outwards and turning inwards? Do your methods incorporate, indeed, give primacy to right hemisphere attention compared to left hemisphere attention? And how about 'beneath the chin' attention modes, placing value on affective, somatic, phenomenological ways of knowing (one client we worked with once said, 'Oh yes, Still Moving, that's all the powerful "stand-y up-y" approaches to change!')?

Encourage Parrhesia

As no change comes without a price, we need to create safe spaces within the process for difficulty to be voiced – making disturbance your friend. How can your change approach incorporate dedicated opportunities for dialogue where people can speak truth and say difficult things, especially to those 'in power'. The irony about becoming more senior in a system is two-fold: first, you become more divorced from day-to-day reality and how results are produced, and second, people will fear bringing you uncomfortable truths. Both these realities potentially render you ineffective at the helm.

Truth pursuit, therefore, needs to be openly invited and visibly encouraged. And not just by seeking truth as correctness ('how are our numbers doing?') but also truth as unconcealment ('what is going on, beneath the surface, that we cannot see or talk about yet need to?'). Here's how I have seen the encouragement of parrhesia being effectively implemented:

- *Encourage the voice of the periphery, the on-the-ground or the marginalised.* Most innovations in living systems happen at their edge and not their centre, as signals about changing contexts are most keenly seen where the system meets the external habitat. So, systems that implement change approaches that build in open, frank and rapid feedback loops between periphery and centre, the on-the-ground and the hierarchy, have a greater chance of adaptation. Secondly, it is essential to get to the voices or opinions that a system is excluding, as what we deny, marginalise or split off often includes what we need to reintegrate for movement to occur. What we wish not to see or hear carries valuable data about the fears and uncertainties that must be faced to embark on improvement and change. Just imagine if the UK's Post Office senior leaders had inquired of their advisors as to why their frontline staff's pleas were being batted away, and rather than rewarding these advisors for silencing inconvenient voices, have explicitly asked them to give these voices centre stage attention.
  Examples: bring in 'wild card' participants into leadership meetings, those not the most senior in the system but with the eyes and ears to the external contexts, and give them a voice in discussions and decision-making; encourage leaders to ask questions such as 'Whose voices are we excluding in this change and why?', 'Who would we least like to hear from right now about the way forward and, rather than ignore them, hear from them?'; set up 'shadow boards' or 'citizens assemblies' to create parallel sense-making fora to the formal hierarchy.
- *Build in open-ended spaces for dialogue.* Frank, honest conversations about reality need encouragement and dedicated space. Otherwise, people might feel that they will be 'holding things up' or 'becoming awkward so-and-so's' if they voice something awkward and challenging to hear. So, effective reality-fuelled change processes contain intentional spaces to enable people to speak, hear and process tough truths; once difficulty and reality are voiced, the catharsis allows for appropriate action to be taken, people feel listened to, and a virtuous circle of trust and truth-telling builds.
  Examples: open-ended 'just talk' sessions set up each month, at which any system member can show up and take the risk to openly share feedback about awkward system truths; leaders venturing out into their systems to hold free format 'town hall' style conversations with their people.
- *Train leaders in the skill of psychological containment.* To accompany the invitation to frank speech, it is vital to prepare the receivers to fully hear and acknowledge what comes their way, as otherwise, the atmosphere

will not have the psychological safety and trust required for voicing truth. Psychological containment is the management and channelling of anxiety towards productive outcomes. More on this in the next chapter, but at the change approach level, investment must be put aside to develop the stature and skills of change leaders to step out of defensive reactivity and openly invite and be comfortable with difficulty and not needing to know all the answers.

Examples: 'fierce conversations' skills training; leadership coaching in the neuroscience of good dialogue and anxiety management.

Take a moment to reflect

⇒ How do your attempts at approaching change build in the mechanisms for parrhesia? If there is a reluctance to go towards frank public speech, what might you/your system fear most in this exclusion? What is the valuable, preserving loyalty beneath the concealment? How can leaders build the resilience, non-defended distance and maturity required to be open to challenge and uncertainty, while still holding course?

Embrace Emergence

Working with what *is* the case is a very different approach to that which directs a system towards where you *wish* it to be, as the Open Space story at the beginning of this chapter described. Whereas conventional change approaches suggest you have a team (more often the centre or the 'tops') set out a clear vision, plan out a path towards that destination, issue communications to the organisation to get alignment to the vision and path, and then put in place systems and processes to change mindset and behaviour, a change approach that seeks to embrace what is has a very different orientation. Fundamentally, it starts with the premise of not knowing: how can anyone set out the destination in unpredictable contexts? The task is to engage the whole system with the unfolding reality of *what is here now* – an emergent approach. The leader's task is not to direct but to create the conditions within which a system becomes (enjoyably) focussed on dynamic, ongoing sense-making and innovation.

As the world around us is waking up to waves of disruptive and unpredictable change – take the 2007/8 financial crisis, the COVID-19 pandemic, climate change and its devastating impacts on many communities, heightened geopolitical war and conflicts creating mass migration/immigration movements, the tilt away from global collaboration towards local nationalism and the coming wave of artificial intelligence (to name just a few things...), can we evolve our change approaches[10] to become more attuned with this context (and how successful change occurs within the living world of complex adaptive systems)? Less controlled, more open-ended. Less linear, more unfolding and adaptive.

I have spent the last quarter of a century advocating this more *emergent change approach*[11]: within an overall loose intention (not fixed destination), you take in intelligence from the boundaries of your system, allow empowered self-organisation within a set of few 'hard rules' and focus your effort on just a few areas with the highest leverage (the 'ripe issues' in your team or organisation or community that will somehow unlock change at the level of the whole).

Such an approach lives or dies on the supply of ground truth – what is. Emergence is not 'laissez-faire' change but an approach so in tune with lived reality that it will 'fan the flames' of a recognisable movement leading to rapid, novel outcomes. Emergent change is there anyway; it's happening all the time in every corridor, conversation, factory floor, financial market and team meeting – the question is, can you harness it?

Be you a leader of a large institution or nation, a local community movement, or a social change campaigner, take heed. Here are the most salient points of an emergent change approach regarding our topic, that of truth pursuit within systems:

- *Work now and next*. When you implement an emergent change approach, you have no fixed long-term plans or solutions but rather 'know enough' to get the current step forward planned, and maybe a little about the one after that, and then remain open to new data and contextual changes to unfold the changes ahead in an iterative way. When navigating the vast Mississippi River, you can only chart your course from one bend to the next, as by the time you get to the next point, reality might have changed again, and you'd need to throw any longer-term plan out the window - the same with emergent change in dynamically changing contexts.
  Example: rapid prototyping, a change approach that builds a partially finished new product, process, or solution, is then tested with people on the ground, the end users and beneficiaries, and is adapted based on these iterative trials. You do not head for perfection, just what might work now, and then head for what next.
- *Go to the ripest of issues*: systems organise around needs, especially pressing unmet ones. Getting out truthful reality is vital in unlocking emergent change where you head to disturbance before comfort. Agents (people, teams) in the system need to get in contact with and voice the biggest tricky things going on for them (truth as unconcealing that which is being, yet hidden). This data is aggregated, and action is prioritised against that which is causing the most disturbance to the whole system's viability.

Example: a change process designed along the lines of Open Space Technology,[12] the group meeting approach described in this chapter's opening story; setting up a cross-system 'ears and eyes' network within rapidly changing environments that assesses and prioritises risks.

- *The is-ness of volunteers*: emergent change rolls forward with lateral networks of enthusiastic volunteers – as you work with the natural energy of the system. No central hierarchy appoints people to working groups (those who *ought* to be involved), but you extend an open invitation to volunteers to help solve the ripe issues. You join the various nodes of volunteers and task forces into networks so that the parts and the whole are in continuous dialogue. In that way, the whole system stays true to its intention, and you can work now and next in a way that is based on regularly updated field intelligence.

  Example: extending an open invitation to key change events and discussions; social movements that originated in specific neighbourhoods are spread to whole communities (see the remarkable El Salvador volunteer ambulance service, reported by Simon Reeve while filming the BBC programme, The Americas).

Take a moment to reflect

⇒ How does your change approach keep its eyes and ears to the ground, tapping into local intelligence? How does it work with those with energy to solve the pressing significant issues? Are you always asking for reality and truth to be brought to the table? What might your system be avoiding if it approaches change in the more classical, ought-to sense, with a central group planning and controlling what happens, being abstracted from reality, and what is the case?

Systems and the Pursuit of Truth, in Conclusion

Through the human being, the universe has created a mirror to observe itself.

David Bohm[13]

Within our systems, be they here and near (my team) or there and vast (the universe), we are always in the process of creating reality and what we see – we are not separate to *les espaces infinis* that Hammarskjöld writes of. At the same time, evolution has granted us humans the remarkable gift of consciousness – we are aware that we are aware and can stand with distance to observe our systems and how we co-create them. I am drawn to this quote from the great theoretical physicist, David Bohm, as it gives us a clue as to why we conscious humans exist – *to help the world see itself.* That's a significant thought. If self-awareness is the starting point for change, then we humans can be change agents for the world. Smart world, then, for having created us.

Can we take this task seriously? In this chapter, we have explored how to deeply see the reality of systems through four essential lenses: the Ordering Forces of Belonging, Time, Place and Exchange. When we can dive into these pools and see how their souls are always present, influencing the degree to which we feel at ease or stuck, present or not present in our families, teams and communities, strong or dizzy in the face of reality, able to give our all or never quite settle in life, then we can harness their power to release change and movement. They are profound truths, the is-ness of our lives together, wisdom channels that lie deep beneath our oughts, four interlocking mirrors we can hold up to our systems to show what's really there and needs attending to.

How do we do that? We do not change systems by giving them commands. We then explored the important requirement to consciously choose an approach to change that enables a system to see itself – an approach characterised by building attentional capacity, encouraging truth-telling and embracing emergence.

All the above deeply draws on our very personal, individual abilities to be fully in this world, or, to quote Hammarskjöld, with everything in this world. This capability is something we can cultivate and nourish, so let's move into the next chapter to see with greater clarity what this ability is composed of and how we can grow into it.

5

Leading Change From *Is*, the Personal Skills Required

> *And I shall not weep from despair, but simply because I shall be happy in my tears, I shall steep my soul in emotion. I love the sticky leaves in spring, the blue sky – that's all it is. It's not a matter of intellect, or logic, it's loving with one's inside, with one's stomach.*
>
> Ivan Karamazov, from The Brothers Karamazov
> by Fyodor Dostoevsky, Chapter 34

As I heard this excerpt from The Brothers Karamazov on Audible, I had to pull over my car to the side of the road and stop for a while. To be still. To fully take in how and why these words about how to be in life had arrested me so. One month prior, for my 10-hour drive from my flat in London to my home in the Dordogne, I had downloaded Dostoevsky's monumental nineteenth-century classic for the journey – feeling it was a work of literature I *ought* to have read by now.

My *ought*-led literary duty turned into hours of pure *is*-based listening, during which Dostoevsky's words flooded through me. (Einstein is known to have said, 'Dostoevsky gives me more than any scientist', and 'The Brothers Karamazov is the most wonderful book that I have ever laid my hands on'.) And this passage above, where the godly brother, Alyosha, had arrived at the lodgings of his logic-driven, taciturn, and sceptical brother, Ivan, had me erupt into great joy. Ivan had been a cold, distant and critical character to that moment in the story. Now, in this little speech to his brother, his true inner nature burst forth.

How to love *with one's inside*, with one's stomach. When I returned home, I rushed to find the physical book and marked out the passage for inclusion in this book – and this chapter. The reason why the words had arrested me so

From Ought to Is: Catalysing Change and Movement in a Polarised World,
First Edition. Deborah Rowland
© 2025 John Wiley & Sons Ltd. Published 2025 by John Wiley & Sons Ltd.

was not so much my relief that Ivan had at last shown he was a real human being. The primary reason was that Ivan's revelation is at the heart of *Still Moving* leadership, a framework of skills my research has consistently shown is highly correlated with enabling successful change. I could substitute the word *love* with *lead*, and you'd get the message – *it's leading with one's inside.*

Successive rounds of my research have shown that our entire capacity to lead a system to a new place rests on our skill to first turn inward – to the inside of our very being. Whereas the *instinct* is to first focus outward on the changes or movement you wish to make happen – how can I get my team to become more aligned with our new purpose, how do I influence my partner to change his lifestyle, how can I implement agile methodology to shift the behaviours in my organisation to more focus on the customer?

So here is another paradox: outer change starts with inner work. In our research, the most successful change leaders did one thing supremely well: they consciously tuned into and regulated their inner mental, emotional, and somatic response to experience as a precursor to being able to tune into and regulate their outer world. They led with their insides.

As Bohm has said, through the human being, the universe has created a mirror to observe itself. We are porous beings – a tuning fork for the outer world, a Geiger counter for the orders I wrote of in the last chapter, a fractal of our families, work teams, communities and nations. What is experienced inside us is system data, not just our personal bundle of thoughts and emotions, needs and impulses.

⇒ Have you ever used your gut to tune into not just what you had to eat last night but to intuit the mood of what is happening around you? Maybe you walked into a room and felt a knot in your stomach, then sensed a funny atmosphere, and later discovered there had been a major squabble between people in the room before you walked in?

The corollary of this interconnectedness between our insides and the outer world is that if we can then *regulate* what's going on inside of us, we will influence what is happening outside of us too. We both import and shape the systems of which we are a part. If the system works through us, then we can work the system.

⇒ Have you noticed how simply shifting your inner mood can change the climate of the people around you – without you having to *tell* people to do so or bend the situation to your will?

⇒ Maybe you began frustrated with a stuck situation in your team that did not seem to help matters, but by you consciously shifting to becoming curious and empathetic about the reasons why things were stuck and creating space for the stuckness to be welcomed, your team then relaxed and moved forward.

When we can master this capacity – using our inner world as an exquisitely sensitive yet potent pivot for the outer world – change can flow with far less effort and prodding, and with far greater ease. We can meet reality more truly and wholeheartedly from where it is, and from this place, not a striving-to-be-other-than-it-is place, we create the appetite and momentum for movement in others. Leading movement – the change that reveals the truth of what is being, yet hidden (Chapter 3), the kind of change that effortlessly takes systems to a different place (Chapter 4) – starts in stillness. Still Moving.

In this chapter, I will take you on a journey through the personal skills it takes to ignite change in a way that works from is-ness out, not the striving ought back. I will begin with some foundations of the philosophy behind the framework, as the eight skills I will share are not some simple tools or recipes to be picked up by rote: they require considerable inner work. I will then describe the Still Moving leadership framework, contrasting it to a predominantly egocentric, ought-imbued shaping style of leading change.

I will weave through the journey reflective pit stops for you to recognise your own inner world, identify your default modes of effecting change, and try experiencing and applying the Still Moving framework. Try it on for size. Visualise your application. Anticipate its impact. Whether you are reading this book to help shift a repeating pattern in your life with others, learn how to unlock change more easily in your organisation, or engage in a different way with a movement within your community, what follows is essential guidance.

As leading change is leading with one's insides, let's begin in stillness and a bit of tuning in.

⇒ Adopt a relaxed yet alert posture; place your feet on the ground, close your eyes or softly gaze at the floor a little before you and tune into your inner state right now. Do this without effort or any need to do it 'right' – the task is simply to notice what you are experiencing on the inside. Pick up any data from your body – areas of tension or ease, warmth or cold; your heart space – what feelings and longings are lodged there; your breath quality – where it shows up in your body and how; any jumping thoughts in your mind. Allow what is the case, to be the case.

⇒ Now, be curious. What most came into your awareness? And what might that be signalling to you about the nature of the events and situations you are currently within? Register what comes to mind, especially anything that might have come freshly to you. That's all it is.

OK, let us go. Allez.

The Heart and Soul of the Still Moving Leading Change Framework

To illustrate the essential nature of how to lead movement from *is*, and not *ought*, I return to the leader I met in my early change career and whom I wrote of at the start of Chapter 2. James was the first leader I had met who understood the difference between leading from ought-led wiring compared to is-experienced reality – though at the time, I did not yet have the conceptual frameworks to articulate this distinction as such. But goodness, did I experience his leadership from my stomach, from my insides. When I became an internal change coach to his leadership team, my mind became grateful as it no longer had to run all the show and could be joined on stage by the fullness of my heart, body, and soul.

Here's a summation of a two-year change experience in which we successfully implemented a turnaround of a struggling retail organisation. The turnaround involved a reorganisation from a country to a regional operating model, a radical cultural change for the customer, a more flourishing and entrepreneurial workplace for employees, and a doubling of ROACE (return on average capital employed) for the shareholder. The story is a good lead into the Still Moving framework. Take note of its salient features and how the story impacts you.

It Was Scary

James could sniff out politeness and 'mumbo-jumbo' speak a mile off. He could tell when we were saying what we were habitually supposed to be saying (to each other and to hierarchy) and instead invited us to say what was really on our minds. One of the ground rules in all our leadership team meetings was to 'Speak from the *I*, not the *we*', 'Don't hide behind collective generalities, where are *you* coming from, what's going on for you?' – I can still hear him asking. Gingerly, we all learned how to bring difficult and risky topics into our conversations, things we might have felt embarrassed or awkward about saying otherwise. He created space in all meetings for us to go off the agenda if necessary and put the undiscussables on the table.

He did this because he knew, systemically, that what was being felt as most troubling for us to face also held the keys to the reality out in the broader organisation that was most being denied and excluded. You cannot lead change when you are out of touch with the operation, the ground truth. Per Heidegger, truth for James meant the unconcealing and re-inclusion of what was being, yet hidden, not truth as the correctness of proposition (he valued systemic insight higher than abstract intellect). He helped us befriend disturbance as the catalyst for untapped energy and movement.

I can still see him with an elastic band stretched out between his hands, illustrating how 'creative tension' propels change. We learned to see reality, especially edgy reality, as always friendly.

It Was Humbling

James brought us all down to be the 'right size'. For him, the reality of the ground was more important than the rarity of the centre, the experience of the periphery more important than the abstraction of head office. Within a very hierarchical and intellectual culture, he dragged the most senior leaders – kicking and squealing – out of their comfortable ivory towers and into the distribution terminals, the retail forecourts, and the noisy customer call centres.

We all got treated the same, and he gave an equal place for everything to be seen and heard. At each European region location we visited as a leadership team, we asked the local team to remove the formal boardroom table for our meetings and set up just a circle of chairs – where we all felt 'the same size'. Our trips to the locations always began with a visit to customer premises, followed by staff engagement, and then we held our leadership team meeting. He valued us being able to speak from the stories of our encounters in the messiness of the operations, not from neat PowerPoint slides containing abstract graphs and clever language.

He did all of this as he knew that truth (including *not* yet knowing something, being in uncertainty, and seeking wisdom from the collective), not intellectual comfort, catalyses change. While natural hierarchies (such as age, length of service, and expertise qualification) were respected, he subverted the oughtyness of status and a priori knowing. He put raw contact with reality to the top of the pile. As Ivan Karamazov later says in his little homily to his brother, 'The stupider one is, the closer one is to reality. The stupider one is, the clearer one is'. We learned to empty ourselves of knowing to better know truth.

It Was Revealing

I felt my insides being turned out many times over the two years with this leadership team. Not physically (though, see scary above ...), yet psychically and emotionally. One of James's 'big things' was awareness at the self and system level. He encouraged us to share our back stories with each other – how our key life events had created the leaders we now were, from what ground did our deepest longings spring. We did this not just to gel together as a team, but to tune into our essential natures and recognise any potential biases and filters we might have on reality.

I will never forget a vivid example of this when he was able to call out, during the humdrum conversation of the team arranging a European tour schedule, how hidden biases and assumptions about hierarchy were still playing out in our thinking and action (to become less culturally hierarchical). We were planning the Italy market visit on May 1st, which one team member pointed out was a national holiday. Rather than seeking a new date to enable the frontline staff a deserved day off, the team rather smugly commented on how dedicated the local team was to give up a day's holiday for the benefit of the senior leadership team. Only James noticed and named that the leadership team was unconsciously still working to a 'serve the hierarchy, not the frontline' mindset, despite their nice words to the contrary. (*But the man that is will shadow the man that pretends to be* – wise words T.S. Eliot[1]).

At the system level, I learned alongside him how to design all larger group encounters in a way that would both reveal and shift the collective cultural reality. There were no staged events, pre-set seating plans, speeches from the senior leaders or fixed meeting outcomes. Instead, we met in a free-flow format, allowing the organisation's cultural dynamics and hidden assumptions to be revealed as they were (the 'system in the room'), not forced into any ought-to state. I also learned how to design these events as transforming encounters where *the process modelled the desired change outcomes*. Another of my vivid memories is of us opening a meeting about how to be more externally facing to the customer with a circle of 100 chairs all facing outward. You should have seen the leaders' faces as they walked in, and the discomfort that was felt and revealed as they sat down to *experience* what it felt to be turning outward.

James encouraged all of this as he knew that change is catalysed through experiential phenomenology, having people *feel from their insides* what the change was about, not by issuing top-down disembodied statements. We designed encounters *that* changed, not *about* change. We learned how to walk (through *is*), not talk our way into movement (where our *oughts* still catch us out).

It Was Liberating

While scary, humbling, and revealing, it felt like this kind of leadership was bringing us all to our true selves. We dropped from acting out of a stylised, manufactured universe into one that became living, emergent matter. When the cloak of our acquired oughts dropped from our shoulders and reality-as-it-truly-is became visible, we became creative and more resourceful. Not from duty but desire. When we realised that *all* of what we experienced had a value and a place, that there was no blame or judgement attached to encountering reality – but only a deeper interconnected meaning that was our task to discover, our active receptivity to notice, reveal, explore and experiment shot up.

McGilchrist would say this was our right hemisphere brain being set free to do what it is best at – explore and understand the world, void of our confabulation. Spiritual thinkers would frame this as touching a collective soul or spirit beyond our own humanity. For me, this kind of leadership was an early lesson in how to *be completely with what is the case.* When deep down you trust that all you encounter and experience can only be helpful, even if challenging and unsettling, you hold your head up and go towards all of life.

While James was no paragon, his approach to leadership infused throughout the organisation a radically different culture, a receptivity to adopt a significant restructuring, and an appetite to deliver a business turnaround (which was actualised). I am glad and appreciative that he helped inspire me on my journey to understand more about these early glimmers of effective change leadership and, not only that, try to 'bottle it up' and codify this for others.

Pause a moment

⇒ Tune in to your responses from this section. What happens to you right now as you imagine yourself fully *leading with your insides*?

⇒ Consider the case(s) where you hope to bring movement and change. Is this a system that is 'up for' a process that might be scary, humbling, revealing, and liberating? What might this ask of you? Include what it may not ask of you.

The Still Moving Change Leadership Framework

Framework Overview

When I left this organisation and turned to external consulting, I was fired up to research what I had experienced. The framework concerning the effective leadership of change I will share has been conceived, honed and validated over two decades, containing four rounds of global research. I have allowed the methodology for this research to remain unchanged to allow longitudinal comparisons. If you want to learn more about the research method, I suggest you read its more detailed exposé in *Still Moving: How to Lead Mindful Change.*[2]

In summary, as it serves this book's core message; our research approach throughout has been an in-depth interview process to gather real-life stories from the field; ethnographies of a system going through change. Then we code these transcribed stories for contextual factors, leader behaviour and success evidence. The coding data is then quantitatively analysed for correlations.

My point is that the data gathering is steeped in empirical reality – the 'is-ness' of how a leader goes about change – and not conducted by questionnaires and surveys, where the researcher and participant can be led by their own *oughts* about the topic (in survey design and response). I can now see how we have followed what McGilchrist describes as the brain's best route to truth. The right hemisphere first has an instinct about reality (what we had been apprehending about effective change leadership). The left hemisphere then abstracts from this and puts what is experienced into a model, language (our coding framework for the research data). Then, the right hemisphere retakes the helm to make sense of the whole gestalt (the transcript immersion and research categories became a newly enriched theory).

While I recognise that all models only partially fit reality, I am confident that this one closely maps the terrain of how to successfully lead significant change (Figure 5.1).

The framework has two interconnected parts: a set of four *Inner Capacities* that guide you on how to cultivate your quality of *being*, and a set of four

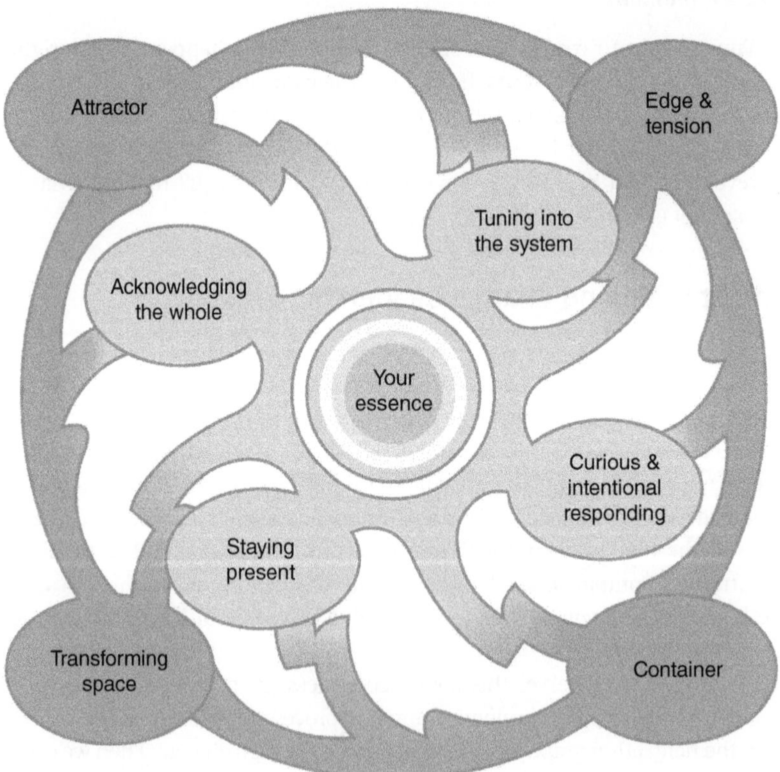

Figure 5.1 Still Moving Leading Change Skills Framework

External Practices that guide you on how to develop your quality of *doing*. Inner state stillness – the capacity to drop out of your oughts to encounter reality, and outer action movement – the capability to liberate others to do the same. The combined presence of these eight leadership skills explains 52% of the reason high magnitude (complex and at scale) change succeeds or fails. In variance analysis, that is a significant swing factor. If you do not attend to your personal skill when leading change, you reduce your chances of success by just over a half.

This success framework repeatedly wins out over a leadership style we have researched called *Leader-Centric*. Leader-Centric is ought-leadership-in-action, a style in which leaders tightly shape and control what is done, driven by their own principles, beliefs, and ideology. This approach to leading change explained 48% of the reason why change *fails* in our variance analysis. *The message is clear: change led through is and not through ought will bring you greater success.*

For those readers already familiar with this framework, I hope you find what follows not just a repeat of my earlier writings. What I aim to do in this section is highlight how these skills are intimately connected with the movement from *ought* to *is,* helping you be continually alert to this distinction so that you can take that journey from the persistent, narrow tug of our *wiring,* towards the fulsomeness of *reality.*

The Inner Capacities – Overview

The inner part leads the outward part.

Julian of Norwich

As the spiral in the Still Moving diagram implies, the four Inner Capacities are the cog in the wheel that drives the effectiveness of our outer action. Without mastering what goes on in our inner world, it will be difficult to fully inhabit what you need to *do* to lead change well. Outer change begins with inner work. The four capacities break down into two pairs: the first pair I have previously described as being our level of personal mindfulness, and the second pair our capacity for systemic awareness. Having now encountered McGilchrist's work, I can see how these two pairs correspond to what he calls two different *means to truth*: attention and perception (both of which are right hemisphere brain function, as opposed to left hemisphere function of judgement and apprehension).

Personal attention capacities: Staying Present, Curious and Intentional Responding.
Systemic perception capacities: Tuning into the System, Acknowledging the Whole.

To illustrate these four Inner Capacities, I will continue to draw from my own stories in the field of change. At the same time, I will incorporate guidance from the writings of the fourteenth-century religious mystic, Julian of Norwich, as an exemplar of how to unconceal the truth of what is being, yet hidden. You may wonder why I have chosen a religious mystic from nearly 700 years ago to be a companion guide on our journey. The reason is that I find her text, Revelations of Divine Love,[3] a remarkable treatise on how to use one's inner state during (an unsettling) experience as a portal to seek truth about the deeper outer realm.

Over a day and a night, when she was close to death from the bubonic plague, Julian had several visions of Christ's passion on the cross. Her remarkable writings show how, when seeking to understand what these visions revealed to her about the nature of divine love, she continually oscillated in her experience between impulsive reactivity (my uncomfortable situation ought to be this and not that!) and creative response (it is this, so therefore ...). On recovery, rather than shaking off the experience as an illusory episode and/or medical inconvenience, with reverence and awe, she spent two decades painstakingly writing up how her inner experience during this short illness afforded her deep systemic insight into her faith. *That's* a commitment to an inner path to truth.

Sixteen revelations flowed from one moment of acute, intentional, present-moment awareness and perceiving. She challenged ought-led conventional Christian orthodoxy – that God is a man or that sin makes God angry – and the startling is-ness of her revelations are still read today. Her inner work has had a far-reaching outer impact.

From Ought to Is is not a book about Christianity, and we do not need to be on the verge of death as a training arena. Still, I will share how her observation and perception process gives gems of insight into the depth (and difficulty) of the practice behind the Still Moving Inner Capacities. Like Ivan Karamazov, she was drawn to *loving with one's insides*. What follows is guidance about *leading with one's insides*.

Staying Present – A *Noticing* Capacity

We have found that this first Inner Capacity is the starting point for all the following skills. Staying Present is our capacity to intentionally and non-judgementally tune into our present-moment inner state – and register what is there without getting distracted or thrown by what we encounter. What is our mind up to? What emotions and feelings seem to be foreground? Do we have any bodily sensations that are pulling on our attention? Do we have any impulses or urges (to do or say something) right now? The capacity is to notice and welcome all that we experience in our inner world (is-response), not wish for our inner state to be other than it is, beat ourselves up about it, *or* feel a need to act on anything (ought-response).

This may sound like an easy task, but Staying Present is rather challenging as I'm sure we have all experienced how our mind's default mode is to either reminisce about the past or anticipate the future, and that studies[4] show that our attention spans for present-moment awareness are a mere eight seconds. Sustained, present-moment attention is a rare quality. But what can become available to us when we master it!

As I have previously said, our inner world of experience is a fractal of what is happening in the wider world. If you are a leader of an institution or team, I will bet you that you are receiving multiple projections from the system around you – people will be (unconsciously) pinning onto you their hopes and fantasies, needs and niggles, sadnesses and frustrations. So, that irritation or impatience you might be feeling inside, or that twinge in your shoulder or tightness in your chest, could signal the reality of the system you are leading. Turning inward to non-judgementally notice what is present for you is not mere navel-gazing – it is deeper, wider reality-encountering. It is crucial to create the time and space to exercise this Staying Present capacity during disturbing situations when the temptation might be to go and 'fix something'.

No, dare to stand still and first tune inward. This response requires humility and yielding to the truth of what is, not reaching for how things ought to be. Try to put aside your ingrained survival codes about how to be in the situation and let things, is-ness, flow. As Julian of Norwich recounts (short text, p. 15): 'This revelation of Christ's pains filled me full of pains'. Yet rather than wish the pain away, she stuck with the task to observe her troubling inner state in order to discover the nature of Divine love – truth as the unconcealing of what is being, yet hidden. How best to do this?

Julian defined a three-fold distinction in her revelatory experience, the first of which is relevant for this Staying Present capacity and the others for the capacities that follow: 'All of this was shown in three ways; that is to say, *by bodily sight*, and my words formed in my understanding, and by spiritual vision' (ch. 9; p. 52).

When you are practising Staying Present, *bodily sight* is paramount. Julian reported that she tried to be accurate about registering what she saw and experienced that day and night. She admits that putting such attention description into words is hard to do openly and fully (though check out, 'My body was dead from the waist down, as it felt to me') – I also find it tricky to be able to write here in this book about my inner experience. But what she does so well is to stay first with the *phenomenology* of her experience, using purely descriptive, objective and non-personally reactive language.

Here's a suggestion for you on how to capture the truth of your inner attention – use symbols or pictures. A leader I once worked with spent a moment each day contemplating her inner state (she was leading a considerable bank institution through the change implications of a serious fraud inquiry). When she got out of the shower each morning, she registered how she felt right there and then by drawing emoji faces on her shower room mirror misted with condensation. This daily act enabled her to remain calm and become curious about what her inner state was telling her about the situation around her. I have often invited leaders to draw images on a flip chart about how they are feeling at that moment, which both relaxes them individually, and, when the pictures are aggregated, can be a powerful temperature check on the mood of the whole system.

When we slow down to notice and name our inner state, we distance ourselves from its power to unwittingly propel us into reactive, ought-led response (when I feel rejection fear and can name it, that act stops me from indignant lashing out at others). Affective processing enables us to touch new, deeper realities about the systems around us (more in Chapter 7 on emotions). Try opening your next meeting with a minute or two of silence, and then invite your team to say what came up for them in their inner state in that moment *as a clue to what is being experienced within your wider situation*. So much of our inner world can be noticed when we stop talking. By Staying Present, especially to that which is felt as disturbing or unable to be disclosed, we can tap into Heidegger's essence of truth – what is being, yet hidden in our situation. Unconcealment could lead to a remarkable revelation about the truth of the system you most wish change for.

Staying Present, pause to experience

⇒ What feelings, sensations and impulses do you have right now? Where do you notice them? How big/small are they?

⇒ Putting personalised interpretations aside, what might your inner state be a symptom of within the situation around you?

Curious and Intentional Responding – A *Choosing* Capacity

Once we are present to our inner state, how do we respond? Well, the next important skill in the quality of our being is to 'hit the pause button' on any autopilot reactivity. Curious and Intentional Responding is the capacity that enables us to slow down the period between how we experience a situation and how we react to that experience, staying open and curious to what arises. When you notice what you are experiencing, are you also aware of the choices you have available to respond? And can you use your intention in the situation to guide which choice you take? Once we oversee our mental, emotional, and instinctual responses to what we experience, we act in less fearful, impulsive, or anxious ways.

Remember my Madame Butterfly experience, when I managed to stay with and not conceal my inner emotional response – a choice guided by an intention to follow that calm guiding voice. I have also mentioned how, in meetings, I can easily get hooked by moments when people choose not to sit next to me and interpret this as an act of rejection, and in that very exact moment, choose to see the same data as a sign of the distance required for leadership – *when I recall* my intention to be a system guide. Our intention is such a welcome regulator of our attention!

Within a nano-second, our brains can tell us to either fully approach (drawn to *is*) or avoid an unsettling reality (lured by *ought*). We continually have a choice point to be either fully with *what is* our direct experience (which might require us to experience guilt if we choose a non-habitual response to our field of loyalty) or to be *chained to our oughts* (where we can stay feeling innocent within our programmed loyalties). Within such oscillation, our intention can gently intervene and keep us heading towards the is-ness of experience, whatever emotions it might trigger.

Back to Julian of Norwich. There is one exquisite moment in a revelation where she contemplates Christ on the crucifix and says that she 'saw this bodily and sorrowfully and obscurely, and I wished for more natural light to have seen more clearly'. How often can we find ourselves wishing for better lighting or visibility in a murky situation? In that moment for Julian, she chose not to make her experience more comfortably bright (how it *ought* to have been). By recalling her 'reason' (i.e., intention) to have God reveal to her his essence, she chose instead to stay with darker obscurity as 'I needed no light but him'. This curious and intentional response led her to see 'God in a point – that is to say, in my understanding – and by seeing this, I saw that he is in everything'.

Now, that's a moment when her inner state skill to override impulsivity helped her contact a deeper reality. How often can we see and understand more than what we initially thought we knew when we are patient enough to stay in ambiguity and mystery, rather than seek the immediate comfort of clarity?

Later, we see another occasion when Julian chooses not to act on an inner state impulse and instead stay with what is: 'At this time I wanted to look away from the cross, but I did not dare, *for I well knew that while I looked at the cross, I was safe and secure*'. Here, Julian teaches us that in a challenging situation, we put ourselves in *more* danger when we look away and resort to the relief of habitual comfort, than when we bravely face the fullness of reality. Being with what is the case – however troubling – is the safest and most secure stance we can take.

When we have mastered this Inner Capacity of Curious and Intentional Responding, we can securely gaze into Hammarskjöld's *les espaces infinis* in steady and unguarded ways – we are unafraid of uncertainty and trying out new things. We approach all that arises in a situation, and, far from bending it to conform to our will, we see experience as a field of welcoming, observable and valuable data about the system within our attention. This is an essential skill if we wish to change a situation, as systems will freeze and resist any movement if they feel they are being held in unwelcome and dismissive judgement.

Can you 'hit the pause button' on experience and generate various response options rather than immediately react? Do you choose the response that goes to the heart of your intention in the situation? Have you done the work to identify your oughts, your instinctual responses to experience, and, with this awareness, put them to one side to respond to reality in more open and less pre-scripted ways?

Curious and Intentional Responding, pause to experience

⇒ What have you noticed about your instinctual response to how I have described this Inner Capacity? What might have made you approach or withdraw from my explanations and examples?

⇒ What might be the oughts (wishes for things to be different, any judgements) beneath these responses?

⇒ If you were to hit the pause button on this default reactivity, can you consider other responses that might more closely follow your intention to learn about this Inner Capacity?

Tuning into the System – A *Perceiving* Capacity

Once we have 'got our own inner house in order' (being able to stay with what is – Staying Present; and respond with an intention, not from ought – Curious and Intentional Responding), we are now a clean slate more able to accurately tune into the system around us. Free from our own story and its reality-distorting oughts, our inner world can fully encounter and register the system's story. A frequent example for me is to consciously put my perfection lens to one side so that I can allow messiness to happen, and, in so doing, see more clearly what is going on in a situation that is no longer being bent (either in perception or action) towards my oughts.

Out of the four Inner Capacities in our research, Tuning into the System was the capacity most correlated with change success. Great change leaders trowel beneath a situation's symptoms to deduce what is keeping its patterns in place. This capacity is vital in generating movement. Without the skill to perceive the invisible causal currents of a situation, you might get busy reacting to events and spinning many wheels, rather than creatively and sustainably adjusting the deeper sources.

⇒ Have you ever been sitting in your team noticing what people are saying and doing, tempted to 'join the fray', yet holding back to contemplate the causes for what you see now as a repeating pattern?

If you answered yes, this is a sign of your capacity to *tune into the system*. You are curious about the underlying structures and dynamics that the visible situation springs from and is beholden to. Recall the last chapter on systems and truth pursuit – it could well be that one or a combination of the Ordering Forces of Belonging, Time, Place and Exchange are invisibly at play. Especially with Belonging, what are the deeper loyalties in your system that would feel like an act of betrayal to move away from?

Whatever your system lenses, this capacity asks that you constantly be alert that your role as a change enabler is not to interpret what you see literally and personally, but to see all you experience as a property of a richly interconnected, not-yet-fully-known relational system. Experience is not chopped up (as our left hemisphere might be tempted to do) into individual parts and isolated events. Instead, all that comes our way is seen dynamically in the round as the visible sign of a deeper underlying causal field (holistic, right hemisphere attention).

Such a mode of attention requires that we use our imaginative and intuitive attention to attain truth and disclose what is being, yet hidden. I found three pointers on how to do this from within Julian's revelations that also chime with my experience and research findings. First, recall her means to accessing truth: 'All of this was shown in three ways; that is to say, by bodily sight, *and my words formed in my understanding*, and by spiritual vision' (ch. 9; p. 52). Let's take this second step: how to tune into the language that the system, as it were, is trying to say to you. When you sit in a team or travel through your community, can you get beneath what individual people are saying to you and try to imagine the few sentences that the system – as a whole – is trying to say?

As an example, I have worked with a colleague who is brilliant at capturing the essence of a group's dynamics via poetry. She sits in silence through the encounter, all the while tuning in to what is being said – and silently not said – and from their moments of truth (she cannot write about oughts as she finds no words come to her), creates sentences that form poems that she reads back to the group at the end of the day. By my colleague bringing to life the truth about their system in such a manner, the group invariably experiences this acknowledgement of their deeper reality non-defensively, and as a release. What they had felt inside but been unable to articulate has been voiced. I have found this imaginative and intuitive mirroring back of reality a far better catalyst for movement in a group than the more conventional route of the moderator 'giving feedback' at the end of the day.

Here's a short poem my colleague wrote while on a leadership programme, on a day when the participants struggled to collaborate across a globally dispersed organisational structure. Once she shared her poem, the words she had captured about the system – and especially the sentence, 'Where do our hearts touch?' – catalysed the group towards quite different ways of relating to their purpose.

> *The dance of near and far*
>
> how do we connect?
>
> how are we together?
>
> we can touch while
>
> each in our own world,
>
> or be far yet
>
> bound by a thousand ties.
>
> where do our hearts touch?
>
> rather than our hands?
>
> *Sytske Casimir*

A second pointer for how to tune into a system is to become like an anthropologist and contemplate a system through its visible artefacts – however seemingly inconsequential. In a strikingly memorable instance of vision, Julian showed us the discerning power of being able to see big things in little things, to have the capacity to spot the vastness of a system's truth within one of its parts: she saw a hazelnut lying in the palm of her hand, as round as a ball and with her mind's eye thought, 'What can this be?' Through her wondering, she saw that in the hazelnut 'is all that is made ... it lasts and ever shall because God loves it ... And all things have being through the love of God.'

Can you likewise take even tiny visible signs within your situation that might easily pass you by and ask the same intriguing question, 'What can this be?' hypothesising about the deeper systemic significance of the reality you are experiencing? For example, I always find it insightful sitting in an organisation's reception area to notice vital cultural signs of the system – such as how people are greeted, the nature of the seating layout, and what – if any – objects about the institution are on display. What aspects of the culture are these visible signs a symptom of? How about the language used around the system? Do you notice how some specific words used are a sign of a culture (that might be entirely out of awareness to those within it)?

Finally, and intriguingly, Julian also *noticed and named what she could not see*, and she drew conclusions from the exclusion.[5] This instinct to tune into 'missing elements' is another feature of the Tuning into the System capacity – effective change leaders notice what is present, yet not seen. They are continually alert to what might be a fact, event, or sentiment about this team, community, or institution that they intuit people are (unconsciously) putting out of awareness; *and which holds a clue to what is needed for movement*. What we split off invariably signals what we most need.

I once worked with a group of leaders to help them identify the new ways of working required to take their company's business practices into its future. In the plenary debrief, I noticed that one breakout group had left a flip chart from the exercise turned towards the wall. By how they stood awkwardly in front of this flip chart, I received a strong feeling that they felt unable to disclose this element. When I invited the group to turn their flip chart around, they did so reticently, yet what became un-concealed was a large heart drawn on the piece of paper. This disclosure led to a catalytic dialogue in the whole group about why it was the case that emotion could have no place within how their organisation was run; they concluded that any feelings-based knowledge was regarded as too irrational, irrelevant and dangerous (some strong *oughts* lurking here!). Rather wonderfully, this dialogue they could now have was full of emotion. By tuning into the system to unconceal what was being, yet hidden, the resulting naming and re-inclusion of a missing element catalysed much movement.

As another example of the power to tune into and include missing elements, James, the leader I described at the start of this chapter, always set aside time towards the end of our meetings to do two things. First, he restated the key discussion points and agreements made. Next, he brilliantly asked, 'And, what have I *not* heard so far in this meeting?' A question that encouraged his team to fully disclose what had been on their minds in the meeting, yet unable to voice. This tuning in to what was being, yet hidden practice invariably led to deeper system truths emerging; vital leadership intelligence. Of course, asking *why* these matters had not been voiced was another system-revealing follow-through question!

Tuning into the System, pause to experience

⇒ What might be your equivalent of the hazelnut? A clue in your system as small as something like how conversations are being conducted, that to date you might have overlooked, yet that you now sense could contain some vital system-wide truths?

⇒ If you had to write a few lines of poetry about the team, community, or institution you'd like to bring movement to, capturing something vital that needs to be brought to light, what might those lines be?

Acknowledging the Whole – An *Integrating* Capacity

The Inner Capacity of Acknowledging the Whole was rarely recorded in our research. Yet, it was *the* defining skill of leaders overseeing large, complex systems going through periods of uncertainty and disruptive change. What is this capacity about? Well, it felt as if these leaders had learned from Julian.

In her revelations, Julian displayed an open-hearted capacity to welcome all of her troubling experiences, including two aspects that prevailing religious oughtyness might have sought to exclude or judge: our physical bodies and fleshly createdness – disparaged elements that she dared put on an equal level to us as spiritual beings; and dastardly human sin – that she boldly proclaimed God held no blame or anger for. The positive re-inclusion of our physicality and sin into her theology was (and still is) a big deal in the face of religious dogma that meted out punishment for both.

We call this Inner Capacity to make an equal, non-hierarchical, unprejudiced space for everything to exist, *Acknowledging the Whole*. Leaders with this capacity can see that all that arises in experience needs to be given a place, especially that which is felt difficult and disturbing.

This is a tough Inner Capacity to lean into as our oughts are continually fluttering through our being, affrontedly whispering to us not to see something that might challenge our beliefs, demanding us to discard that which does not fit with our theories of what is acceptable comportment, and tempting us to think disparaging thoughts about people or situations that hold very different oughts to our own. Pffff. Our survival stitched cloak of loyalties is there for a reason.

What follows is a tricky question: how can we reorient our deep wiring to be able to, as it were, move beyond conscience? To put our judgements and indignations to one side to hold a meta-place? This is a question I do not feel entirely adequate to answer, yet I'll offer a few thoughts here as, without the radical allowing stance of this fourth Inner Capacity, change and movement cannot flow. Beyond our individual agency, the deep conscience of a system will get upset if we disavow and exclude any element, and, consequently forever put obstacles to movement in our pathway. (When Theresa May, a past UK Prime Minister who struggled to 'get Brexit done' said, 'If you believe you are a citizen of the world, you are a citizen of nowhere', while literally correct, this statement put a shuddering exclusionary and divisive thunderbolt through our nation's capacity to unite and move freely ahead.)

Acknowledging the Whole is an Inner Capacity that asks us to *befriend guilt and loneliness*, as the affiliation systems to which we belong will become indignant with us if we dare put their oughts on an equal footing to others. Mandela putting on a Springbok rugby shirt in post-Apartheid South Africa sparked 66,000 whites in the rugby World Cup stadium to erupt in adoration. Yet, his act caused consternation among the nation's black majority, for whom the Springboks were the ultimate symbol of white minority supremacy. Ouch. What a brave man.

The prophet Isaiah (54:2) asks us to 'Enlarge the site of your tent, stretch your tent curtains wide, do not hold back; lengthen your cords, strengthen your stakes'. Now, I'm no theologian, but this text offers further guidance for this Inner Capacity to Acknowledge the Whole.

Like Mandela, can you imagine holding a wider place for your team, community, or institution, one that *calls upon the wider context* within which your system is situated, inviting and welcoming others? In a sense, making your own system a little 'smaller' in its place within the swirl of much wider dynamics? Can you bring something into your 'tent' that might be troubling from this wider system – an awkward market reality, disturbed client systems, an external investigation, or any ought conscience field that positively clashes with your beliefs? Invite positive regard towards other systems that might be challenging for your own system to face – negative media journalists, an aggressive competitor or vocal protest groups in your industry? What is their (deeper hidden) value to you? This is lengthening your cords.

At the same time, you need to strengthen your stakes (otherwise, the larger tent would collapse), which, in the context of this Inner Capacity's practice, I take to mean *becoming clear and firm about the wider principles and purpose* for your greater acknowledgement and inclusion. Mandela's bold gesture changed the world and became a significant step towards one-nation building – a prize worthy to transcend tribal loyalty. Maybe your welcoming of an aggressive competitor is necessary for the customer to ultimately benefit, or your re-inclusion of a past upset from your system's story a sign that you, too, in the present are not without sin or shadow.

Resolution that releases movement from stuck situations always requires that we identify with something bigger than our own crusade. In systemic work, all has a place.

Next, Rumi's oft-quoted words:

> Out beyond ideas of wrongdoing and rightdoing,
> There is a field. I'll meet you there.
> When the soul lies down in that grass,
> The world is too full to talk about.
> Ideas, language, even the phrase *each other*
> Does not make any sense.

Most often you hear just the first two sentences of Rumi's poem: *out beyond ideas of wrongdoing and rightdoing, there is a field. I'll meet you there.* This opening certainly speaks to what Acknowledging the Whole is about.

But *how* to do so? I take his sentences that follow as guidance that *we best cultivate this capacity non-verbally.*

If I look back on how I have helped leaders best experience this capacity, it is when I have invited them to simply 'set up' or represent the elements of their system with physical artefacts. They visualise their system and then use chairs or post-it notes or blocks to represent their people, divisions, any influencing factors, such as challenging market context climate change, and they then place all these elements within a spatial map in the room. I invite them, in silence, to 'visit' each and every element they have placed (especially those felt most troubling), standing alongside each one, fully taking in and acknowledging its place in relation to the other elements and the whole.

This experience can have a profound, almost softening impact on the leader. It helps them to more acutely sense a wider system's reality and intentionality, and in so doing, enables them to be seen and felt by their people as a leader who can transcend partisan oughts and stand for something bigger. They become a living embodiment of from *ought* to *is*.

To round things off, I will say that this Inner Capacity naturally flows through us when we can find within a route to a faith that trusts that nothing is amiss in our lives and that all experience – including the most difficult – needs to in some way be embraced within a whole. Just notice how humankind needs to erect memorials in places where horror has been encountered, or how people without any 'religion' as such come to bow their heads and pray before extreme hardship and distress, lest we forget.

McGilchrist notes how the brain's right hemisphere predisposition is to believe, as to understand experience fully, nothing can be excluded. Can we, too, adopt a disposition towards the world *as if* some guiding mystery or Divinity existed? Such a stance would undoubtedly help us become more open to encountering a world beyond our own knowing and belief realm, our oughts. To that extent, Acknowledging the Whole is Julian's third step to discovering truth, *having spiritual vision*. Her most famous words can conclude the section on this Inner Capacity.

All shall be well, and all shall be well and all manner of things shall be well.

Acknowledging the Whole, pause to experience

⇒ Sometimes we innocently exclude things to make things well in a system. What troubling elements might you, unknowingly or knowingly, have excluded in your case requiring change and movement?

⇒ Imagine your equivalent 'Springbok shirt' gesture; what might that be?

⇒ If you deeply imagined that 'all shall be well' in your situation, within that trusting holding energy, what might that embolden you to do?

The External Practices – Overview

Let's now move to the outer skills cog within the Still Moving spiral framework of effective change leadership. If the Inner Capacities are your 'to-*be* list', the four External Practices are your 'to-*do* list'. Now that your Inner Capacities have resourced you with the predisposition to notice, regulate, perceive and be inclusive of wider realities, how do you now take others on the journey to become freer of their oughts and more receptive to what is?

Recall my insights that the most successful approaches to change work with the natural energy of dynamic, ever-changing reality, not those that try to prod and exhort a system fixedly towards a different place. The former achieves pace, creativity, and commitment, the latter only top-down, ought-led compliance. I now share the four interactive skills we have consistently seen in our research to distinguish leaders in the successful change approaches. All four practices will help you bring the system you are leading and guiding into greater contact with is-ness – what is being, yet hidden. If you can master these skills, change will flow more effortlessly.

Attractor – A Pull Towards *Purpose* and *Meaning*

All living systems are being compelled toward a purpose and set of patterns that sustain their survival. Whether it be leaves photosynthesising, beavers building river dams, bees busily honey-making, or birds flocking in formation to migrate to warmer climes in winter, nature magnetically has in-built codes that get transferred and passed on through generations, adjusted when external conditions dictate.

Likewise, in human systems, we are attracted to the goals, scripts, and intentions that ensure the continuity and survival of our institutions. Just as gravity and black holes are examples of 'strange attractors' in the physical universe, exerting magnetic energy on all matter, so are purpose and meaning-making effective leadership practices for generating alignment, commitment and belonging within our human systems. This is what we call Attractor leadership.

Leaders who are effective at this practice create a shared intention, atmosphere, spirit and meaning for their teams, institutions and communities, to enable flow and loyalty towards that system's mission and viability. They do this by connecting with others on an emotional level, setting the context for how elements of the system's life fit together, and visibly working beyond personal ambition to serve a higher purpose. They work *with* (is) and not *on* (ought) the system to create a compelling and distinctive narrative that binds people together – who are we, why do we do what we do, what's the point of us?

So, what about when things need to change? The risk of intense loyalty to a system's narrative is, of course, 'head in the sand' behaviour when a challenging new *is*, or reality, comes their way.

The Attractor leadership skill is *not* about creating and adhering to a one-off inspiring 'vision statement' from on high and then cascading that through a team, organisation or community (ought-style). Leaders who are effective at Attractor leadership *continually tune into the reality* of their context and never cease authoring the system's story (the whole system becomes right hemisphere in its attention).

Future direction is necessary for change, but the more that this realisation of a new requirement can come from today's lived reality, the glimmer of future-truth-in-the-now, and not from ought-led imposition, the greater the take up of the need for and speed in change.

One leader I worked with in fact refused to launch a 'vision and mission statement' as he knew that the task was a waste of time in continually changing contexts. Instead, he implemented a process through which the various divisions in his organisation regularly gathered to share their stories about new market and customer intelligence, technology innovation and changing investor sentiment, so that they could make ongoing decisions about how to adapt and change. These ongoing sense-making and adjustment stories were regularly shared across the organisation.

To help us find future solutions in the living present, I also like to work with the phenomenon of *positive deviance* when mobilising change. A concept derived from the field of Complex Adaptive Systems and initially coined via nutrition research of malnourished children,[6] positive deviance exists when there is an anomaly, uncommon practice and behaviour within your system that is *already heading in the right direction* (future solutions are always there if you are close enough to dynamic reality to sense it!). Positive deviance is a very effective Attractor tool as the story for change comes from within current practice, not external imposition.

One leadership team I worked with had figured out that their organisation was making or losing money based on how their local teams stepped outside their country boundaries, and cooperated along the transnational river systems of their distribution channel. These small networks of teams were certainly 'positive deviants' as the cultural ought was to stay within the loyalties of national boundaries and adhere to the country hierarchy. Instead, they had dared to step out of these 'must do's' and create new rules for supply chain decisions along the networks of rivers. This novel joined-up thinking based on system realities became the catalyst for completely restructuring the whole entity into regional (following the rivers) and not national boundaries.

When leaders introduced this new organisational model, they created visuals of their organisation as a network of rivers containing 'flags' of irrefutable profit and loss data of raw materials transportation along the various river tributaries. This reality-capturing, ground truth picture energised their teams for change much more readily than if they had created some lofty vision statement sentences. Moreover, this stand for a radically different regional future even avoided antagonising the national fiefdoms previously existing within the country's senior leadership. Loyalties shifted more readily when the new direction had sprung from empowered community-sourced realities and not external prodding from the hierarchy towards an ought.

Attractor leadership *tunes into the system* (notice its attachment to one of the Inner Capacities) to notice shifting realities, unconceal potentially constraining oughts within a situation, and, via skilful purpose-building and meaning-making skills, inspire a system to move with greater ease towards its destined future.

Attractor, pause to experience

⇒ As you reflect on your case where you wish for movement, are you aware of an anomaly – some uncommon behaviour/practice somewhere within the life of your team, institution or community – that might be heading in the right direction?

⇒ How might you create a compelling story for your desired movement in a way that works with the reality of what is present and coming towards you?

Edge and Tension – Make Disturbance Your Friend

Nature shows us how flow *and* dissonance must coexist to create growth and multiplicity, and that these contrary tendencies of order and disorder also need to be part of one and the same creative process. The resistance a rock creates in a stream to form an eddy is aided at the same time by the very force of the stream. Both flow and rock are partners within the stream – nature continually evolves due to the resistance it carries within itself.

This generative, non-duality feature of the living world corresponds with my research into effective change leadership, where successive studies have shown that leaders need to create an equal balance of stability and chaos, structure and disruption – *within the same transformative act of leadership.* While Attractor leadership creates magnetic alignment and flow, Edge and Tension creates dissonance and disruption. Can you imagine being able to hold both the forces for alignment and discord simultaneously?

While all four of the External Practices are strongly correlated with success and need to work in combination, Edge and Tension came out as the single most potent skill for catalysing successful change: this disruptive skill is the bow of a ship leading the charge within the rolling seas, the rock within the stream causing disturbance and new patterns to flow.

What does Edge and Tension look like, and why is this skill so vital as a change catalyst?

Leaders who have mastered this skill can cleanly name what is; they talk straight and confront challenging issues – especially firmly held assumptions and ways of working people hold that are acting as a handbrake on change. They describe this reality with respect yet without compromise, have constancy in times of turbulence (where the temptation might be to seek comfort rather than keep the discomfort of significant change on track) and stretch the goals and limits of what is possible. This skill does not stop with seeking out truth; great Edge and Tension is about *amplifying* people's experience of reality. Given Chapter 3 on the transformative punch of *is* to catalyse change, you can understand why this skill is essential to master if you wish to effect movement and release from stuck patterns.

Back to my story of James at the beginning of this chapter. With his leadership team's increasing confidence in their ability to notice and name truth and shift the culture to one that could bravely look at itself and its patterns, over time, edgy moments started to become transformative, and not dangerous encounters.

I supported one of his team in designing a large-scale engagement event for their Southern European region. The event was entirely themed around passion for the customer. Emboldened by the art of designing experiences to *model* and not just *talk about* change, we had created an utterly counter-cultural event. One hundred leaders from within this normally rational, intellectual, and in-control-of-what-happens culture were about to go into an event where the room was going to be lit with red lamps, venue staff were to hand out strawberries dipped in chocolate, and passionate music would be playing in the background. Within such a setting, the leaders were to spend the first morning in a free-flow design, sharing stories of their most passionate experiences.

On a preparation call two weeks before the event, one of the design team members expressed vehement opposition to the design, saying that we would 'lose it' as participants would react in extreme discomfort to the experience. What happened next on the call was a beautiful display of Edge and Tension leadership.

After a moment of silence following this voice of opposition, the head of the region (the leader I was supporting) said something like, 'Thank you, Sarah, for your comments; they are very insightful. And do you know what, you have completely 'got' what the event is about. How you have anticipated the participants' response to the design is *exactly* the purpose for the event; well done! If we do not create this discomfort, we will not get to the truth of the culture change we all need to go on. We will not change the design. We will continue with it as is'.

Another moment of silence followed. Thankfully, the leader who had been in opposition visibly relaxed. She saw how her reaction had not been treated as irritating personal resistance but as a systemic signal for the necessary transformative path for her organisation to embark on. She left the design call as one of the conference's strongest advocates.

In this instance, the region's leader had not disallowed discomfort *but had worked with it as data.* To do this Edge and Tension so well, he had used all the Inner Capacities – being present to what is, responding with curious intention and not defensive reaction, tuning into the system beneath what was being said, and giving a valued place for all that arose – including welcoming disturbance. He also combined his Edge and Tension skills with Attractor in his appeal to purpose.

In all my decades of experience in change, this straight-talking Edge and Tension skill, far from spreading panic, defensiveness and resistance, builds open-eyed commitment to a change journey and greater credibility to you as a leader; far better to get the truth and any associated discomfort out early, as then people are free to choose whether they are up for the journey or not, and the upfront disclosure builds in time for people to both psychologically assimilate change implications and become resourced. It's a disservice to your team, organisation and community not to be open about truth. If you have any in-built ought wiring to be polite, not rock the boat and keep people innocent and protected against reality, I'd encourage you to loosen your loyalty to such codes if you truly wish to bring about change (I've had to learn how to).

Edge and Tension, pause to experience

⇒ How are you with the fierce naming of truth?
⇒ What awkward realities are not currently being faced in your system, and can you imagine yourself bringing them to light? Remember, difficulty and disturbance are usually a systemic clue, not a pathological problem.

Container – Channels Energy

In Chapter 3, I wrote about the interrelationship between truth and trust. To lead change from reality (and not ought), creating a climate that can tolerate and embrace the emotions that accompany awareness and disclosure becomes critical. Perhaps if the UK's Post Office had had a more affirming and self-assured leadership and oversight structure, there would have been a greater preparedness among its managers to get to the bottom of the accounting system problems, and over 900 frontline staff would not have had their lives and livelihoods destroyed.

Container skill is another vital ingredient in the cocktail of effective change leadership. Leaders who possess this skill can take the anxiety likely generated through Edge and Tension leadership and channel that into productive energy for movement. I have seen too many changes fail because leaders have not paid enough attention to – and at times, quite frankly, not cared enough about – the human dynamics of change.

Great change leaders dedicate energy to the following: they remain personally non-anxious in challenging conditions; are affirming of others in the pursuit of working from reality, not posturing or self-protection, building ownership, trust and confidence; they put in place structures and processes that create psychological safety for people to speak out about difficult topics, using high empathy and dialogue skills; they promote webs of interactions across a system that build resilience and spread change; they set and contract boundaries with clear expectations and ground rules so that people know what to operate on and how, giving permission to take risks to try out new things.

That's quite a list of both personal and process skills. But without this set of Container leadership practices, it will be nigh on impossible to help your team, institution, or community embark on a journey to face what is, dare loosen loyalties to oughts, and be fully resourced to walk a new path.

In Still Moving,[7] I wrote of the miraculous containing energy of my adopted mum and dad that enabled me to walk the scary journey towards tracing my birth family. Their parenting had a spaciousness, an at-one-ness with it all that helped me loosen the settings of my oughts. Dropping out of our oughts to head towards what is can be pretty disconcerting, as the experience feels you are losing all the familiar coordinates that have until now kept you safe. You find yourself flying through the air from one trapeze swing to another. Gasp. There's a reason we stay within our familiar boundaries – either those we know consciously or carry unconsciously.

Back to my story of the European region's restructuring (from countries to rivers) and cultural change (from internal sophistry to external customer passion). Some might say we did not do enough to contain the scariness of the very different, truth-seeking culture that James brought to the business. However, one thing that I know helped significantly was training all managers in the skills of courageous conversations and emergent change.

Aside from working as a change coach to the leadership team, my other primary responsibility was working with a super team of leadership development professionals to bring in a suite of dialogue and systemic perception tools that helped people learn to work more creatively and courageously with reality. This capability-building investment built people's capacity to get alongside all the challenging elements associated with the change, to work from complete data, not inferential opinions, to examine the deep mental models that were keeping the organisation where it was (the systemic oughts), to make sense of ambiguous data in changing times, and to see the journey they would personally need to walk along to remodel the business – helping them to become aware of their own back stories and free of any loyalties that were leading them to unhelpful patterns in the new context.

If Edge and Tension was the boat's bow and Attractor its guiding navigational North Star, these Container skills became the oars rowing the vessel through the choppy waters of change, keeping the system safe (enough) to steer against the countervailing tides of ought and be open to new seas.

Container, pause to experience

⇒ What are the moments in your life when you felt most fully challenged and resourced to escape stuck patterns and take a new path? What was that like? What was present to help you contain and channel your anxiety?

⇒ As you now consider the situation or system you most wish change for, how are you planning to let others know they have your back? What acts of containment do you feel would help enable people to accept and face reality and so catalyse change?

Transforming Space – Changes the 'Now'

You might have already registered hints about the nature of this final External Practice through the above illustrations. That would be natural, as Transforming Space is not an entirely distinct skill but an extra special ingredient you can add to the cocktail to spice everything up. Whether you are doing Attractor, Edge and Tension, or Container leadership, if you deploy these skills in a way that has the present moment be an *experience* of the desired change, a chance to see and shift behaviour in real-time, then you would be practising Transforming Space.

Do you create shared purpose by taking your teams out on customer journeys, or by issuing a customer-valuing vision statement? Do you draw attention to poorer-than-expected performance by visiting struggling sites or simulating people's current unhelpful routines, or do you just stare at the numbers? Do you create psychological safety by modelling disclosure and vulnerability, or merely asking people to 'speak up'? Are you walking, not just talking the change?

Leaders with this Transforming Space skill make and take opportunities *in the here-and-now moment* to draw attention to a system's repeating patterns and collective dynamics, acting to unconceal that which might be being, yet hidden. For example, you might intervene in a conversation where people are talking about the need to become more innovative, yet the dialogue feels 'same old, same old' – the usual people are talking, or when new ideas surface, they are shot down. You would also be attending to the physical environment for a transforming encounter, for example, changing the layout of a meeting room to remove hierarchy if the change goal is to reduce power distance.

Given that phenomenological experience is the fundamental given natural fact (no one can dispute my subjectively lived and interpreted reality), catalysing change and movement through creating spaces in which people can *live, embody, and not talk about* the desired change is the most direct route to leading from what *is* the case. When we remain theorising what change needs to look like, we will likely be using old logic and familiar routines to get to new places; only through encounter – not abstraction – can we truly know the terrain. Yet our oughts can still flood in to fill the available space, driving out the new before any change has a chance to take root. The skill here is to be absolutely tuned into the present moment – using all the Inner Capacities – *and to be able to both notice and name what is present as a way to keep tension in play as data,* rather than use discomfort as a reason to dismiss what is unsettling and revert to type. Let me illustrate.

Drawing from a learning experience I had when training in group relations with the Tavistock Institute, I encountered a compelling process that helps a group move from *ought* to *is*. I have since used this frequently with leadership groups who wish to drop into a deeper reality about the truth of their patterns and interactions, dislodging what is unhelpful to their purpose, revealing what is being, yet hidden – and so catalysing change. The activity is situated within a clear frame to develop the capacity to be with what is and not what ought to be, and encourage the capability to notice and name that.

In short, we set up chairs in a room to form two intersecting curving lines that together make up a spiral shape (if you look down on the chairs from above). People are invited to choose their seats upon entering the room. Then, the facilitator frames the 45' task – usually along the lines of 'to learn how we are co-creating the system that we experience' (a suitably ambiguous statement of task). Throughout, the facilitator carefully moderates the process and conversation, ensuring that the task and time are followed and modelling the skill to non-judgementally notice and name what is occurring within the live group dynamics.

This seated spiral activity is one of the best exercises I have experienced to enable a group to truly see themselves in discomfort and uncertainty, when our default routines (ought codes) tend to get amplified. Often, the group wishes to move out of the discomfort of the seating structure by rearranging the chairs back into one big circle where they can all see each other, or, after a while, individual group members ask that they swap chairs with one another so that they can find a place that makes them feel OK. They might remain in such oughty debates for the first 20' of the activity.

Gradually, the group starts to notice how the pressure of their personal and collective oughts is pulling them away from simply being able to sit with what is the case – the unusual and intense seating arrangement and ambiguous task. The conversation starts to drop into a level of honesty and truth-telling not previously encountered within the group – they 'get real' with each other. Moreover, members begin to make connections between the difficulties and patterns they are directly experiencing in this seated spiral activity with how they are leading the wider system outside of the room ('our tendency here to want to wish discomfort away is precisely how we are not facing the whole difficulty of what our change is asking of us back in our workplace!').

I would not advise running this exact activity if you have not had some group relations training, or if you only have one day (it is very revealing to run this spiral activity at the start of each day of a multi-day get-together so that the group sees how it is growing in its capability to notice and adjust its patterns in real-time). However, I hope it helps illustrate two crucial principles of this Transforming Space skill: design and use encounters to provide a phenomenological experience of the movement you wish for (a 'living laboratory' of the desired change) and hold the experience in a way that keeps people in the turbulence of staying with what is. Do not sit around in the usual way debating what needs to change. Even inviting people to stand up and hold a conversation in which they walk towards each other when they agree with a statement, and walk away from each other when they do not concur, can help a group drop out of the tightness of ought-led routine and become freer to express truly what is on their mind.

Transforming Space, pause to experience

⇒ Can you imagine designing an encounter in your system that models the context and movement you wish for?

⇒ How might you set that up intentionally and transparently, using a combination of the Inner Capacities and other External Practices you have read about in this chapter?

This chapter has been a guide to the personal leadership skills it takes to catalyse change and movement in a way that can both unconceal deep wiring, and build the awareness to access full reality; moving from our hidden *oughts* to resourced *is-ness*. We started with the underpinnings of the Still Moving framework: this kind of leadership is predicated on facing and working with truth and reality, however disturbing or unsettling, and flows naturally when underpinned by a belief that *all shall be well* - we encounter all reality with clear, compassionate and trusting sight. In that respect, we need to *lead change with one's inside*. The quality of our outer actions and encounter with reality rests entirely on getting our inner state into the right place. The inside leads the outside.

We then took a journey through the Still Moving framework, starting, naturally, with your Inner Capacities, the quality of your being: becoming present to the moment, responding to experience with curiosity and intention, paying attention to the world through a systemic and not personalised lens, and taking a radical meta-stance beyond conscience to include all that we experience. These four inner state skills help you drop out of your oughts and become a powerhouse to encountering the world as it is, not conformed to how we wish or imagine it to be.

Next, we visited your quality of doing, the four External Practices that, when combined, help you catalyse movement in the systems around you in ways that enable a collective loosening of the oughts: finding purpose and future direction from within what is currently present, speaking difficult truths and working with the necessary disturbance in change, channelling anxiety along creative pathways and transforming the moment through experiential encounter.

At the heart of this approach to leadership – and you might have noticed a small circle in the middle of our Still Moving spiral framework, marked 'Your Essence' – is the task of finding our unique self and natural authority. We next move to discover and work with soul as the deepest of our resources to accompany us on our journey from *ought*, to *is*.

6

The Journey of the Soul

His soul swooned slowly, as he heard the snow falling faintly through the universe, and faintly falling, like the descent of their last end, upon all the living and the dead.

James Joyce, The Dead
(from the Dubliners' short story collection)

So ends the 1914 story of what Dan Barry of the *New York Times*, on the centennial of its release, has acclaimed as being 'Just about the finest short story in the English language.'[1] I wonder how I can still bring this lyrically melancholic line to mind, 48 years after my final school year when I studied Joyce's The Dubliners.

The Dead is the final short story in the collection.[2] In this concluding sentence, the central character, Gabriel Conroy, stands beside his hotel room window, looking out onto a Dublin square where the snow is falling thickly. It is the night of Epiphany (the twelfth night after Christmas when it is said Jesus was revealed to the Three Wise Men), and Gabriel silently reflects on his own epiphanous journey taken that evening. A journey which saw him shake off the cloak of his unsure, controlled and restrictive self (a microcosm of many men in Ireland at the time, including Joyce) to rekindle all his naturally passionate, uninhibited, tenderly protective manhood.

The short story in its entirety is an *ought* to *is* passageway and merits a brief examination here, as it beautifully illustrates the depth of the inner work needed to facilitate this movement to bring greater ease and truth contact to our lives.

From Ought to Is: Catalysing Change and Movement in a Polarised World,
First Edition. Deborah Rowland.
© 2025 John Wiley & Sons Ltd. Published 2025 by John Wiley & Sons Ltd.

The evening had begun with the reluctantly dutiful Gabriel showing up with his wife, Gretta, at his aunts' house to head up their Twelfth Night celebrations. One of his tasks for his aunts was to give an after-dinner speech – an obligation we hear him inwardly obsessing about all evening, rendering him unable to relax or enjoy himself. How would he come across? Would he get things right? He notices himself getting frustrated by the inner judge of his insecurities and inhibitions, not just for this occasion, but for his comportment in life in general. His oughts, the codes that ran his life, might have secured him familial and nationhood belonging, but these loyalties now felt suffocating. Gabriel and his wife eventually leave the dinner and, after walking across Dublin city through the heavily falling snow, where the swirl of troubled Irish history envelops them as much as the cold, wet flakes, find themselves in a hotel room.

There, for the first time in a while, child- and duty-free, and having witnessed his wife striking a beautiful pose at one point in the evening, Gabriel deeply wishes to break out of his restricted self and make love with his wife. Far from folding into his embraces, however, Gretta sobbingly recalls to him for the first time her memory of a passionate love affair she had when young with a youth called Michael, who had died aged 17 a short while after she had rejected him one night. His enduring love was now arresting her due to a soulful song she had heard sung at the party that evening, her response to which had caused her to look so alluring to Gabriel.

As she later lay sleeping on the bed, Gabriel, initially shocked at his wife's truth disclosure and its many years of concealment, ponders the role of the countless dead in people's lives and observes the reality that everyone he knows, himself included, will one day only be a memory, as Michael remains a shade for Gretta. As 'generous tears filled Gabriel's eyes', he found in this healing truth a profound affirmation of life – passion from the past *can* continue, the living need not be bound by external pressures and inner trapped pain but instead boldly and passionately carry forward the ever-ness of who they truly freely are.

Turning to the window, Gabriel hears the snowfall, and the story expands past him to encompass Ireland, the universe and all the living and the dead.

I still find the final paragraphs of The Dead profoundly affecting. So, what are we looking at here, and how is Joyce's masterpiece relevant to our journey through this book?

Our souls, that sense of our uniquely entrusted essence beyond the tangible, which will survive us as memory, are essential companions on the passageway from ought to is.

In a sense, they *are* the journey. Soul work is ought-releasing work. When we can uncover and fully accept our souls, loosening ourselves from any trapped loyalties, we begin acting from who we know we freely are.

When we are in touch with such truth, our distinct is-ness, we better manage our lives as we head towards greater congruence between our character and our path. This chapter aims to show just how much our souls are instruments for this movement from *ought*, to *is*.

Our Souls Guide Us Towards What Is

Throughout Joyce's story, one of the first (in English language literature) to be based purely on inwardness,[3] you hear the presence of Gabriel's inner voice. This firm yet inviting companion beckons him across the course of the evening to recall and reclaim the depths of who he essentially was before the cares of the world and repressive Irish society took him away from that unique self entrusted to him, his I.

I could imagine this soul resource sitting on his shoulder, whispering into his ear, 'Come on, Gabriel, cast aside those fleeting and superficial possibilities of being and doing which you toy with[4]!' When stiffly and unsurely delivering his 'foolish' speech at his aunts' dinner, I can imagine his soul morphing into an invisible guest beside him, poking him exhortingly in the ribs, 'Go on Gabriel, crack a joke, tell them about the one when you … .' You almost languish alongside his soul as it slowly and thankfully swoons at the conclusion of the story, with Gabriel's journey of self-recapture and more easeful union with the wider field of Ireland's souls accomplished, job done.

This journey to break free of our loyalties to oughts (the conscience codes that secured our early belonging yet now unwittingly run our lives) to venture towards the essential truth of who we are (the is-ness of self before attachment) can be a liberating and enlivening experience. Over the course of almost 16,000 words, we are privileged witnesses to Gabriel's experience of such an inner soul journey. The brilliance of Joyce's writing is that as we read the story, he invites us to think and feel differently about ourselves too – as if Gabriel's soul is calling out to ours from its depths, 'Come take a trip towards truth too'.

Can you recall epiphanous moments when you put your conditioned self aside and felt you had truly woken up to your soul, to your true, unique self?

Now in the Dead, we accompany Gabriel throughout just one evening. This kind of soul journey tends to take a little longer than that in our lives. Yet the story highlights that we cannot make this journey to travel from our wiring to our essential self via overt striving and ought-led approaches. Gabriel could only free himself from his inner trapped pain after he had softened into his wife's story and paid attention to its wider import (Curious and Intentional Responding and Acknowledging the Whole). This quiet, inner softening is also why we can enjoy the letting go-ness of the Saffire

Rose poem in Chapter 3, and need the quality of being and doing skills I wrote of in the last chapter. These skills are an essential resource in your backpack – and are learnable.

But nor can this journey from *ought* to *is* be accomplished solely through more conscious, trainable methods. In this chapter, I will summon a deeper, more out-of-awareness support for you – the essentialising workings of your soul. Without recapturing this special kind of inner subjective truth about who we are, we can feel quite wobbly and defenceless in the face of reality. We will strive for truth to fill a hole, not because it is essentially good. Souls ground us and bring the healing faculties of ease and grace to our lives.

The eagle-eyed among you will have spotted that tiny circle at the centre of the Still Moving skills framework from the last chapter, entitled, 'Your Essence'. This chapter is about that tiny circle. While this soul quality, unlike the skills in Chapter 5, is not trainable, it *is* knowable.

In the pages that follow, while I cannot write like Joyce, I wish to take you on a soul journey alongside me. We will explore the nature of soul and its deep origins in our ancestral and wider systemic realms and then dive into the elements of soul that bring us into greater contact with truth and reality – loosening the grip of our oughts. You will have a chance to do your own 'soul summoning' and consider soul's vital role in bringing inner freedom, insight and ease to your life – once you can free yourself of any trapped systemic loyalties. This section is about *living* with soul as a resource.

We will then move on to *leading* with soul, looking at the impact this soul-level contact can have on our capability to catalyse more effortless change in the systems we care for – which also have soul. As Joyce evocatively captured the duality of Ireland's oppressive/playful soul through the snow metaphor in The Dead, can you discern and imaginatively describe that intangible yet defining collective character of the systems you wish change for? During this section, you can turn to your cases and, with more awakened soul resource, plan what steps you wish to take to bring greater ease and flow to whatever team, community or institution you have in mind and within your heart.

Soul-level leadership suffuses our steps with a radiance that gives life to others.

At age 18, in my final school year, my soul was not yet in the fullest of its powers. Yet I do not doubt that the deep internal stirrings that reading The Dead drew forth in me accelerated my soul's faculty to alert me to the me of me. On the cusp of adulthood, I did not yet consciously know of my birth story and origin. Still, in the depths of my being, I heard the enduring love of my Irish ancestors' souls silently calling out to me and beckoning me to come and meet them one day – all the living and the dead.

⇒ I wonder, what silently being, yet hidden part of your soul might you be softly hearing now?

A Little Soul-Summoning

I sensed a mild apprehension as I set out to cover the nature of soul – a feeling that accompanied me in Chapter 3, as soul is as ineffable a notion as truth and reality. Yet thanks to the holistic, phenomenological knowing of our right hemisphere brain, we instinctively know what *soul* means – we know it when we experience its affect ('as generous tears filled Gabriel's eyes').

Before I offer my reflections, I invite you on a little soul-summoning activity of your own.

⇒ First, a moment of attention purifying. Whatever you do best to bring your mind to a quality of non-judgemental, present-moment attention, do that now (it might be breath focus work, closing your eyes to turn inward and scan your body for any sensations, paying attention to the sounds and scents in your current surrounds – however foreground or background).

⇒ Next, look around your current surroundings and take in its objects into your awareness. With the eyes of your heart lingering on each one, notice how noticing these objects impacts you on the inside. (Your eyes might linger on a photograph of a now-departed family member, an item of well-worn furniture, a piece of art, a pet animal or a treasured object you brought back from a holiday that meant so much.)

⇒ Reflect: which object has most arrested you, tugged at your heart, brought the most vivid of recollections, moved you on the inside, maybe made you do an inward gasp?

⇒ Silently register these soul-level stirrings. What is their quality? Try intentionally maintaining this quality of soul attention throughout this chapter.

I wish I could hear your reflections now, yet, somehow, I can hear the response of your soul awakenings within me as I write. (I did the activity too and alighted on a piece of Cornish sculpture, a memory of little gifts I gave out to those present for my 60th birthday celebration, an event that revealed to me how much I am loved.)

While it might feel challenging to put the nature of soul into words, what follows is my attempt to do so in a way that has my right hemisphere brain watchfully overseeing that the reading can remain a felt, lived experience (I cannot always loosen my loyalty to left hemisphere, cognitive valuing oughtness).

In her Revelations of Divine Love, Julian of Norwich says that the soul sees (truth), contemplates (wisdom) and marvels (in delight, love).[5] As I delight in 1960s and 1970s soul music, with its emphasis on soaring vocals, call-and-response singing, rhythm and improvisational additions with pure joy from the horns section, I might even suggest you stream some

James Brown or Aretha Franklin to get yourself into the zone while you read. Start with Sam Cooke's Bring It on Home To Me, deemed the first record to define the soul experience.

So, here's my take.

The Nature of Soul

Immediately, the following words come to mind when I imagine soul: Longing. Enlivening. Touching. Mates. Heart and –. Mystery. Ghost. Presence. Grace. Spirit. Inspiration. Eyes. Pools. Depth. Pulse. Essence. Truth. Wrenching. Searing. Surrendering. Outbreath. Departed. These words, for me, have soul qualities – visible signs or affects; they move me on the inside. So how to comprehend the source concept of *soul* itself?

Etymology and Locus

The modern English word *soul* etymology derives from the Old English *sáwol,* which comes from the Old High German *sêula, sêla.* The Germanic word is a translation of the Greek *psychē,* ψυχή – meaning *life, spirit and consciousness.* Soul entered the world when, 1.5 million years ago, it is said that our human species became aware that it was aware.[6] So, the Greeks believed that the soul gives the body life, vitality and awareness.

Philologist Max Muller notes that soul is the Gothic *saiwala,* saivs, a word of uncertain origin but most likely denoting the sea, the tossing sea within us, 'heaving up and down with every breath',[7] and the supposed stopping place of the soul before birth or after death; if so, it would be from Proto-Germanic *saiwaz.*

The Hebrew word for soul is *nephesh,* which means, *breath.* In Islam, the Koran uses two words for the soul: the immortal *rūḥ* – translated as *divine spirit, consciousness, the breath of life,* which drives the mortal *nafs* – translated as *self, essential character, psyche.* In Hinduism, *Ātman,* or soul, is conceived as the first principle, the *true self of an individual beyond identification* with phenomena (we could say here, oughts).

For Christians, the human soul is *God's dwelling place within us*; soul contains the spark of divine life. 'Between God and our soul there is nothing', wrote Julian of Norwich. In *Mirror of the Simple Souls,*[8] another early Christian mystic, Marguerite Porete, says that soul must give up reason, whose logical, conventional grasp of reality cannot fully comprehend God and the presence of Divine Love. Sounds like a travel from *ought* to *is,* towards a right hemisphere path to truth? Soul is another form of knowing the world, a more mysterious and sacred route to our knowledge of what essentially is, a higher faculty than intellect through which we can encounter the divine realm.

A key point of distinction throughout the millennia of contemplation of the nature of soul, is that between a belief that soul is separate from the body – humans are an incarnated soul, we are the soul's temporary dwelling place, versus the non-dualists who believe that soul *is* the whole living being, mind (soul) and matter (our bodies) are not separate – and so we have animated bodies. Even ancient Greek minds could not agree on this, with Plato favouring the former (dualism) and Aristotle the latter (non-dualism), in De Anima stating that the soul is the *'first actuality of a natural organic body'.*[9]

Non-dualists include the physicalist (and Christian) Nancy Murphy, who in *Bodies and Souls, or Spirited Bodies,*[10] puts forward a strong case from sources as wide-ranging as scripture itself, evolutionary biology and neuroscience to claim that mind (soul) and matter (body) are not separate; our soul is the highest faculty of our physiological minds that produce consciousness (see also the thought-provoking book, *I am a Strange Loop,*[11] by Hofstadter, for the physiological explanation of soul). Murphy claims that it was only when Rome took over early Christianity, and the likes of Constantine hi-jacked the formal religion and church with early Greek dualist thinking, that we separated soul and body and were taught that our lives were meant to be a preparation for soul's immortality.

A radical view (for a Christian). Yet I warm to it as a natural extension of physicalism is that we can embrace the whole of the physical world as having soul (what is so special about us humans, who, in any case, share the same DNA with the living world?). Aristotle and, subsequently, the thirteenth-century natural theologian and philosopher Thomas Aquinas, maintained that plants, animals, and humans had nutritive, sensitive and rational souls, respectively. Souls are forms of living things. This thinking seems to me a far better strategy for our positive relations with Earth and the rest of her inhabitants.

Soul and the Experiencing Field

Whether we believe that we temporarily carry or have embodied soul, I think we can all agree that we can experience and feel what soul is about. McGilchrist calls soul the *presence beyond the tangible.*[12] I can relate to this definition, and believe that soul is the spiritual, animating principle embodied in all human beings, collective bodies, life and the universe. We sense 'something' is in us and around us, even if we cannot put that presence into language or a box. I know that I, my dog, the different client systems I work with and the Dordogne landscape with its millennia of ancient history, all have their distinct entrusted soul.

The ancient Greek philosopher Heraclitus said all things are full of soul; the psyche is in everything, the mind is everywhere, the world is conscious and limitless, 'you will not find out the limits of the soul whatever way you travel, so deep is its logos'.[13] Panpsychists believe that everything material, however small, has consciousness or soul – the mind is across all reality. The British philosopher Galen Strawson claims that all physical matter is some form of energy and 'all energy … . is an experience-involving phenomenon.'[14]

While physics might give us the mathematics of the universe, this science of matter does not explain the mystery of its causality or actualisation. Philosophers such as Schopenhauer and Bertrand Russell are known for challenging the reductionists who claim that all matter can be reduced to inert maths, devoid of consciousness. But even eminent scientists such as the evolutionary biologist Sir Julian Huxley have written, 'Mind or something of the nature of mind must exist throughout the entire universe. This is, I believe, the truth.'[15]

Soul is, therefore, embodied phenomenologically in experience; it is intensely felt as real – even if that reality cannot be objectively and independently 'proved'.

Here are some moments when I have or have had a sense of the me who is experiencing my life. Singing my heart out during worship. Treading gently through graveyards. Kissing my mum farewell as I leaned over her coffin. Indi (my dog) and I staring into each other's eyes (he can hold the deepest, longest of gazes – and not just for getting food). Hearing Bach's sonatas and partitas for solo violin (yes, not just soul music). Drinking in a sunset. That wrenching visit to a place that has meant so much to me, for what I know will be the last time. An inner aching when I feel commitment cloaking me.

When I am in such soul territory, I am deeply conscious in the present moment, fuzzily alive, being touched by a presence inside and through me without any need (indeed, capacity) to explain or justify. But here's what soul territory does: it moves you. And this book is about how to bring movement to stuck places. Soul work can be the very deepest of catalysts for the acceptance of what is, awareness of what might be and hence, change.

Soul Work

Accessing our soul, though, that tossing sea within us, is no easy ride. Hence the expression, 'Dark Night of the Soul' – that moment of crisis when we thought we had arrived at some self-enlightenment or breakthrough, but then realised that we were far from attaining that truth or state we were searching for. Of Porete's 12 names for the soul, the last one is *oubli*, forgetting. I like this insight that one part of the soul is its capacity to forget itself. Awareness and the divine can easily pass from mind, as our long stories of conditioning are never that far away. So, we readily lose touch with our souls, our animating essence, when our oughts flood our being – as did Gabriel get sucked into the obsessions of petty conventionality, early twentieth-century Dublin.

Soul-searching work is therefore a journey that can entail two steps forward and one step back. Rather, we should not assume linearity at all, as I imagine soul work as moving upwards through a spiral. When we look down on a spiral, it seems like a circle, yet there have been ascending steps; you do not end up precisely in the same place. We were unconsciously born into our souls, yet it can take some time to consciously discover what we primally knew at the start of life, releasing ourselves from any unhelpful inherited entanglements. We find ourselves back at our beginnings, but now with added textures and layers from our life's journey. Maybe some of us know the core truth about who we are at a very early age, but I took a little time.

Whether at the outset of life or later in years, you know when someone has been on such a soul-awakening, accepting, and cleaning-up journey. They appear real, centred, and free of need.

I believe that one of life's most potent paths to inner freedom is to spend time getting to know and then acting from our souls – including accepting the nature of its impact on others. We'll learn more about how to do that as we move through this chapter, but the journey, for sure, demands our capacity for devoted, patient and steadfast attention (and, dare I say it, a spot of humour and lightness along the way ...).

Pause here for a moment of 'soul searching'

⇒ Bring to awareness your top embodied 'soul experiences' when you felt an internal riptide of longing, yearning, intimacy and hope.
⇒ How was it to do that? What was your somatic (inner bodily felt) experience of recalling this memory?
⇒ What quality of attention and reality perception are available to you when you are in contact with your soul?

So, what can we draw from this excursion into the nature of soul that holds relevance for this book - how to move from the rigidity of ought to the flow of reality contact when seeking change? From effort, to ease? How can we be with our lives a little less exhaustively and drop into soul as an enabler of truth and movement?

Living with Soul

> *As soon as we have a point of eternity in the soul, we have nothing more to do but to take care of it, for it will grow of itself like a seed. It is necessary to surround it with an armed guard, waiting in stillness.*
>
> Simone Weil, from Gravity and Grace[16]

Such beautiful words by the French thinker and activist, Simone Weil. Like Dag Hammarskjöld a decade later, she suffered an untimely death, yet also, and very thankfully, her notebook writings were later compiled into a compendium that remains a source of spiritual guidance and philosophical wisdom to this day.

Her words here invite us to find within ourselves that sense of everness that binds us to all the living, dead and those who will follow (and for her, some form of divinity). From that moment when we can find that seed of eternity, our souls are at ease in our life; our remaining task is to attentively protect this growing shoot of inner soul contact, defending it against the swirls of our fleeting worries and obsessions (I can imagine a sequel to The Dead, to find out how Gabriel Conroy might have done that ...).

In this section, I will draw out four elements about the nature of soul that enable us to seek, take care of and act from this the most nourishing of resources for our capacity to be with what is: soul as our unique, essential *character*; soul as our *calling*, a natural (not ought-led) authority to follow; soul as our *connector* with wider fields; and soul as our contact with the reality of *fate and mystery* in our lives.

Soul as Our Unique, Essential Character

> *My father's eyes – at last I see,*
> *the sparkling eyes that are,*
> *me*

Soul is the unrepeatable person we are. Akin to a term coined by the followers of medieval philosopher and theologian Duns Scotus, your soul carries your *haecceitas*, or 'thisness', that which makes you *your essential self*. The poet Manley Hopkins, greatly influenced by Scotus, called this process of individuation – how we become who we uniquely are – one of 'selving'.

While fluid, our essential selves – our souls – form a unique whole over time. They are the deep truth of us. Discovering the self that has been uniquely entrusted to us can be a life's work, and is not always a pretty process, but the uncovering can bring such a release from our oughts. There are many paths one can take on this journey, but I am struck by the oft-said insight that our eyes are the window to our souls.

Paolo Coehlo went a bit further; 'The eyes are the mirror of the soul *and reflect everything that seems to be hidden*; and like a mirror, *they also reflect the person looking into them*.'[17] The line above about 'my father's eyes' is from a poem I wrote shortly after meeting my biological father for the first time. Within the year, I had also had a reunion with my birth mother, and another poem followed, containing this line about the moment we first walked towards each other across that Dublin hotel reception:

'Our Irish eyes locked-tight, blue-grey'.

I'm no Manley Hopkins, yet I have included these lines here nearly 20 years since I wrote them as they speak to me about how I was discovering the deeply inherited essence, or soul, of me. What I was discovering predated the codes shaped in my early familial contexts as a solution to my belonging needs; this was something more primal. My father's eyes were literally my eyes (including the right one that slopes slightly), and while I had never consciously known him to this point, I discovered in his eyes my own playful, roving charmer self. In that hotel reception, my mother and I could not stop drinking in each other's eyes. We were making up for that lost time 42 years prior when the mother-infant gazing attachment process had been so mercilessly severed. I felt my untethered soul able to gingerly put one toe on the ground, for once.

Everything about my ancestral system, my inherited soul story that to this point had been hidden from plain sight, as Coelho writes, was now being mirrored back to me. I would go even further; my soul was guzzling it all up with one large fat straw. The final shape of the whole of me that was peculiar to me was taking form. The last lines of The Dead were coming home to roost. I had, of course, already acquired a wonderful crib of values from my adopted mum and dad through their love and upbringing, for which I will be eternally grateful. Nonetheless, this felt like something else.

Over the last 20 years, I have become more alive to the fullness of my soul, that unique life force, the self that has been entrusted to me and no one else. You might be picking up some of that life force through these pages – the rawness and the polish, the less sure and the sure, the untethered and the anchored, the wild abandon and the controlled calm – all the glorious is-ness of me.

And this reclaiming of my entrusted soul enabled me to do two things. Firstly, break free from my loyalty to be perfect and please others – two strong ought conditionings formed in my upbringing to secure early belonging as an adoptee. Of course, I still feel the effects of these impulses of perfection and pleasing, yet they no longer unwittingly govern my life. Secondly, I feel loosened from my systemically inherited loyalty to non-attachment.

Since meeting my biological family, it feels like I have moved across that loyalty threshold and feel blessed to move into the new territory of putting more of my toes firmly onto the ground (they certainly wish for that). Eeek!

To declutter the oughts from our life and meet reality in its fullest expression, we need to journey to find the nature of our uniquely entrusted soul, that which the forces that led to your life long for you to reclaim.

Pause point to consider the nature of your soul

⇒ What steps, significant people, events or landscapes were present at your birth and among the ancestral forces that came before you that have bequeathed you your essential character or soul? (Consider those elements that feel affective, troubling, stirring – still mysteriously present in your psyche.)

⇒ How might you describe the resulting soul that all these forces have entrusted to you, and no-one else? What might these forces also have required of you (your hidden loyalties) that you might wish to seek blessing to move beyond?

⇒ In Philip Pullman's great Trilogy, *His Dark Materials*,[18] he drew from Plato's theory that each human has their own 'daemon', an attendant guiding soul we carry through life. He created these external attending souls in creature form for his characters (such as a snake, bird, moth and animal); if you chose a creature to be your daemon that represented all your soul qualities, what creature would that be?

Soul as Our Calling, Our Natural Authority to Follow

> *Mild he lays his glory by, born that man no more may die.*
>
> Charles Wesley

I see soul as an active agent in our lives. Yes, it defines our essential nature, or (th)is-ness, but soul also asks that we *potentialise* this. If soul, as the Greeks claim, is the actuating cause of life, then it can have what Jungian analyst James Hillman writes of in The Soul's Code[19] as a *calling*, a deep intentionality as well as a character. Soul, once summoned and understood, can determine our path in life.

The above line of Wesley is my favourite from the Christmas carol, *Hark! The Herald Angels Sing*, and when singing it, the experience always brings tears to my eyes and has me raise my right hand. Christ was born *that* man no more may die. Putting aside any fleetingly vainglorious ego needs (ought strivings ...), mild, he knew what his essential task was on earth. He was born *that*.

Likewise, Manley Hopkins writes about how every mortal being (even stones, bells, and wells) has individuality *and* purpose in the beautiful short poem When Kingfishers Catch Fire. Our unique nature, our soul, carries the seed of something hidden within itself that it wants to propagate, cultivate, use and proclaim, 'Crying *What I do is me: for that I came*'. (line 8)

In just 10 words, Hopkins has captured how we can all find that path (what I do) that matches our essential nature (is me) *and* which holds an authority to follow (for *that* I came). Finding our soul's calling is not about straining and striving for some ought-led outer-conditioned goals but rather serenely seeking that which accords with the reality of *what is me*. Our souls have intentionality *from* our individuality, from our unique selves. Our purpose comes from our natural is-ness, not our conditioned oughtyness. It would be doing a profound disservice to the great sweep of forces that created our life – and animated our soul – if we ignored our is-ness and sought to become something we are not.

Now, it can take a while to be attuned to our soul's calling and to one that is free of unhelpful loyalty attachments. The calling is always there, and we deeply feel it tugging at us unconsciously. Still, we are often pulled away from this calling by our conditioned oughts or inherited ancestral systemic loyalties that need not be ours to carry – our calling needs to be cleaned up a bit.

Take what I now know was the deepest defining feature of my inherited soul that individuated my self – my untetheredness. My ought-led self tried to override that first actuality in my life, the wrenching of mother-infant attachment and no known father, and so in earlier years, I sought a life where I could attach myself, velcro-like, to a single company, relationship, home and nation. But that just never felt true. That life did not fit me.

So instead, I turned out living the life of what one friend and mentor has called an 'air plant', an organism that can find home and succour anywhere with no need to put down singular roots (someone recently called me, in a positive sense, very 'plural'). Untethered at one level yet attached to a wider field at another. My soul's journey over the years since I started to meet my biological family enabled me to loosen that hidden loyalty to non-attachment; in a sense, I found a blessing to move into new territory. Now, my soul can exquisitely hold the seeming untethered/anchored contradiction together simultaneously. Reconciling my life between these two polarities fills most waking moments of my day.

Far from seeing the untethered part of my soul as a 'bad' thing, however, I now know I have simply been following my soul's inner code as a natural authority. I arrived at this realisation partly due to my innate curiosity about the me of me and partly because I wanted to find out why I always felt a little 'odd' within a seemingly more conventional way of living one's life. This impulsion also brought me into contact with several deep soul guides and coaches – I could not have made this journey alone.

But the result of it all is that I have turned the primal is-ness of my untetheredness into an asset for working in the field of whole system change, where you need to be able to hold a neutrally detached, catalytic yet temporary place. While untethered to many things in life, I have nonetheless, at a broader level, anchored myself deeply in my faith and the field of researching, consulting and educating in the field of change.

As my life began in change, so shall I help the field. For that, I came.

Born that. For that, I came. Can we follow, not just find our soul? Be true to, not shy from our is-ness? One friend said, 'We need to honour our resistance'. By this, he meant that very often, physiologically, the soul says 'no' to what might be fleeting oughts. We can somehow viscerally feel in our bodies when we are not following our soul's authority and making compromises. The term 'soul', John Cottingham, the English philosopher, says, 'very often points us not just towards the selves that we are, but towards the better selves we are meant to be.'[20]

Can we dare follow our soul as our highest, most whole potential self, moving across any unhelpful loyalty thresholds? If we ignore our soul work, we miss out on a powerful invitation to our true life's party and forego any radiance we could bring to others around us, who could benefit from that contact with calling.

Here's a further bit of soul work for you.

Pause for a moment to reflect on your calling, your soul's natural authority

⇒ Spend time pondering the declaration, '... for that I came'. What words would precede that, for you? (And notice if your oughts shout out too loudly ...)

⇒ Without needing to have your calling clearly articulated as yet, now write up three words, 'my soul's calling' on a piece of paper. Stand up and place that piece of paper somewhere on the floor around you, where it feels like it has resourcing energy for you (you feel stronger and more stable, even if only imperceptibly so) – often this is behind you, maybe slightly to your left or to your right.

⇒ Fully feel yourself leaning back into that soul support. How does that feel, the presence of your soul having your back?

⇒ Now write up on a separate piece of paper the words, 'where I most long for change' (this might be about your life or a work situation), and place that on the floor in front of you. Facing that situation with your soul's calling as a resource, does anything feel different as you look on this situation? What is that difference?

⇒ Sit back down and reflect: looking to your future life, what may you be called towards? Which oughts might you need to loosen your loyalties to in order to fully arrive at your calling?

Getting acquainted with our soul's character and following its calling, free of unhelpful attachment, enables us to live the life uniquely earmarked for us. As Hammarskjöld said in his journal, 'At every moment you choose yourself. But do you choose *your* self?' Once we can exclude the superficial and fleeting possibilities of our being and doing, and release ourselves from any unhelpful inherited loyalties, then can we cast anchor 'in the experience of the mystery of life, and the consciousness of the talent entrusted to you which is your *I*.'[21]

As we begin acting from who we know we freely are, we discover an inner ease and radiance which benefits others and the causes we have chosen. Soul work is not selfish work.

There are two additional features to soul's nature that take us from the personal realm into the collective: soul as our connector to wider fields and soul as our contact with fate and mystery.

Soul as Our Connector with the Deep Truths of Wider Fields

> *I am alive, alive to the depths of my soul, and in touch somewhere with the vivid life of the cosmos.*
>
> D.H. Lawrence[22]

While our souls might be our essential character and calling, we are not alone in life with them. Lawrence evokes how our soul energy vibrates with the soul energy of much wider fields. Like the animals we share our landscapes and biology with, we will die from the loss of this powerful soul need to belong and find our home in the universe.

The inspiring South African psychiatrist, poet and environmentalist, Ian McCallum, calls for us to better understand and reinforce these evolutionary bonds that interconnect us with all life. Remembering where we have come from 'is to rediscover that original church within oneself and to remember that the wild areas of the world are the landscapes of the soul and that creatures who belong there are soul makers.'[23] I am sure we have all been touched when situating ourselves within wild soul-scapes of nature, wherever we live and have travelled.

We do not need to belong to any organised religion to sense that 'original church within oneself'. The natural philosopher Schelling coined the notion, *Weltseele*, or world-soul,[24] by which he meant an all-encompassing primordial energy flowing through the universe that continually renews itself as it encounters a difference within, like a vortex arising in a stream. He claims that our souls arise similarly and that nothing is distinct from anything else.

While our souls might define us, they do not divide us. Souls have inherent 'attractor' energy that can summon and align wider fields – so what a resource they are when we wish to lead movement within our communities, teams and organisations. Like invisible pheromones in the living world that lay down their scent to summon and affect surrounding matter, so do our soul energies act as waymarkers – inspiring and guiding movement, creating alignment and belonging. We know what it is like when we are in contact with wider soul-scapes.

I feel my boundaries become a little fuzzy, and I melt at my edges. I am sure many of us have had that experience when gazing at a night sky full of infinitesimal stars and galaxies. Or experiencing a piece of music when you need to close your eyes, your entire body tingles from your scalp to your toes, and you feel you, the audience, the music and the location all dissolving into a single wholeness. Or visiting the resting places of your ancestors when you feel compelled to whisper a sentence or two to those who came before you, and who made you, possible. When I visited my biological paternal grandparents' graves earlier this year, my guide said that the whole section of the graveyard where they were buried was a 'village' of their neighbours and friends. I felt compelled to take in their entire community, too.

Through soul, we know we belong to a wider universe and that at the level of the psyche, we are all deeply interconnected and of one. We meet soul within the tugs of fields far wider than us.

Our soul's gift is, therefore, not just our own essence and intentionality, our character and calling, but a tuning-in capacity to sense a presence beyond the tangible in all that we encounter. This presence unifies us within a larger field and fuels our kinship and belonging. If we are not in contact with our soul, we cannot be at home in the world.

And neither can we deeply sense that world. I will share more in the next section on *leading with soul,* but this soul-led capacity to sense a presence beyond the tangible within wider systems is a critical skill for encountering reality and catalysing change. I wonder how, if senior leaders in the UK's Post Office had been able to summon the soul energy of the centuries of history behind the institution, they might have tackled the anomalies of a modern-day IT system a little differently.

All our organisations and communities carry a collective soul inherited and shaped from the landscapes and events of their origin and history. You will not be able to *Tune into the System* around you (see last chapter) without accessing its energy. Soul level, one could say, spiritual, intelligence enables us to get in touch with not only ourselves but also the entirety of the *vivid life* surrounding us – present, past, and what is to come. This inherent system energy is a potent mobiliser to summon when seeking to catalyse change.

Pause for a moment, to slip into a wider soul-scape

⇒ When have you been in tune with the soul energy of a wider field (including the legacy in the present moment of significant past events and people)? What was that like, and what enabled that connection?

⇒ If you were to map the 'vivid life' of the system you now wish change for, who and what are its 'soul makers' (from the past, present and even future)? Can you touch the 'original church' within this system?

Soul as Our Contact with Fate, Mystery and the Unknown

> *This is what I believe: That I am I. That my soul is a dark forest. That my known self will never be more than a little clearing in the forest. That gods, strange gods, come forth from the forest into the clearing of my known self and then go back. That I must have the courage to let them come and go. That I will never let mankind put anything over me, but that I will try always to recognise and submit to the gods in me and the gods in other men and women. There is my creed.*
>
> D.H. Lawrence, from an Essay on Benjamin Franklin[25]

Soul brings our conscious self to the right size. In these evocative words of Lawrence, he describes how a large part of our soul contains deep unconscious workings that cannot be seen and are not ours to control. We are not totally in charge of our soul's journey of selving. Rather, the soul takes its time with us; our task is to listen patiently, welcome in the forces that help us discover our character and our calling when they come knocking, and, equally, bid them farewell when they choose to leave.

Soul work, as Weil writes, is a waiting and attending game.

I like Lawrence's metaphor of the known self being able to open and close the door to these unconscious guides, and that each of their visits enriches ourselves. The arena of that known self might not be totally in our control, but can we be open to some divine visiting presence from within? It's a bit like putting up an 'all mysterious and unexpected visitors welcome!' sign on the door to the home of our soul. While, as Weil suggests, we need to put up guards around our 'point of eternity' within, there still must be swing doors to our psyche for the comings and goings of sacred guides. As we get to know these divine mysteries inside us a little more, and encounter them in experience, we can learn to recognise their calling card and follow their path for us.

In a sense, souls can see the whole of us, including our oughts which run our lives and take us away from who we essentially are. They do not wish to battle with them but rather help bring them to our awareness so that we can consciously choose how to live our lives without their grip.

Gabriel Conroy could easily have been angry with his wife's concealment of a prior love to their marriage, and jealous of that love that preceded him. Yet, far from getting 'hissy', he courageously submitted to the is-ness of this disturbing truth disclosure, as that prior love had gifted him his wife's arresting pose earlier that evening that had rekindled his passion. His soul was pointing him towards the more profound revelation that what was causing him pain was also catalysing movement, a recapturing of his self and his first love for his wife. A far worse suffering would have been to stay in moral outrage.

Out of embarrassment, I could have readily fought to suppress my choking emotions during my Madame Butterfly experience or, in fear, run out of the opera (I did see my escape route). Yet, I kept the door open for whatever invisible forces were coming my way from deep in the dark forest of my psyche. Both experiences show how our souls are essential coaches for us to learn how to befriend and trust in the forces of fate in our lives and not fight or flee from what comes our way.

When we fight fate, we stay stuck in our learned coping routines. When we surrender to its forces, we release movement. Our souls can give us the big, wide-open arms to bring all of life on. This is such an essential skill if we wish for change, as otherwise, we will discount anything that feels new and unsettling. When we are in contact with our soul as a resource, all that comes our way can be an enriching encounter.

Back to being resourced by fate, the analyst James Hillman makes a convincing case in *The Soul's Code* for there being a pre-existing 'acorn' of our psyche planted within us from at least birth, if not before. During the very formation process in our mother's womb, our soul is taking shape, already knowing who we will become. We carry transgenerational, system souls.

Before the fact of my birth mother's pregnancy with me became visible, her parents put her teenage self alone on a ferry from Dublin to Liverpool to escape the shame of unmarried motherhood in Catholic Ireland. What she must have been going through. And a full seven months before I was taken from her arms, my pre-natal blob of dividing and growing cells was being cast out and tossed, untethered, across the Irish sea.

As I got to know my birth mother and heard of the fate of her parents, I picked up generational floods of displacement. As Lawrence writes, 'Far back, far back in our dark soul the horse prances'. Just how far back? I'm not going to attempt to answer that unanswerable question, but I do hope I am getting you acquainted with these thoughts:

- *That soul predates our oughts,* so getting to know our soul's code is a worthwhile, if not essential, journey to take if we wish to break free of our limiting loyalties to our conditioning and awaken ourselves to a more primal truth and reality in our lives. While our oughts might have bought us secure belonging in early survival groups, our souls can give us the freedom to break out and follow that original self that has been uniquely entrusted to us and us alone.

- Getting to know our soul is a challenging developmental exercise in *surrendering to mystery and not knowing* (understanding that small circle in the centre of our skills framework is not mechanistically writing up your espoused values or life goals) and
- The agency we have in the journey of our soul's selving is one of being able to *notice, recognise and welcome visitors from a realm quite alien* to that which we already know.

I found it illuminating to discover that Lawrence's 'My Soul is a Dark Forest' credo was written in protest response to Benjamin Franklin's attempt, which was as follows:

'That there is One God, who made all things.'
'That He governs the world by His Providence.'
'That He ought to be worshipped with adoration, prayer, and thanks- giving.'
'But that the most acceptable service of God is doing good to men.'
'That the soul is immortal.'
'And that God will certainly reward virtue and punish vice, either here or hereafter.'

Can you sense the difference between Lawrence's earlier credo and the one above? What is that? I discern a vivid distinction between recognising and submitting to the deep divine forces contained in my soul, welcoming the workings of those 'strange gods' with reverence and deep respect, and the imposed duty to worship one great big God who exists outside of me and who imposes rewards or punishment on my soul according to my deeds. Soul as the guiding God-mystery within us versus soul as God's servant. Creativity, spontaneity and engagement versus dictate, obedience and dominion.

One could say, *is* as contrasted to *ought*. Or enabling versus imposing change. More in the next section on *leading with soul*, but again, just as our soul flourishes when we welcome in fate and not knowing, so does the deeper field of whole systems relax when it can re-include missing or unexpected elements (I once asked a team to invite more into their aware-ness a new 'awkward' industry regulator, to see it less as an intrusion but more as a partner – which visibly relaxed the atmosphere in their meetings and created some breakthrough thinking).

If we can get used to the workings of fate in our lives, we can be more alive and alert to the unexpected, emergent and sometimes unwanted expe riences within our teams, communities, and institutions as indicators of what most needs our attention to release movement.

Pause for a moment to reflect on the workings of fate within our soul's journey

⇒ How has this section impacted you?

⇒ Can you recall moments when you have overridden an impulsive reaction to a new unsettling experience and instead trustingly sought an inner guiding soul voice within the situation, beckoning you on to discover something vital about the nature of yourself in the world?

⇒ Does the team and community you work within have the capacity to welcome in the unexpected moments as 'truth and reality signs' knocking at your door, rather than points of discomfort to defend against or recover from?

To recap this section on living with soul. Soul is a tremendous resourcing energy in how we live our lives: as our essential unique character, through soul we get in contact with our own is-ness, the truth of I, enabling us to see our oughts and any inherited systemic entanglements more clearly; as our calling, soul can help us learn to live our lives with greater congruence and ease, less governed by oughts and hidden loyalties; as a connector with wider fields, we can be contained within and able to shape systems around us; and as our contact with fate and mystery expands, we become more reverent to welcome in the unknown and unexpected.

What a resource soul is. Can we take seriously the task of knowing, accepting, and acting from our souls? This task not only brings us a more easeful life; it is a prerequisite for being able to lead change and movement in less effortful and more fulfilling ways.

Leading from Soul

In this section, I will plop soul – our character, calling, connector and contact with the unknown – firmly at the centre of the Still Moving leading change skills spiral and highlight how it enables us to lead change with greater depth, wisdom and radiance. Soul work powers up our Inner Capacities – our quality of *being*, and it animates our External Practices – our quality of *doing*. This all adds up to soulful leadership. When you can act from who you truly are and know that your leadership is coming from this source, not only does that feel better for you, but you invite others into truth and reality alongside you.

Soul Work Powers Up Our Inner Capacities

Soul work is the gymnasium of our inner state. The stirrings of our psyche produce a rich inner workout that pulsates through our being, a heart pumping blood through the muscles of the Inner Capacities. If we believe that catalysing change begins with working with the reality (not projection) of a system and that working with such reality starts with inner work, then dropping into the territory of the soul is, pardon the pun, a 'no-brainer'.

When we engage with soul, we build our capacity to be present with ourselves, respond intentionally to experience, and perceive reality around us in more complex and less simplistic ways. We welcome all of life's experiences with wisdom and generosity. All inner state hallmarks of successful change leadership. I see this as a magical reinforcing loop (see Figure 6.1). The more we engage in soul work, the more we power up our Inner Capacities, and the more we do that, the richer our soul work becomes. The External Practices, what people can see us doing, should be grateful for how we learn to lead with our insides.

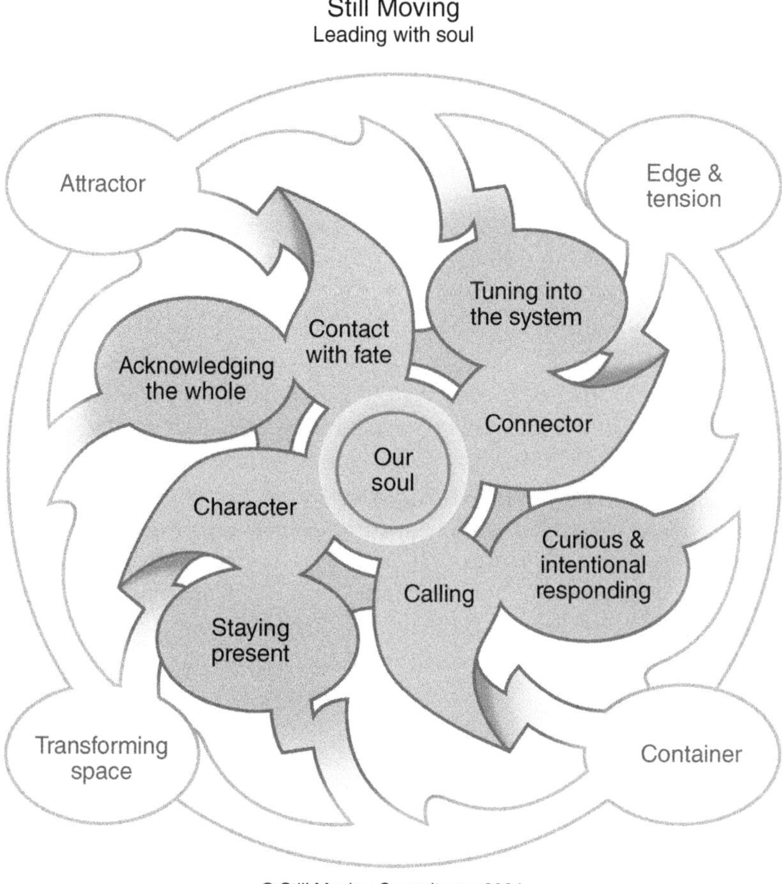

Figure 6.1 Leading with Soul as the Gymnasium of Our Inner State

Discovering Our Character – Staying Present

Soul moments are present-awareness moments. The fluid process over time to scoop up these moments and see how they point us to our unique, essential character asks us to be alive to our inner state in discerning, non-judgemental and welcoming ways, Staying Present. The soul's discovery journey, including Porete's moments of forgetting and coming back to awareness, is brilliant training ground for our ability to sit with and notice our inner experience (which can be easily distracted) - the starting point for effecting change.

At the Still Moving practitioner masterclass I wrote of in the Introduction, one of the participants introduced a 'soul exercise' as an experiment. Before sending us off to complete the activity, he happened to mention a recent story he had heard about a baby monkey that was taken from its mother at birth, and that immediately began howling in deep grief. Everyone chuckled and rose for the activity, but my soul whooshed from having a casual interest in the exercise to being utterly present and nowhere else.

As we walked into our smaller groups for the exercise, my whole body pulsated with resonating awareness. The experience became a great exercise in welcoming the (unsettling) present moment and exploring its territory. Willing to be entirely in the moment and not distracted, I had a better chance of seeing what was there and could see the truth of my soul more clearly. This moment of complete perception enabled me to share with my colleagues the true nature of my soul in the richest way I have ever done.

As a childless adoptee, I had never either received or given that sustained mother-infant gaze. This reality has left me both profoundly rootless at one level, and free at another to work *with* this untethered sensation and contribute my non-genetic memes into the field of disruptive change. A fantastic community of Still Moving change colleagues and practitioners now contribute to and take from this field.

The soul's nature keeps our inner state on its toes (even when asleep, are we alert to its visitors in our dreams?). When we are alive to present-moment experience, that state of awareness mulches the soil in which our soul grows. Exploring our psyche asks that we notice and register our inner state with all its rich contours, including those moments that come unbidden and those we summon.

Once we have sharpened our sense of our essential self, what we register in our inner state awareness can be more easily sifted into 'what belongs to us' – which is ours to deal with, and what belongs to the system – which is valuable data that can be brought to the attention of others and our leadership of the situation. When you are feeling 'out of character,' it is likely you are picking up projections of the system around you (I once worked with a leader whose soul was imbued with patience, who could then tune into any restlessness inside of him as a sign of impatience within his team – helpful insight for him as their leader).

Soul work stirs up our inner state. We can either suppress that sensation and take our experience to be somewhere else, or, take the perturbing feeling as a great training ground in Staying Present to what is. The more we are present to our inner state, the more that capacity enriches our soul's process of selving. Staying Present, and soul work, are such mutual bedfellows.

Following Our Calling – Curious and Intentional Responding

The soul's journey to discover our natural calling (for that I came) enables us to live our lives through intention, not reaction, thereby giving us a super development experience in the Inner Capacity of Curious and Intentional Responding. Every moment of every day, we can respond to what comes our way, either on autopilot or consciously intentional. Our calling – that natural authority of our soul – enables us to 'hit the pause button' on experience and respond to all that comes our way from a more centred, imaginative, and less impulsive place.

I return here to how Dag Hammarskjöld used his private journals while Secretary General of the United Nations – a significant public position of world power – to capture and reflect on his inner experience and spiritual compass. I do not doubt that the soul-led way in which he did this (by writing poetry and examining his faith, not day-to-day grumblings about his job and the people around him) helped him show up as a leader who could serve the geopolitical system around him free of any unprocessed inner needs and neuroses.

How often do we stop and notice our inner state (Staying Present) and *intentionally regulate that* to lead more effectively in our outer experience (Curious and Intentional Responding)? Just look at this journal entry of Hammarskjöld, the most soulful description I have seen of how to be in curious and intentional response.

> To have humility is to experience reality, not *in relation to ourselves*, but in its sacred independence. *It is to see, judge, and act from the point of rest in ourselves (author's italics).* Then, how much disappears, and all that remains falls into place. In the point of rest at the centre of our being, we encounter a world where all things are at rest in the same way. Then a tree becomes a mystery, a cloud, a revelation, each man a cosmos of whose riches we can only catch glimpses.[26]

Soul work leads us to that 'point of rest at the centre of our being' when we are so at ease with who we are and why we came, that we are available to access reality independent of our strivings. This humbling capacity ensures we are free to meet the essential (sacred) character of all experience that comes our way. We do not get personally muddled up in what we see. We have no impulse to bend reality to our will but instead, open it up to its most fulsome truth. Our souls do enable us to marvel, as Julian of Norwich says.

Just imagine, what would it be like to experience a leader with that unwavering capacity? We will be seen, we can blossom, we will want to disclose, and we will rest assured that all that we bring will in some way have value. If we, too, as leaders, can hit the pause button on any innate reactivity and, with humility, show up to what we experience with soul-led compassion, curiosity and intent, then people around us relax and can do likewise – enabling movement.

With the soul-powered Inner Capacity of Curious and Intentional Responding, all that comes our way (people, emails, meeting dynamics, unexpected events) is inherently a revelation, not an inconvenience. And with revelation and awareness, comes movement.

Connecting with Wider Reality – Tuning into the System

When we are in touch with our souls, we are in touch with wider fields. From within our distinctly individuated eddy of Schelling's Weltseele, we connect with all of life: while we might be unrepeatable, we are not unreachable. If we can source that interconnected soul level of our being, boy, can we see the undercurrents surrounding us. Now, we need to have our distinctiveness; otherwise, we would all blend into one large soup and become the proverbial fish swimming in the water, unable to see it is swimming in water. The entire universe is held together through union and distinction.

But if we have touched depths in ourselves, so can we see the profundity in what we encounter in others and wider fields. If we have taken the time to recognise our patterns and purpose, so can we spot a system's interlocking order and intentionality. Not only that, but we can also be clear, truthful, and compassionate about what we see, as our soul work requires that we be honest and easy on ourselves. As my yoga teacher says, when I am wobbling in Vrksasana – tree pose – seeking inner balance, I need to both acknowledge the wobble and be able to smile.

I have worked with one of the world's most soul-led systemic change practitioners, Judith Hemming. Through using an approach called systemic constellations, she can see how whole systems contain souls drawn from their collective past and their founding stories, that transcend the lives of their individual members. As another practitioner in the field, Racquel

Schlosser, writes,[27] institutions, teams, communities, and nations all carry memories and qualities that affect the daily functioning of people within them in the present day. Leaders need to surface, and work with, the collectively held, unconscious dynamics that exist alongside tangible structures and functions, as this meta-reality will have different operating rules to any conscious mission or set of values.

I once worked alongside Judith with a group of leaders from a large energy institution that needed to reinvent itself completely. This reinvention meant the historically profitable flow of money between this institution and their shareholding municipalities would become a thing of the past. And yet, their home nation had benefited for decades from this flow of wealth, including being able to fund the manufacture of steel that had armed their military during the Second World War (and bombed the nations that were now part of its expansion plan). In its then-current state, this company meant far more to the country, than just being an energy supplier.

When Judith, through her soul-led tuning into the system skill, uncovered this ancestral story of exchange and troubling events and enabled today's leaders to name and face this reality (including how its hidden operating rules and loyalties in a changed world were now holding them back), it felt like the senior leadership team issued one large collective out-breath; from this place, they found their way to be at ease with both the benefits and costs of reinventing their business model.

Soul work is a prerequisite for system work. The soul, Julian of Norwich says, *was made* to see truth. Leave this extraordinary reality lens behind at your peril when you are seeking to get beneath the surface of what is going on in your team, community or institution. Without soul-level seeing, you will struggle to find out what is causing stuck-ness. Just as our soul contains our deep individuating essence, this process of selving is always working its way through the systems we encounter.

With soul-seeing perception, you will bring an aesthetic eye to read the intonation of a leadership team's dialogue – that might otherwise appear humdrum; a compassionate eye to a community that is struggling or in conflict – that might otherwise appear aggressive; a spiritual eye to an organisation that feels lost and devoid of meaning – that might otherwise feel hopeless and in need of rescuing; and an eye of laser-like clarity to see the entanglements of a group that is unwittingly stuck in defensive routines of denial, cynicism and splitting – that might otherwise appear bewildering.

All such systems are in some way on their distinct soul's journey. The task of a change leader is to, mole-like, burrow into them to find out what they are about.

Our souls gift us a perceiving capacity to view reality beyond the obvious. A route to understanding truth beyond the mechanistic and reductionistic.

A means to tune into the reality of a system that can provide a startling reframe of what is being experienced – Tuning into the System at its most potent. While our oughts close shut the doors of our perception, our souls swing them wide open. The whole of our inner state becomes a seeing entity. We can answer Paul's prayer to the Ephesians that 'the eyes of your heart may be enlightened' (1:18), and through this soul-level perception, help others to rewrite old scripts and seek new paths too.

Our Inner Capacity to Tune into the System will be a much thinner one without engaging with soul.

Soul Knows About Darkness and Mystery – Acknowledging the Whole

> *I wake and feel the fell of dark, not day,*
> *What hours, O what black hours we have spent,*
> *This night!*

Gerard Manley Hopkins

As mentioned, soul work is no easy ride or walk in the park. We will encounter these 'Dark Nights of the Soul' that Hopkins, the trainee Jesuit priest, wrote of so searingly in his bleakest set of poems as he struggled to find union with God. We might not like the strange gods that come unbeckoned into the clearing of our soul's dark forest, and feel ourselves welcoming them through gritted teeth. Or we might like them a lot and become bereft when the magic of their nourishing presence becomes but a fleeting visit, and we realise that the presence of our *haecceitas* is not stable. We thought we had just grasped our unique calling, but after this initial illumination, there it goes again. We return to feeling bound by the comfortable familiarity of a deep ought's convention.

As the soul's journey is towards wholeness as well as individuation – the union of elements within us and between us to the wider (sacred) field – it asks that we find the space large enough within ourselves to embrace the opposites and the contradictions, the welcome and the unwelcome, the ease and the struggle. If we choose to take this path to the ultimate reality, the is-ness beyond our oughts, we will require the highest intensity piece of soul equipment within the Inner Capacities gymnasium; that which builds your muscle to Acknowledge the Whole.

This Inner Capacity is a standout skill for leading significant change. Once you have felt 'the fell of dark' soul work, it becomes easier to approach the turbulence necessary for transformation. As a leader once said to me, when I was researching leadership effectiveness at PepsiCo in the United States, 'Deb, every great leader needs to have had a "dark alley" experience'.

Now, you do not need to engage in intentional dark experiences to cultivate this capacity, but struggle and inner turmoil help to bring out the fullness of what it is like to enter unknown – even unwelcome – territory. This is soul work.

To illustrate, I recall working as a change coach for a large company that had realised it needed to make dramatic changes to survive a marketplace revolution. During my initial conversations with the CEO, he said one thing that struck me vividly. He said that he needed to take all his senior leaders for a 'walk into the woods' where they would get lost and disoriented, a little frightened and unsure, catalysing a shake-up of their inner state *so that* they would by necessity, start to read and respond to their environment quite differently, and in so doing, shed their old ways and discover new paths. Lawrence's metaphorical 'dark forest' was to become a reality.

We designed an intensive development process for his leaders that was far from straightforward training, but one that took them on a deep soul journey to facilitate their entity's change. This involved challenging work with all four of the systemic Ordering Forces: Belonging and loyalties to old ways of operating required a dramatic and sad ending; the sweeping forces of Time became prominent as we both honoured how the previous 120 years had made them the company they were now, and created vivid awareness of the rapidly approaching different future; various units and prominent individuals were going to have to get used to being in a different Place, which brought much turbulence; and we kept the eyes of their hearts on seeing and acknowledging the painful costs and consequences of the necessary changes, as there was significant human impact.

All this deep, collective soul work built a robust inner capacity to Acknowledge the Whole. Leaders became more comfortable with being in discomfort. They spent days (literally) walking in the woods to find meaning within their disturbance (both for their organisation and themselves). They became more at peace with the difficult leadership decisions and acts they had to take. Soul work built their capacity to be with, and not shy from, turbulence. In return, the institution's soul benefitted from this experience as the fate of the enterprise could now be acknowledged and realised (a breakup after such a long history).

It can be an agonisingly unsettling liminal step between knowing what to do to bring about desired change, and then doing it. Yet you need to hold this discomfort, Acknowledging the Whole, otherwise there is always a temptation to retreat. When we have encountered the depths of our soul's journey, we will be far better equipped to continue along the path.

Pause for a moment to reflect on how you can cultivate soul-infused Inner Capacities

Taking into your full awareness your stuck situation where you would like to bring greater flow and movement:

⇒ How can you pay more present-moment attention to your soul's stirrings within the situation (taking periodic moments to tune into yourself) to cultivate greater calm and perspective? *Staying Present*

⇒ Take the person/situation that most troubles you and where you are finding yourself in judgemental reactivity; how can you find that 'point of rest at the centre of your being' to loosen your interpretation of reality, and switch to curiosity about what is presenting itself (and discover *in you* why it has been troubling)? *Curious and Intentional Responding*

⇒ Can you begin to look more compassionately and wisely at the stuck situation by tuning into the deeper soul stirrings of the system, so that you can perceive and help people talk about what is truly going on? *Tuning into the System*

⇒ Where is the darkness, the unknown and the mystery within your case, and how might you swing your soul's door wide open to receive and integrate that? *Acknowledging the Whole*

Soul Work Animates Our External Practices

Our soul work is primarily connected to our Inner Capacities; they stimulate and require each other. With these two inner elements powered up, you will de facto have more animated External Practices – your leadership behaviour will be suffused with insight, depth and radiance, a phenomenon at Still Moving we call *being before doing*.

However, before I conclude this chapter on the soul's capacity to release us from our wiring and better receive reality, facilitating the journey from *ought* to *is*, I will share some final observations and vignettes about what soul-level leadership looks like across the four External Practices - the quality of what we need to *do* to lead change well. This section aims to give you some practical ideas on approaching your cases soul-fully (Figure 6.2).

Attractor Leadership – Holding the Narrative and Soul of the Company Through Time

Narrative coherence is profoundly settling when we are in incoherent and unsettling times. Attractor leadership skill is about drawing people within an entity towards an aligned purpose, and fostering belonging and loyalty to this entity by constructing meaning for its work in the world. You know you have Attractor leadership when people feel appropriately proud to be part of a

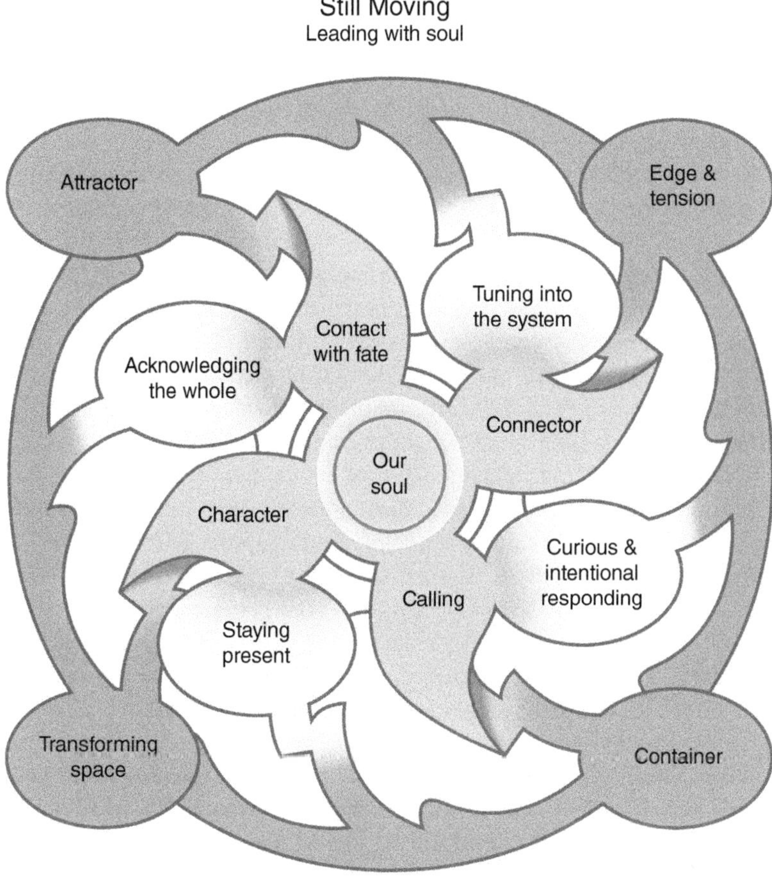

Figure 6.2 Soul Work Powers Up Our Inner Capacities and Animates Our External Practices

system, they feel what they do together deeply matters, they can contribute directly to the system's purpose, direction, and beneficiaries, and, if any change is required, it is always positioned as part of an unfolding story of becoming. (This reminds me of a powerful soul-level Attractor question that helps you co-create vision and identity for an entity: *who are we trying to become?*)

I once worked for the global food and beverage company, PepsiCo. The fact that I am still in contact with previous colleagues almost three decades later, speaks to the soul of the place. I loved my time there (I only left due to my relocation from the United States to the United Kingdom for personal reasons).

At PepsiCo, joining mattered. The system's soul took great care in welcoming new hires and inducting them into PepsiCo's (then) 120-year story.

As head of Organisational and Leadership Development, I was responsible for the onboarding programme *Experiencing PepsiCo*. Even as I reflect now, I notice how important the word 'experiencing' feels. As I have earlier said, soul is encountered phenomenologically; the reality of soul is a subjectively lived experience. Here's a flavour of this programme.

We held Experiencing PepsiCo, I recall, several times a year, scooping up all new hires in that previous period, primarily centred at the 'headquarters' (which was Richmond, London, when I ran the European programme, and Purchase, New York state, when I ran the global US programme for the most senior of hires). This mattered because we believed buildings and places carried memory, charge and energy. Touring the location was always built into the programme, and many stories were recounted about the people who had worked and the events that had occurred there. In a sense, it felt like we were joining a tradition, not a company.

Here's the main thing, though, that stood out for me. For programme pre-work, every participant was invited to read *not* the facts and figures about the company and its products, *but every recorded speech of PepsiCo CEO's past and present*. You felt the past was speaking to you when you read their words. The voices of long-gone leaders had been honoured and respected, as it was recognised that each of them had made the next period of PepsiCo's story possible. Nobody was excluded, whatever their performance record. They were all beads in the long leadership necklace of the system's soul.

Participants reported this was one of the most touching and instructional parts of the programme; they were also joining this line of leadership (note here how system soul was drawing on the deep Ordering Forces of Time and Belonging). They could discern deep patterns and meta-codes from across all the CEO speeches that compellingly conveyed the enduring character and calling of the organisation. Clearly, the institution had an 'essential life' that transcended those of individual leaders. I can still recall how the then-current CEO would join the programme in person, giving time to each new hire, looking them in the eyes, welcoming them to the institution, and then sitting down informally to open a dialogue about what they had deduced about the soul of the company – no need for any formal mission statements.

Story, including past stories, matters to the soul of a system. All the living and the dead. Without the inclusion of past stories, there can be no future story. (I once met with a newly incoming CEO of a renowned champagne house – tough life being a change coach – and the first thing she did was take me into a cellar, not to drink her product, but with white-gloved hands, show me the 150-year-old notebook of the house's founder where he had noted down the essential notes and character of his champagne. She used this little book to catalyse the future changes she would lead.)

How can we keep a system's story alive and sustained over time, including any troubling events that we might wish to exclude? That's soul-led Attractor leadership. We will always be pushing water uphill if we try to bring change without story.

Edge and Tension, from a Place of Deep Respect

Edge and Tension leadership is the ability to talk straight, name reality, and challenge assumptions. Truth charges change. But there are many ways in which this can be done, some more skilful than others in taking people with you, and encouraging them to speak up too. We know from dark nights of the soul that all big journeys through life will entail disturbance and facing our fears. Movement is eeek-y territory. How do we engage people through this journey to self- and reality-awareness without creating denial and excessive anxiety? Soul-led truth.

At PepsiCo, I will never forget being trained in the *Art of Successful Pushback*. I can no longer recall whether these guidelines were for general leadership. Still, the soul of the PepsiCo Human Resources function was known to be characterised by bold, business-led coaching of the 'line leaders' (our internal 'clients' who ran the various business divisions). With these guidelines, we intended to enable our leaders to be the most outstanding leaders they could be, and at times, this meant reducing their blind spots about their behaviour and its impact on their organisations. 'Telling it as it is' conversations were highly valued (I had to learn how to stop saying 'sorry' when I did this, my first piece of helpful feedback on arrival as an English woman in New York, when my ought to please others was still in charge ...).

The *Art of Successful Pushback* was created to help us know how best to challenge leaders and hold up the mirror in a certain way. I cannot recall all the steps (I think there were six), but here are two that I do, and, funnily enough, they carried the system's soul for me.

The first 'rule' was to '*recite the loyalty oath*'. This did not mean we were to convey sugar-coated truth via sycophantic fawning, but the need to communicate to our leader from the outset our genuine, deepest acknowledgement of our commitment to their success in the role. We were not there to beat them up or make ourselves look good, but to demonstrate how much we cared about what was at stake in the situation. Because of the depth of our care and commitment to the entity's purpose and their leadership success, we needed to say 'x, y, z' (whatever the difficult truth might be). This pushback rule acutely required us to connect with our own soul energy when coaching leaders in the business.

And I recall the last rule as, '*Never forget whose candy store it is*'. After we had stated our commitment and then delivered the message, and before inviting them to respond, it was essential to show our respect for the different places and roles we had within the system. We were the support function; they were in charge. Our Edge and Tension guidance was to come from a place of respectful truth-telling advocacy, not from a controlling, superior power grab. Here, you can see the soul-level energy of the Ordering Force of Place being acknowledged with the deepest respect. System souls become unstable when people become either 'too big' or 'too small'.

The fact that we had these 'rules' for delivering Edge and Tension (I could now call them *parrhesia* guidelines) and that we all came to know and understand them, conveys how important the character and calling of the HR function meant to PepsiCo leaders. At the systemic soul level, and as a change enabler, I was also learning about the importance of respect and reality-acknowledgement when holding challenging conversations.

Systems really do respond to truth and transparency.

Containment – The Fiercest, Most Compassionate of Holding Energies

Without the skill of Container alongside Edge and Tension, the heat might get too much. The turbulence of alchemy requires an intense heat-bearing crucible. Container leadership is that crucible, and it means being bold to put yourself out there and become vulnerable in difficulty, so that you can help others through the anxieties of change.

At one peak experience in my time with PepsiCo, we needed to redesign and implement a new organisational model across the entire international beverages division, within just six months: 190 countries, simultaneously. Talk about organisational anxiety. The whole system had the potential to become adrenalised, and business continuity was at risk. I learned so much about soul-level Container leadership in that period.

First, it was recognised that while functional expertise was required from Human Resources, Finance and Communications, the line leaders would front the restructuring. I had never seen that before. They stood up and took accountability for the tough change process and all its communications; no one from the business would 'throw bricks' at the support functions if things went off the rails. One of the key mantras for the restructuring was 'leader-led'. The senior line leaders asked of their direct reports too that they devote at least 50% of their time to figuring out the new structure and then communicating and implementing that – even when they knew there would be a personal impact on themselves.

Second, I spent significant time helping the senior leaders get into the 'right place' to face and front this significant disruptive change. They had to do their own soul-searching to find that point of calm within themselves that the uncertainty could be faced, and that a good new organisational solution would emerge. If they were not assured, nor could the system around them be.

At one of our regular leadership team meetings devoted to helping the team manage through the change, I read out a chapter from within a book[28] by Charles Handy, a deep-thinking British leadership coach and philosopher. The chapter was headed, 'Last month we closed a factory'. I read it out in its entirety. The room went silent. The messages spoke deeply to the need for senior leaders to confront and let flow the emotions they would feel in implementing difficult change. But more than that, Handy's words reminded them of their almost God-like responsibility while impacting people's lives during tough restructurings. The intervention created an affective response in the senior leaders that enabled them to hold the emotional reactions of their organisations through the change.

Brave, compassionate, soul-level leadership went such a long way to helping the whole of the organisation feel that they would be taken care of, that their leaders would not shirk their responsibility in difficult times, and that the change process was inextricably linked to changing the work of the business for the better. This is hallmark Container leadership – and soul-level infused with a character and a calling that genuinely went beyond just taking out inflated cost. The organisation was able to go through fire together. The trust, clarity, and commitment built through soul-led leadership were key to ensuring that all the mini 'dark nights of the souls' could be successfully navigated.

Transforming Space – That Spine-Tingling Moment When You Know It's for Real

One of the most soul-led examples I have had of Transforming Space skills comes from another organisation. To recap, Transforming Space is about the capacity to bring change into the here-and-now moment, living the change you wish to see. Either through intervening in a conversation to name any incongruence between *what* is being talked about and *how* it is being talked about (you notice in a discussion about innovation that the same old voices are dominating), or through designing physical encounters that embody the desired change; at all times, your goal is to create a felt experience of the change you desire. You literally, transform the space.

At the soul level, this means accessing and working with the deepest realms of current experience. The sitting-on-the-edge-of-your-seat type moments that are poignant, devoid of artifice, heart-thumping, and so absolutely real.

Here's the story. I was working with a team trying to make a breakthrough in their vision and strategy, yet they realised that their team dynamics were getting in the way. My client was the recently arrived (one year in post) team leader who, try as he might, could not exhort his team to become more cooperative with each other. The whole team was frustrated and knew it had to try something different.

I and a colleague took the team away from their office environment and into a place that, while challenging to work with practically (a farmyard barn with straw bales for insulation), nevertheless reminded them of their essential humanity within the community their company served (rural producers of renewable energy).

The most transformational element was the process we ran to invite them to talk openly about what it felt like to work within the team. We asked them to design and perform a three-act play; a drama that depicted the team of the past, the team of today, and the team they most wished for in the future. The goal was to increase their capacity for truth-telling, which we had diagnosed as the root cause of their lack of trust and poor cooperation. Often, we can speak truth more easily when told through a story, picture or drama. The team volunteered themselves into three groups, one for each act.

I will not go into the story details here, but the whole morning was filled with the bravest and most vulnerable of leadership moments. One hour preparing their three acts, and then it took two hours for the teams to perform and, critically, process the affective impact of delivering and receiving such a vivid picture of themselves as a team. The truth. The loss. The shame (they acted out their own and their colleagues' behaviour on the stage). The longing. The team forgot the discomfort of straw bales ('Senior leaders ought not to be at such a lowly venue!'). This group of leaders became utterly transfixed with the unfolding of an experience that resulted *in a changed team*, not a set of actions about what they had to do differently to become a better team.

My colleague and I did not have much to do to facilitate – apart from designing and briefing the process, and a nudge through the morning here and there, we could have gone out to milk the cows. When you have the wheels of Transforming Space oiled with soul, movement becomes exquisitely and sacredly effortless.

Pause for a moment to reflect on how you can animate your External Practices

Taking again into your full awareness your stuck situation where you would like to bring greater flow and movement:

⇒ How might you enliven your situation by tapping into and working with the deep system's story of its becoming? *Attractor.*

⇒ What aspects of reality most need to be named in the current situation? How might you name this truth from a place of genuine commitment to the system's success and with the deepest respect for each person's role and place? *Edge & Tension.*

⇒ What process might you need to introduce to ensure adequate time and space to reflect on the inner turmoil that any change might stir up? *Container.*

⇒ How might your approach to the situation be in complete congruence with your desired end state, becoming the change you wish to see? *Transforming Space.*

In this chapter, we have been on a journey to discover the soul of soul; the deep sense of our internal essence that, while uniquely experienced, also connects us with wider realities, the living world and even the divine realm. Soul is our entrusted character, our calling that existed before our oughts came along to wire our patterns and run our responses to experience.

Getting to know, reclaim, accept and act from our soul can bring greater ease to our life as it frees us from our loyalties to those oughts (whether from early life conditioning or inherited from our systemic ancestral realm) and provides us with a grounded core at the centre of our being. We can go to that inner place where we most belong, and where we are most ourselves, and from that place, we can unobscure and take away all the unnecessary ways of being and doing that we toy with that take us away from *for that I came.*

The soul is like our tracker in the landscape of life, keeping us alert and attentive to stay on the path towards the ever-ness of who we truly freely are. This is soul work – containing an inherent struggle between the path and our distractions, both grounding and, at times, elusive. It is often invisible and undertaken in humble, unsung ways but usually evident to anyone with eyes to see or hearts to feel.

Soul work can be contagious. Once in contact with soul at the centre of our being, we can lead movement towards greater ease and truth in the systems we live and work within. And this can happen anywhere or from any level in our lives and workplaces – you do not need to be a CEO. From wherever you live and lead, I am reminded of some final words from Julian of Norwich[29]; 'For the soul is highest, noblest and worthiest when it is lowest, humblest, and gentlest'.

Soul can knock on the door of our deepest, most emotional realm. In the next chapter, we head to understanding the role of our emotions in guiding us towards truth, and hence, movement.

7

Emotions and Movement

Attention without feeling is only a report.

Mary Oliver.

Emotions respond immediately to the truth of things. They are the most alert form of attention.

James Hillman.

In this book, we are exploring the value of heading towards truth and reality as a catalyst for movement. Change starts by acknowledging what *is*, not by striving for what we believe or imagine the situation *ought* to be. This approach requires us to loosen our loyalties to the deep oughts that secured our early belonging needs, and have since governed our life, as these imprinted codes distort our capacity to know what is real. They inhibit us from discovering and actualising our deep soul's calling – our truth, our highest potential self.

Along the way, we have been looking at the vital role our *attention* plays in enabling us to move from the hold of ought to the wider lens of what is, to travel from being governed by our wiring to seeking out a more spacious reality. How we bring the world into being, our attentional skill, really does determine the quality of our thoughts, the ease of our being, the grace of our actions – and even our physical health.

This chapter is about our emotions' very special role in that attentional process. If the soul is our grounding ballast and beckoner for our journey to reality, our emotions are our truth messengers for the ride. Yes, emotions perform basic, impulsive, biological survival needs: fear keeps us from danger, anger guards our boundaries, joy keeps us procreating and sadness enables us to bear loss.

From Ought to Is: Catalysing Change and Movement in a Polarised World,
First Edition. Deborah Rowland.
© 2025 John Wiley & Sons Ltd. Published 2025 by John Wiley & Sons Ltd.

Yet, as Hillman indicates, at their highest and most complex, emotions are of social value and have a purposeful, revelatory role: guilt can be a sign of our growing, necessary maturity to break free of unhelpful, ought-led loyalties; shame a tough yet tender teacher to approach and not avoid deep learning; unflinching love a sign of our capacity to stand alongside it all, no longer irritated or in judgement of what comes our way – the ultimate test of our capacity to be with what *is*, not how we imagine the situation *ought* to be.

Emotions Allow Us to Be with Difficult Things

While I do not aim in this chapter to give a complete education on emotion identification and regulation (I will point you to some excellent resources on how to do so), I will spend time looking at the role that emotions play in our physiology and our lives. I will show how they accompany our passage-way from *ought* to *is*, illustrating how emotions such as fear, anger, sadness, grief, guilt, shame, joy, and love can be our most valuable of guides as to *the truth of things*.

My grief and anger outpouring during (and a little after) my Madame Butterfly experience was a great gift to my soul's journey from *ought* to *is*. Talk about becoming more alert to truth. These twin emotions opened up a long-buried primal wound and catalysed my personal journey to discover who I was and where I had come from. The wrenching of grief put me in conscious contact, for the first time, with the deep loss of my birth mother and the exquisite nature of love. The shuddering of anger with the injustice of forced adoptions and, dare I say it, the seeming inability of my mother to have stood up for keeping me. Not that I would have wished for a different life, but these emotions of grief and anger needed to be faced to release me from an inner entanglement with my inherited, systemic past.

And facing emotions in such a way is also essential when we embark on change in the workplace. I can still see the face of an erstwhile, extremely taciturn leader coming to this realisation for the first time in his 35-year career. He and his colleagues were taking their company through an unprecedented change process in which their manufacturing plants would have to either close or reform. As this realisation hit, the organisation's emotions, understandably, were running high. Through our transformation programme, he learnt how his feelings were a vital leadership sensing agent and a container for those he led. He even scurried off between training modules to experiment with setting up 'anger rooms' for his local teams in the plants (weekly meetings offered for staff to show up and 'vent' their displeasure). His eyes glistened with deep emotion when he returned to report how these encounters had enabled his organisation to work through their sense of injustice, face difficulty, and accept the new reality – and how he had needed to learn to confront his own intense fear at convening them.

I would find it hard to write a book about the journey of us moving from *ought* to *is*, from our defendedness to our wholehearted openness to what comes our way, without including and emanating emotion. And for you, the experience might end up like reading a report devoid of feeling, to which Mary Oliver so succinctly alerts us. But would mere report move you? I don't think so. My aim in conveying the emotions through my work and personal stories is not just to illustrate the concepts in this book but also to stir your soul and pathway in some way, as our emotions play a pivotal role in catalysing change – personally, interpersonally, and systemically. The clue is even in the word; put a • after the letter *E,* and you get the word *E • motion.* Emotions enable movement.

I feel no fear (now) at expressing emotion – though it took a little while to share my own story in public without my feelings overwhelming me. In this chapter, I will show how our emotions are a resource, not an embarrassment; a direct route to truth, not an irrational inconvenience; a flow of honesty, not a flight of fancy. We wouldn't have them in the neural network that flows through our entire body otherwise. Fundamental to our physiology, psyche, and humanity (and companionship with other living creatures), emotions are messages from our instinctive selves, the voicings of our soul that enable us to be with very difficult things, which is what the world of *is* will require of us.

For this journey from ought to is, and to continue supporting truth and reality, it is essential that we learn how to bear the consequences of the emotions that arise out of awareness.

In this chapter, I aim to fly the flag for us bringing the life of our emotions more squarely and wisely into our lives and workplaces. And this flag does need flying, at full mast, as collectively society puts out many oughts that can censure, belittle, and mock our emotions, rupturing us of our humanity; 'It is not civilised to show anger, lust and shame', 'Emotions are illogical, and reason a higher faculty to knowing what is true', 'Emotions have no place in business'. Perhaps, in our personal, familial settings, we learnt to belong by staying loyal to oughts such as, 'Don't show emotions as they are a sign of weakness, chin up!', 'Always pretend to smile so people don't ask you what is really going on'.

So, we have quite an inherited context to override. As in previous chapters, this one will give you ideas and encouragement along the way; specifically here, for how you can bring a greater emotion-rich punch to the situations in your life where you most wish for change and movement. Another resource for your *ought* to *is* back-pack.

Pause for a moment here

⇒ Reflect on your most challenging change case right now that you have agency in influencing.

⇒ Fully take in all of its challenges, complexities, and mysteries – what top emotions are you feeling in this situation? (Don't be 'polite' with yourself – anger, shame, disgust, or desire have just as much a place as joy, sadness, and anticipation.)

⇒ What truths about the situation, including your own and the system's story, might these emotions be messengers for?

⇒ On a scale of 1–10, where 1 = not very much and 10 = all of the time, to what extent are emotions and their processing given time and space in this situation?

⇒ What might become possible by turning up (or down) the emotions that you sense are present?

Emotions can be complex and confusing. Let's start by exploring what they are and why, exactly, do we have them.

What Are Emotions?

An emotion is a complex state of feeling that results in physical and psychological changes that influence thought and behaviour. Such feelings bring physiological arousal (heart rate, stomach churning, hand tingling), conscious experiences (pain, memory), and behavioural expressions (facial movement, hand gestures, approach or avoid action). An emotion can show up as a temporary and passing response to an experience (happiness at seeing a sunset), a longer-lasting mood (sadness at leaving something or someone behind), or a more enduring temperament (a personality predisposed to anger or melancholy).

Since emotions exert such a potent force on our mental state and behaviour, it is hardly surprising that theories abound about them. Researchers and neuroscientists, philosophers, theologians, and psychologists have all proposed various theories of emotion that seek to explain their purpose, causes, processes, and effects.

Above, for example, I have stated that emotion *precedes* physiological change and *influences* thought, yet certain theories contend the opposite: that emotion is an *outcome* of physiology (see the James–Lange theory,[1] developed by philosopher John Dewey) – we feel our heart beating wildly, and so we feel fear – and that emotion is a *result* of thought (see Lazarus Cognitive Appraisal Theory[2]) – I encounter a roadblock, and the way I think about the situation will influence the emotion, 'I will now be late, gosh that makes me angry!'

Another prominent theory that combines these two processes is the Schachter-Singer[3] two-factor theory of emotion, which contends that both physiological arousal and cognition produce emotion. In their paper 'Cognitive, Social and Physiological Determinants of Emotional State', Schachter and Singer argued that emotions are not just bodily sensations and physiological changes, dumb responses to situations. Rather, while physiological changes or bodily sensations accompany emotions, cognition is the key factor that accounts for the variety of emotions and our ability to distinguish and identify them. So, emotion is an outcome of, not an input to, thought. Our minds cognitively interpret and label a physiological response to a stimulus, resulting in an emotion. Emotions are not just impulsive survival reactions but purposeful responses to our world.

Millennia before in de Anima, the great thinker Aristotle likewise argued that beliefs and expectations about one's situation, our cognition, and non-cognitive elements, such as physical sensations, constitute the emotion. In his view, most evidently set out in the Nicomachean Ethics,[4] correct emotions are a large part of virtue – a courageous person when in danger, is neither fearless nor overwhelmed by fear. Likewise, his analysis of anger in the Rhetoric[5] states that this emotion requires certain accompanying moral beliefs about the wrongness of contempt and spite as well as beliefs about how we should be treated. Without cognition alongside emotion, our feelings could remain unguided reactivity.

It has taken us two millennia to catch up with Aristotle, but we now have a more nuanced and complex theory of emotion. Still, there is debate as to whether we access an emotion first and then cognitively understand it (the 'primacy of affect', see McGilchrist 2009[6]) or that thinking must occur before experiencing an emotion and a physiological response, but what we do know for sure is that our bodily sensations (our somatic states), our emotions and our thinking all play an interlocking and contributory role in how we both become aware of and respond to what we perceive as reality. Artists, musicians, writers, and poets have all found their fullest expression through the language and effect of emotions. What a world we would miss without them.

So, merely uncontrolled, limbic brain reactions, as any other basic animal survival responses, or higher-order mental faculties, passionate states of the soul, purposeful responses to our world? Having touched on defining emotions and their processes, I would say the answer is a bit of both. While rooted in basic survival needs, through our social nature, humankind has for sure taken emotions into more evolved places.

Let's now look at some theories as to the why and the wherefore of emotion that will guide our capacity to fully encounter a reality decluttered from our oughts. We need to feel resourced, not threatened, by the emotions that will inevitably appear along this journey. Knowing their function can sharpen how we attend to and appreciate their role in our lives (and certainly enhance our Inner Capacities of Tuning into the System and Acknowledging the Whole, see Chapter 5).

Emotions Are Fundamentally About Survival

The most acknowledged theory of emotions is that they have an evolutionary origin, and so are biologically based processes. Naturalist Charles Darwin proposed that emotions evolved because they were adaptive and allowed humans and animals to survive and reproduce. Seated primarily within the amygdalae of our limbic brain structure, feelings of love and affection lead people to seek mates and reproduce, whereas feelings of fear compel people to fight or flee the source of danger. It was important that our female ancestors learnt the difference between these emotional responses and went to the cave with a healthy male waiting for a snuggle rather than the one with a big hairy bear waiting for a meal.

Emotions motivate people to respond quickly to stimuli in the environment; via the autonomous nervous system, emotions get the body to react to either maintain positive or change negative circumstances. Joy kept our ancestors heading towards hunky, gorgeous mates for procreation; disgust made sure they spat out decaying and harmful animal flesh, and anger motivated them to defend their territory from marauders intent on carrying off their child-rearing-aged females.

Darwin's particular contribution to the relationship between emotion and their survival value came in his study of the universality of our facial expressions of emotions. Also studied by Theophrastus in antiquity, Darwin showed[7] how we all tend to express happy smiles, sad frowns, angry glares and shameful blushes. Such a common, non-verbal expression of emotion helped improve our collective chances of success and survival. Nowadays, with the proliferation of emojis available on our smartphones, everyday expressions of emotion save us much time when typing social media messages. I have also used emoji faces printed out onto round 'lollipop sticks' as a helpful resource at leadership conferences to get people identifying and sharing their predominant emotions when going through significant change processes – an experience that can feel as much a survival experience as those of our ancestors in challenging landscapes.

The primacy of the survival value of emotions has subsequently led researchers and psychologists to agree that there is a basic set of universal emotions that originate in subcortical brain structures,which have evolved within the human species to help us deal with the world. Ekman's[8] theory of six basic emotions is well-known; following in Darwin's footsteps, his six emotions are based on us having common facial expressions for fear, anger, contempt (disgust), sadness, surprise and joy. Psychologist Robert Plutchik[9] believed that humans can experience over 34,000 unique emotions. Still, we usually experience eight primary ones that are rooted in survival goals – his model contains anticipation and trust in addition to Ekman's six. Most of these basic emotion theorists agree that these emotions interact with each other and with cognitive processes to produce an emotional experience and survival-led behavioural output.

Further support for the theory of the survival value of emotions is that we share these basic emotions with our fellow living creatures. Many studies have shown how they lead to similar physical responses and facial expressions in animals (I am convinced my dog knows of shame when he bows his head slightly in submission while looking up to me with adoring eyes, pleading that I keep him within my life despite him having run off for an hour in search of deer).

Being in the grips of an emotion instantly makes us intelligible and commonly human (and beyond human). Therefore, an emotion's principal intention is to connect our animal nature with the world in which it is embedded and inform us of the truth and reality of a situation so that we and others we care for can survive. Pure, basic emotion unclouded by oughts puts us in true and direct contact with the matter of things.

Our Emotions as Pathway to Movement Beyond Survival

So, how can we work with our emotions as a direct route to access and be with what is, bringing reality to the foreground of our attention? This task can be problematic, as you might have already picked up by now that, given so many of our basic emotions – such as fear, anger and disgust – are about *avoiding* a situation, they might compel us to not just stay 'safe' within a survival context, but also a social one.

When we encounter a new and unknown situation in our regular life, one that does not conform to our current belief system – let's say our workplace informs us of a new process that will require us to work quite differently, our biochemistry will tell us this is 'danger' rather than 'opportunity'. Our oughts will keep us sticking to the known rules of our conscience groups; we will gossip in our team that this new process sounds ridiculous and seek relief by only *approaching* people and situations that reward this loyalty. Why would we leave the security of the flock and keep heading towards what is new/different/challenging, risking the fear of becoming an outcast, followed by guilty feelings of disloyalty or grief of loss for what came before?

No wonder change is so hard to pull off. Somehow, we need to be able to risk survival to move to a new place.

The above workplace situation is not a life or death one. Still, I have certainly felt many times in my career that my belonging within a company or client contract was at stake when I dared to initiate change or uncover an uncomfortable truth. This need to risk survival and head towards the discomforting feelings accompanying a new, seemingly dangerous path is also why I find the approach-avoid categorisation of emotions unhelpful. Such labelling tends to connote only *approach* emotions, such as joy and anticipation, as positive and welcoming; whereas *avoid* emotions, such as anger, shame or grief, are consigned to negative, dangerous, 'no-go' areas.

Only yesterday, I was working with a team undergoing a significant leadership transition, stuck in being unable to face the problematic emotions accompanying their big decision. The team member who had been in the primary leadership relationship with the firm's Managing Partner was exiting this role and handing the baton to a colleague previously within the 'rank and file' of the company. They had tended to stay 'happy smiley' about the situation ('better not display how I am feeling as that would indicate weakness or non-support for the transition'). However, it was not until their feelings of fear of being unsafe in the situation ('Yikes, I've never done a big leadership role before!') twinned with their sadness at what was being bade 'farewell' to (the Managing Partner and his co-leader had been together, through thick and thin, over 10 years) were able to be expressed and witnessed, that they felt released to move ahead and fully execute the transition decision.

Far from denying and hiding their troubling emotions, facing them enabled change to flow.

How have I learnt to overcome our biology and welcome in the more difficult-to-bear, as well as 'positive' emotions, recognising *all* of their alchemical value in bringing us to see truth, and hence catalyse movement in our life and work situations? I am indebted in the next section to both my systemic teacher, Judith Hemming, and to Jungian analyst, James Hillman, for introducing me to five different levels of knowing, or ways to experience emotions: our somatic, bodily sensations; our psyche; the systemic, collective; the wider archetypal; and beyond to the divine realm.

All these levels of knowing reality are valuable sources of attention. They are emotion-rich pathways pointing us to fields of truth beyond the safe prisons of our oughts. Emotions might be primarily rooted in survival, but as a human species, they can be used for so much more.

Our Whole Body as a Sentient Being, and Capable of Regulation

I will never forget seeing one leader I was working with collapsing from his standing position, slowly and gracefully (also extremely tall, this was quite a feat), and ending up slumped on the floor. We were in the middle of an experience with 40 of his colleagues to tune into the reality of the change impact about to hit their organisation. The group had set up a physical map of their entire change landscape – little boxes on the floor to represent both their internal elements, such as their various organisational divisions, and external elements, such as changing customer needs – and were now walking around the room, in silence, visiting each part of the landscape. Their task (which, to be honest, was met with quite a degree of incredulity) was to register how this somatic-based tuning-in process could enable their inner state to pick up signals about what was most needed to be faced in their change.

This leader had fallen to the floor beside the element of their organisation that would have to bear the highest cost of the change – old technology plant closures. At first, none of his colleagues registered his dramatic movement. Still, gradually, they all ended up standing around this part of their landscape in varying degrees of wobbliness and shiftiness. When invited to speak, the collapsed leader (who confessed he had started on this exercise quite cynical) spoke of how his body had started shaking when he visited this element, and, without any cognition involved, his body needed to lie down beside this part of his organisation.

So, what was going on here? This leader was quite startled by the emotional intelligence of his body. Free from any oughts about how to comport himself during a senior leadership meeting, his somatic response to stimuli brought a revelation to them all about the grief that was not being adequately faced in their change process. To that moment, all their attention had been on the prize and not the price of the forthcoming change. In a very rational organisation, their loyalty to logic had disabled them from meeting the reality of the emotional turbulence coming their way.

The methodology we were introducing in this experience, systemic constellations,[10] is one of the most powerful processes I have encountered in my change career to help individuals and groups move from the rigidity of conditioned, ought-led attention to a resourced, revelatory and direct encounter with truth – and all through using the instrument of our entire body as an organ of perception. While challenging to our oughts, beliefs and neuroses (this leader only collapsed because his blood sugar levels were too low, as he had not eaten breakfast!), there exists much scientific evidence about how our entire bodies are sentient beings capable of telling us truths that our cognitive brain might be in denial or delusion about.

While our mind might buzz with oughts and ought-not-to's, our body stores more primal truth – especially the pain of repressed emotion or denied reality. In my view, nobody more than the neuroscientist and pharmacologist Dr Candace Pert, in her groundbreaking book Molecules of Emotion,[11] has comprehensively shown us how the biochemicals in our body are the physiological substrates of all our emotions. Her miraculous opiate-receptor discovery proved how our whole body is a sentient being, capable of holding, storing, and processing emotion.

While the two amygdalae in our limbic brain structure are the seat of our emotions, Pert showed us how peptides, the information molecules found in the autonomic nervous system, and their receptors, are the molecular underpinnings of our feelings and sensations, thoughts, drives and 'perhaps even spirit or soul', *and are distributed throughout our body on each cell.* For example, the entire lining of our intestines is lined with cells containing neuropeptides and receptors. This could explain why we feel emotions in this part of the anatomy: gut feelings. Excitement and anger increase gut motility; contentment reduces it.

What's more, Pert showed that the flow is two-way; emotions both originate in the body and flow up to the brain, where they get perceived and explained, and, via the workings of the sympathetic autonomous nervous system, can originate in the brain and then trickle down to the body. The mobile brain moves throughout our body, and emotions are felt as bodily sensations. (For exactly where the different emotions are felt within the body, see a recent study, *Bodily Maps of Emotions*[12].) Emotions might well be embedded in our physiology, but far more holistically than earlier theories, she contends that our emotions bring our whole body into a single purpose, integrating systems and coordinating mental processes to produce behaviour.

If you wish to read a short, mesmerising story about the whole gamut of human emotions and how they show up through our bodies, I also highly recommend Stefan Zweig's *Twenty-Four Hours in the Life of a Woman*.[13] In this stunningly written prose, Zweig gets inside the head of a respectable English 'lady' who is recounting to a stranger how, 20 years prior, at the age of 40, she had had an intense night-and-day experience with a man 20 years her junior, whom she had met in a casino in Monte Carlo. I do not wish to do a 'spoiler' for your reading of the story, but here is an excerpt from several pages during which Zweig has her recounting, in exquisite detail, the emotions she read into the young man when she first saw him across the roulette table: 'During that hour I did not, even for a moment, take my fascinated gaze from the ever-changing face and all the passion ebbing and flowing over it. I kept my eyes fixed on those magical hands, their every muscle graphically reflecting the whole range of the man's feelings as they rose and fell like a fountain'.

Not only do our bodies carry and convey deep messages of emotion, we can also use them to regulate our feelings. Have you ever tried changing your physical posture and found your mood changed? I once worked with a very somatically and emotionally astute Chief Financial Officer who, by changing his office meeting furniture from a sit-down to a stand-up table, not only changed the efficiency of his meetings (also numbers driven; he found it reduced meeting times by a half), he also shifted the atmosphere of the meeting conversations to greater courage and truth-telling.

I have always found my body a remarkable resource for processing difficult emotions – not just contacting but also facing and moving reality. My yoga teacher, for example, has always helped me with hip-opening postures to release deep-seated emotions such as grief. Back to Pert, in this passage from *Molecules of Emotion,* she sets out the scientific case for how the biochemistry of emotions, held within our bodies, enhances our capacity to encounter truth.

> Since our sensing of the outer world is filtered along peptide-receptor-rich sensory way stations, each with a different emotional tone, how can we objectively define what's real and what's not real? If what we perceive as real is filtered along a gradient of past emotions and learning, then the answer is we cannot. Fortunately, however, receptors are not stagnant and can change in both sensitivity and in the arrangement they have with other proteins in the cell membrane. *This means that even when we are 'stuck' emotionally, fixated on a version of reality that does not serve us well, there is always a biochemical potential for change and growth (writer's italics).* (p. 146)

So, our biology need not impede change – we can override our purely impulsive, conditioned modalities and have agency over how we experience our lives: our bodies help us break out of our rigid scripts. Through consciousness training, we can direct this process (e.g., meditation or breath work, I enjoy yoga – a form of moving meditation, but any activity that helps you bring pure present-moment attention, such as walking in nature or creating art). Through visualisation, we can even alter blood flow from one body part to another. Of course, you might also simply try having stand-up and not sit-down conversations.

While our ought-filled minds might deceive and delude us, our bodies truly are a gift to our capacity to be able to tune into *and* regulate our emotional response to experience – widening the lens of our perception and influencing our construction of truth towards one that more closely meets reality as it is, not as we imagine or fantasise it ought to be (so often after a walk in nature, I return with regulated emotions, and quite a different perspective on the reality of a difficult situation requiring my attention).

Our bodies might be the receptors of our emotions, enabling us to register and even regulate them, but from which depths do emotions ultimately arise? Can we learn to discern which reality realms they are truth messengers from? Do they come from us and our family of origin, the collective systems we are social members of, or even wider places? What truths, what aspects of reality, are our emotions trying to tell us?

Emotions as Truth Messengers for Our Personal Realm

Emotions from the personal realm are those that are felt as intense and as ours; they belong to us, our familial life and our origin story. The fear I felt when I gingerly announced to my adopted parents that I was tracing my biological mother and father was about the sheer terror of anticipating a second abandonment from love. The dread was commensurate to the degree of attachment I had formed to those who had scooped me up and become my parents. The fear was definitely 'mine' from my story of origin.

When we initiate change in our lives or the workplace, it is crucial to know if the emotions we are experiencing arrive from this personal realm, and if they do, then they are ours to take care of. We need to be careful that they do not colour our perception of what we see in situations or have us recruiting others to attend to them, as then our own needs and story might be getting in the way of us seeing and attending to reality with a clean eye. So, if I feel fear in a situation where belonging might be under threat – for example, if I am not being asked to contribute to a project – far from me reading the situation as a culture of unfairness (which would be known as 'disowned projection'), I know that the fear belongs to me, and I will take care of it.

(Having said that, it is always invaluable for teams going through change to invite each member to share their stories of origin. By getting to know our colleagues' 'hot buttons', we can provide support and a listening ear for those inevitable moments when challenging personal emotions surface under anxiety.)

Another primary emotion I often encounter from my personal realm is guilt – there must be something deeply flawed in me, as otherwise, why would my mother have given me away? How I responded to this emotion to secure future belonging became my deeply engrained ought to please and not offend others. This drive has also brought me feelings of shame throughout my life, as my fear of offending anyone can quite literally have me beating myself up for even a seemingly minor transgression.

While renovating my house here in the Dordogne, a large sheet of plastic from the building work caught a gust of wind one day and sailed through the air and across the field towards a neighbour's house. It took me until the following day to go and retrieve it. When I next met my neighbour, he muttered words about the laziness of my builders and how the plastic that day had been an eyesore from his garden. I dared not confess that it was my fault and then felt so terrible at not being able to do so – and I so envied my friend who was with me when it had blown away and who just laughed the whole incident off.

I wish that shame need not visit me so often; that emotion definitely comes to me from the personal realm. When leading change, again, I had to learn how to take care of any feelings of guilt that I sensed were coming from this realm so I could become robust in making difficult decisions with human impact. With my instinct for shame, I had to learn how to stop saying 'sorry' so often in situations that did not require an apology (though I do believe that this emotion always kept me open to my learning, creating a culture around me that valued taking responsibility for one's action).

But hey, our personal emotions give voice to the truth of our soul. They are reminders of who we are, where we came from, and where our souls wish us to move. I have experienced such mad rushes of joy after running a masterclass on change, delivering a keynote speech at a conference, or steering a leadership team through a tricky transformational experience. It's not pride, I feel. I don't do it for any adulation or recognition (and I am lousy about posting about my work on social media). But I get such an intrinsic buzz when, together with the group in the room, I can somehow respond to their transformation needs and stories and bring a message about change through my talk, action and presence that moves the room and leaves people in a different place (an experience *that* changes, rather than *about* change).

The joy that has me dancing inside on my journey home and, dare I say, reaching out for a little celebration of whiskey (I am Irish, after all) is my soul crying out, 'What I do is me: for that, I came'. Joy is the most exquisite of emotions that can tell us when our calling and our path are in synch.

Sometimes, our personal emotions seem to come from nowhere, without any external referent (plastic-gate, leadership workshop); no thought or memory has even called them up. Hillman refers to such emotions as those that do not seem 'caused' by the world 'out there.' Back to emotion as *E•motion*, he refers to the distinction first made by Aristotle between *locomotion* – motion in space as between yourself and the world – and *motions that are alterations*. Somehow, the soul is going through a process of change for its own sake or is decreasing or increasing its capacity.

Maybe it is down to my own *ought*-to-*is* journey over the last two decades, but over time, I can track how my predominant emotion of fear (of rejection, of offending) has moved through melancholia (what might have been, with family, with having children) to one of contentment (be that in joy or when I am feeling sad). Such deeper alterations in our emotions without external reference can signify changes in our subjective soul and correlate with what Jung has called the process of individuation, the soul's disclosure through time of its organic nature.

What messengers and truth markers our emotions are for our life, our capacity to effect change, and our soul's journey!

Pause for a moment

⇒ Can you recall highly charged emotions (both more positive and enabling, as well as those that might be less comfortable and potentially disabling) that can come to you from your personal realm? What truth about your life might they be carrying?

⇒ When have you been most 'surprised by joy'? In what way might this emotion have been giving your soul its voice, calling you towards what your soul most longs for you to do or become?

The experience of our emotions brings our attention to the workings of our internal life, and we need to recognise when these feelings 'belong' to us. But our capacity to tune into our emotions as unadorned messages from reality becomes enhanced when we can also learn to recognise them as visitors from realms beyond our own lives.

While today it can feel like we are increasingly living within a 'culture of me', our emotions can be signifiers of much wider fields. Learning to recognise this distinction is essential for us to become 'the right size' in relation to what is truth, move beyond our ought-led version of reality, and desist from using what we are feeling as hooks for others to respond to us personally. Sometimes, our emotions are just not all about us.

Emotions That Belong to Our Systemic Realm

Emotions that arise from our systemic realm are those that, while intensely felt by us, point us to truths or the is-ness embedded in our surrounding situation. You can tell these emotions are systemic and not personal in that they are a little trickier to shift (take our feelings of sadness that lingered during the COVID-19 pandemic). As these emotions don't 'belong' to us, we have to do a little more work when we wish to influence the reality that gave rise to them.

There are no organisational issues that don't touch us at a personal level – even if our conscious minds strain or pretend otherwise. When the leader in my story above fell to the ground, his body carried an emotion that belonged not to him but to the communities within the organisation he was responsible for stewarding. His grief might well have also come from his personal realm (we were not in any therapeutic relationship, so did not enquire), but what we worked with at this moment was how his emotion was a startling and valuable truth signal about the dynamics being felt by others within his context. Yes, he personally *felt* grief, but he was *carrying* it from the system. This direct contact with the systemic reality nudged him and his leadership colleagues to give far more time and space within their change process to working with the turbulent human dynamics of a significant transition. Tuning into systemic emotion in this case also helped the leaders restore the reality of an exchange imbalance; they started to become able to say, 'I am sorry that you are paying the price'.

Our emotions are embedded within the political, social and cultural worlds of the communities of which we are a part. Sitting here in France, I recall the 'gilets jaunes', a grassroots citizens' protest movement coming from mainly rural and working/middle-class populations who were enraged at the government's planned tax increase in fuel duty, which quickly morphed into a broader anti-establishment movement. Our emotions are a conduit for context.

When we are leading change across a system, tuning into the feelings of our inner state becomes a critical leadership responsibility, as it helps us to know what is being felt and experienced within the wider collective. For example, if we are feeling anger and rage for no apparent personal reason, it might be that the system (unconsciously) feels there has been an injustice – a reality is being, yet hidden. That is invaluable data that we might ordinarily miss if we only interpret the feeling personally (am I still furious about what happened in my upbringing?) or try to bat the emotion away as it is not 'seeming' to be angry in an organisational context. Yet, what a clue your emotion might be holding about a hidden dark truth in your organisation that our ordinary cognition would simply not register. An unacknowledged profound injustice could have your organisation or community stuck in the grip of unprocessed shame.

I was once coaching a leader who was naturally predisposed to having a cheerful temperament, yet no matter how hard she tried, she could not dispel the feeling of sadness when with her new team. After a deep exploration with her team, we found out that one of their members, before she arrived, had tragically died and that there had been no space to mourn. The grip of unprocessed grief made moving forward very hard for this team. (Death might be an extreme case, but I have also found many instances of past upsets and injustices, such as clumsily carried out people exits or a hurtful disservice being done between a company and its community, as originating causes for systemic feelings of sadness, anger and guilt.)

What we get stirred by emotionally is valuable system data that acts to support truth. Yet this is intelligence of a nature not often sought in regular organisational discourse, where 'data' remains the left hemisphere brain's focus on financials, work project status, culture survey findings, customer behaviour and other in-awareness performance indices. System data from the more unconscious, or felt yet unexpressed, emotional realm can reveal deeper hidden vectors that exert a strong gravitational pull on observable reality; whether we dare 'go to' such places will dictate whether change and movement can flow with ease.

I have also noticed that, even if an astute leader registers such systemic emotional data, the noticings, more often than not, remain a private affair. If Dag Hammarskjöld had lived longer, I often imagine what a difference it might have made to the quality of the collective leadership held within the United Nations, if he had chosen to share parts of his private journals with his colleagues.

Do *you* ever ask your team members or fellow collaborators in your community movement, or whatever system you are close to, to openly 'check in' with how they are doing? Not seeking social niceties about how they spent the weekend or checking if their work is on track, but to inquire into how they are genuinely, deeply feeling at the moment *so that you can all pick up signals about what is being felt within the wider environment*? If you do this, do you sometimes discover they are all experiencing similar emotions? Well, that's because what they are experiencing is about the system, not themselves. It can be quite a relief when this is acknowledged. (I am currently coaching a team whose individual members all felt that the fear they were personally experiencing in this team only belonged to them and that they were not being brave enough; it was such a relief when they discovered it was being collectively held.)

Not only can emotions from the systemic realm alert us to truths that require our attention, but they can also signal the steps to take to shift the situation and, in particular, take us to those exquisite places where we might need to risk survival and break free of our loyalty to oughts for the desired movement to flow.

I once coached an internal change team of a large professional services firm. Their brief, from the partners (the most senior leaders within the company), was to help transform the culture towards one that listened more to the voices of their frontline staff, those with the most operational contact with their clients. In this meeting, I recall, the team had brainstormed a whole list of initiatives they could take to help enable this cultural change, and it was now decision time as to what to do and how to relay that decision back to the partners, who were their clients.

I invited the team to look at each initiative (sticky post-it notes on a flip chart) and register how each initiative made them feel. After some to-ing and fro-ing, I noticed that one team member had turned very silent, almost immobilised. When he spoke (and I can recall this many years on), he said, 'This idea here (one of the initiatives) is the scariest thing imaginable to do (we all held our breaths, expecting him to vote for another initiative), and ... that is why this is the one we must do!'

Here was an instance of how a typical 'avoid' survival emotion, fear, far from being a sign to run away from something within the system, was working its magic to alert people to the deep truth that significant change will always feel a little dangerous. Of course, fear also needs to feel well-resourced so we don't freak out if we choose the scariest path. Still, a degree of fear might be the lighthouse alerting us to brave the choppy waters accompanying the passageway to leave behind our safe conditioned oughts ('don't upset the partners'). Nothing ventured, nothing gained. (For an excellent little guide to fear and what to do when things feel like they are falling apart, I would highly recommend the book *The Places That Scare You*[14] by Pema Chödrön. While written with the personal realm of fear in mind, the insights also work across to the systemic realm.)

When we have learnt to work with our own primary emotions, we can work with the meta-feelings of a system, as we become less porous to other people's anxieties and can work with them collectively as data, not triggers for us to rescue anyone or sweep feelings away. I encourage you (with others) to go through them, wallow in them, inhabit them, and then hold them with distance so all can discern exactly what valuable truth they bring about the system you are in that most needs your attention. Emotions bring an unguarded intelligence to our system work; let's not let our oughts put the feelings part of ourselves out of commission. Try making emotions a discussable item in your team, community, or institution, and see if they can be collectively acknowledged and treated as helpful and not unwelcome data, a vital intelligence to release what is causing difficulty and pain, and, in so doing, effect movement.

Pause for a moment

⇒ Consider a situation within your workplace or other social setting where unhelpful patterns persist despite good intentions and effort at change.

⇒ What emotions do you most register about this situation that you now feel are about 'the system' and not you? What is the range and depth of these emotions?

⇒ What, maybe out-of-awareness, truths are they alerting you to that you could investigate further?

⇒ How might you bring others within the system into exploring this situation with you, via all of you sharing the emotions you most carry about the situation right now?

Emotions as Universal, Irreducible Archetypes

Emotions that arise from the archetypal realm have no 'emotionality' trailing them; we both feel and recognise them, yet we are not so caught up in their costs and consequences. When we experience them, our bodies and feelings give us clues about reality realms far more reaching than our personal lives and those of the local communities we live and work within.

So, what might we be carrying when we experience sadness, joy, anger or shame? Where might these emotions originate? What are we touching when we feel archetypal emotions? What do they make us familiar with? What do they make us part of?

Before Hillman's writing on the soul, his doctoral thesis[15] on Emotions set out his view that we can enter into archetypal emotions existing within fields far wider than us. Influenced by ancient thinkers such as Aristotle and, more recently, Jung, who defined archetypes as recognisable and timeless 'forms or images of a collective nature which occur practically all over the earth as constituents of myths and at the same time, as individual products of unconscious', Hillman defined an archetypal perspective on emotions as;

> that view which holds emotions to be primary and irreducible, transhuman and ubiquitous, of major value and forcing 'unconsciousness' on their subject—from this archetypal perspective, emotions are the theme of earthly life. They keep us all alike, give us all equal opportunity to be sane and insane, victims of our rages and hatreds, of obsessive jealousies, shames, and disgusts, of our wild hopes and longings. And they do not belong only to psychology. Literature, art, crime, politics and social education are all theatres of emotion, to say nothing of the daily round of the family household. When Shakespeare's plays were performed at the Globe Theatre, royalist and commoner alike were amused: cripples, fools, scholars, monks, soldiers, and nobles all attended, wept and laughed, submitting to the same emotions. *We can thank emotion for our shared humanity (writer's italics).*

Without a doubt, emotion is an interior psychological condition – we feel rushes of happiness or can be overcome with grief. Likewise, emotion physiologically exists deep inside the skin, the hippocampus, the hormonal system and the animal body; residing, as Candace Pert discovered, in the core of our cellular being. Hillman's contention, however, was that this psychological and physiological fact does not necessarily make emotions, 'ours'. Can we also entertain the notion that an emotion we are experiencing might not spring from our own lives but be embedded within the wider world's soul – we visit *them*?

When our emotions arise from the archetypal realm, they are there to make us theirs; sadness might not belong to me; rather, I might belong to sadness. We are enrolled into joy, fear, anger, or disgust so that our brief yet no less consequential lives can use the gift of this emotion within humanity through time.

And so can I enter the vast pool of compassion when I join the archetypal realm of women the world over who might have wished for a child yet were unable to; guilt and loneliness oft-visited chambers when my soul reaches out to fellow adoptees far and wide; and how can I dance and sing within both metaphorical and now, more often, actual pubs and bars when the twinned emotion of melancholic joy I feel tells me I am part of the psychic heritage of Ireland.

Compassion, guilt, loneliness, melancholia, joy. I could add courage (of the hero), cruelty (of the ruler, even the best surgeon), shame (of the fallen), and love (of the passionate). All meta-feelings arising from archetypal realms of our shared humanity that are universally understood, imprinted and hardwired into our psyches.

So, why is our capacity to discern when the emotions we are experiencing are arising from archetypal, not personal or systemic, realms valuable for the messages in this book? How has this awareness enhanced my journey to move from *ought* to *is*? In what way can archetypal emotions be a resource for catalysing change and movement? Here's what I believe:

- *Archetypal emotions make us the right size*: as I came to realise that the grief, shame and anger that often came to me were about being an adoptee and not about being Deborah Rowland, these emotions somehow came less to define me. My ego no longer needed to be caught up in them; I started to feel I could be in service of them and not the other way around. As that happened, I could see reality less cluttered with my needs and projections and more able to see and hold a 'wider tent'. Paradoxically, when my ego quietened down, I could lead and take on more challenges.
- *They can take the 'emotionality' out of emotions:* emotions arriving from the archetypal realm gift us a detached capacity to see what is going on. No longer our personal responsibility, or with emotionality trailing them, they can bring insight and ease to our being in the world. When I feel the

fear of trust and inclusion under threat in my client work, my presence as a coach no longer feels panicky and clingy (transference from my personal realm) but measured about what might be being hidden or excluded within my client system (insight into a more universal state) – fear becomes wisdom about reality, not a cortisol trip.

- *They can bring a sudden perception of the essential nature of things*; when we can discern emotions arising within us as archetypal, they shine a light on the invisible background of life; they are a psychic sense for reading the environment. When a colleague or member in your community suddenly has an outburst of passion – maybe anger or love – what might that be signifying about your institution's or society's broader mission and place in the world through time? In Hillman's words, can the emotion's arrival have 'moved the psyche to a deeper and epiphanic connection with the world'?

- *Directing us towards a beneficial transformation:* so, with humility, ease, insight and connection, if we can discern when and how our emotions arise from the archetypal realm, we should not fail in our capacity to void life of our self-defining, autonomous, reactive, and stuck patterns, and instead welcome such universal emotions as protective angels to help us move across important thresholds.

How might this show up in the workplace? Here's one example. From my career over the years working with leaders stewarding their organisations through change, I have often experienced the anxiety that can reside at the so-called 'top' of a system, the most senior leaders. This is where responsibility and complexity combine into a potent and often deleterious force on one's spirit and competence. The more senior you rise, the more you leave behind the safe flock of your peers and, in so doing, cross over the loyalty thresholds that had once guarded your secure belonging. The prize can be more significant – in status, recognition and reward – but so can the price – and not just in hours worked or role intensity, but also the pressure on the psyche.

What I have found in this key threshold moment is that when leaders arriving at the most senior level can truly get alongside the twin meta-feelings of guilt and loneliness, emotions that belong to the archetypal realm of top leaders the world over and through the annals of time (not just their institution or system), and especially accompanying those leaders introducing change, they become more effective in the role.

One leader I worked with was promoted into a very senior role that made him the boss of people who had previously been his peers, and he was now seated in the so-called 'C-suite' of his organisation. In order to sign up for a new global change programme, he had to leave behind his loyalties to his old team and visibly lead a change that was to significantly impact his old division. He started feeling bad about this seeming act of betrayal (emotionality trailing him). Still, to fully take up his new place in the system, once he had had the epiphanous insight that guilt and loneliness would be the necessary archetypal emotions to bear within his new place (he had not done anything personally 'bad'), he could ease himself into the role and fully take the decisions necessary for his company to have a flourishing future. Not only that, but he also used this realisation skilfully, even sharing it with his previous peers so that they too could be released from their projection-laden hold on him and step into greater autonomy and maturity.

Archetypal emotions worked their magic to secure a beneficial transformation. Job done. Deep bow. And to emotions – guilt and loneliness – that our oughts might ordinarily have warned us away from as personally awkward complexes, problems, negative intuitions and re-enactments of early life traumas. So not in this case. And I say 'chapeau' to the brave leader who could fully register and work with his emotions as a resource, not just for his growth but also for his organisation's progression (and, by inclusion within this chapter, all of us as change leaders).

Pause for a moment

⇒ Bring an important change case to mind, one that feels embedded within wider systems (you have a mission that is shared with other institutions the world over; you might be a unit comprised of team members coming from quite different geopolitical systems whose loyalties are greater than those to your institution). Can you recall a moment when you felt an intense force of emotion yet without becoming 'emotional'?
⇒ Can you relate this emotion to a universal, archetypal realm – having nothing to do with your own or the system's story?
⇒ What truth and transformation might this emotion enable within the situation?

Emotions as Truths from the Divine, or Sacred Realm

> *I can only love, honour and respect those outside of my group if I rise above conscience.*
>
> *To love purely is to consent to distance.*
>
> Simone Weil, Gravity and Grace[16]

Emotions that are felt as a deep disposition towards the world – such as meta love, courage, awe and reverence – more like a state of being than an emotion per se, are likely to emanate from the divine or sacred realm: a realm where all is well. I find it hard to describe in words, but let's say that we might recognise those moments when we have had an experience richly expressive in feeling that connected us with the broader landscapes of creation, leading us away from ourselves to all that lies beyond us in time and place. To be within this complete-contact-with-all-reality (past, present and future) realm requires a true meta-stance, or consciousness, open to what the English poet William Blake called, 'divine influxes'. A predisposition, as Weil (often named the 'saint of outsiders') states, to put aside the loyalties contained within the boundaries of one's conscience group and, standing with distance, be able to *love purely* and embrace it all.

In Zweig's *Twenty-Four Hours in the Life of a Woman*, there is a game-changing moment when the respectable protagonist, Mrs C., on waking up in a grubby hotel room to find a half-naked stranger sleeping beside her, moves from her intense feeling of fear-drenched shame at imagining what people would think of her (personal and systemic emotion) to a quite different state of emotion: 'I was overcome by the kind of emotion – ridiculous as you may find it put into words – the kind of emotion one might have in church, a rapturous sense of wonder and sanctification'. And this intense, embrace-it-all emotion had arisen as she contemplated the purity and beauty of the young man's face as he lay sleeping.

As the quality of her attention shifted, so in an instant did an emotion visit her from a realm quite different to that of conventional societal mores; and what is more, her capacity to welcome this type of emotion led her to take action that day (generous and inclusive) far different from that which would have come from a personal or systemic realm (get the h—l out of here!).

Does what I am writing about here sound a bit like 'woo woo' and a complete flight from 'the real' world? I don't think so. If you followed me through Chapter 3 on the nature of truth and reality, then you'd be with me in entertaining the notion that there is more to what is real than just what we can logically and objectively prove. Back to Zweig's Mrs C., now aged in her 60s, she relates to the stranger to whom she is now confiding this past story that, 'In those ten hours, I had come to know immeasurably more about reality than in my preceding forty respectable years of life'.

If we believe that some sacred realm runs through all our lives and landscapes, then we will be open to Blake's divine influxes and see a reality that is immeasurably more complex and infinite and devastatingly clear and straightforward. And what a punch having this kind of disposition brings when we are trying to catalyse change and movement in stuck, fixated places.

I felt and recognised such emotion, a pure state of compassionate seeing, yet distanced being, when reading the transcript of an outstanding leader of change whom we had interviewed for our most recent round of research. He was leading his entity through dangerously challenging changing times in their marketplace and the world, and he and his senior team had to make some tough decisions; decisions with change impacts that led to significant disgruntlement in his organisation, where various divisions were feeling alienated and put aside. While his senior colleagues were prone to batting away these concerns to 'keep on course', this leader seemed almost possessed by a stance, a deep emotion, a predisposition, that stood for something else.

Here is an excerpt that illustrates his fierce compassion, through it all, to not be swayed by his convenience or present-day needs, and instead be alongside *all* his organisation – those he was close to, and those who were now coming to join. He was holding a meta stance – in this instance, challenging his team when they had been dismissive of listening and responding to cries for help from one division (regarding whom he had previously berated his team for 'treating them like orphans'):

> And I always try, in these big leadership moments, to do the thing that I will be proud of when I look back at all this in my 70s, so to speak, or if my mother was looking over my shoulder. Or begin with the end in mind: picture your own funeral. I tend, at these big moments, to try to step right back and say, okay, from first principles, what is the right thing to do here?
>
> How can I connect into that, because that's where the power comes from. It's not from slightly self-interested organisational positioning, or how do I emerge from this looking personally impressive or whatever. None of those things really stack up when you get into seriously difficult territory in life.
>
> That's what I was connecting to, so I said to my team, 'We have compelled 1,500 people to come together, in some cases, slightly against their will. Are we really now not going to give them the tools that they will need to make a success of it?

I can almost hear in this passage Jesus with his disciples, chiding them when they judged or ignored segments of society who were slightly outcast or going through difficult times. But this is what we are talking about: the capacity to be kindly, wholeheartedly with what is the case, acknowledging and honouring all that comes our way – each person, event and experience – however challenging. Such skill requires holding a fierce and containing compassion, one that stands for radical inclusion, sniffing out and eradicating judgement - not hopping up and down *with* emotion, but *through* emotion, allowing the more sacred realm to flow into our soul so that we can be with the excitement and the fury, the sorrow and the mourning, the folly and the ecstatic desire of our lives (go Mrs C!).

Given our normal human impulses, holding an unflinching love that dares the unguarded inclusion of everything can be a challenging and exposing place; yet, it is the foundation for this work of leaving behind our oughts and heading towards a reality within the largest of tents. Now, I am not asking us here to become saints. However, I am asking that we all raise the love level when we come to acknowledging what is: the more distant and detached, yet fiercely held and all-seeing love that comes from the divine or sacred realm.

To be fully in the world of is, not confined by our oughts, open to ours and others' lives precisely as they are, trusting that things are OK, that we are inherently whole, means making an equal, non-hierarchical, unprejudiced space for everything to exist. That takes a whole dollop of love, a pure unconditional love that can stand alongside everything and say yes to it all. While within the day-to-day realm of belonging-fuelled human love, we can say that our loyalties make love 'blind', not so in the realm of sacred love that wishes to know the truth of it all.

In this divine realm, not to love is a bias against reality.

Pause for a moment

⇒ Can you recall a moment when you felt an emotion beyond the personal, systemic or archetypal realm, one you felt you were carrying from a more sacred place?

⇒ What kind of contact with reality did this meta-energy enable? A clearer and more compassionate eye, one that engendered a deep trusting feeling that all will be well?

⇒ What kind of ease, movement and change did that initiate within you and the situation?

Emotions Serving the Movement From *Ought* to *Is*

I hope by now you have taken in some food for thought (and feeling) about how emotions directly serve our access to truth, and, in so doing, enable movement; how they can alert us to *what is*, dislodging us from comfortable yet rigid oughts. In this final section, I will do two further things: first, introduce the distinction between us having primary and secondary emotions, showing how our understanding of this distinction alerts us to whether we are in *ought* land or with *what is*; second, through a short story, feature three specific emotions that are most likely to accompany the journey between *ought* and *is* – guilt, grief and joy.

(For a more comprehensive explanation of a range of emotions, I highly recommend *The Language of Emotions: What Your Feelings are Trying to Tell You* by Karla McLaren,[17] in which the author invites us to empathise with how fifteen different emotions each have their message, need and purpose in our lives.)

Primary Versus Secondary Emotions

The distinction between primary and secondary emotions was a revelation to me. It helped me to see the difference between emotion states that serve movement, and those that keep us stuck. What follows draws from a book, *Acknowledging What Is,*[18] which contains conversations with Bert Hellinger, a highly innovative psychotherapist and founder of the systemic constellations approach I have touched on in this book, and passed on to me through the teachings of Judith Hemming.

Primary emotions I have referred to in this chapter – such as fear, anger, shame and sadness – are pure, uncluttered feelings that evolved within the human species (and beyond) to enable survival and adaptation. A primary emotion faces truth and gives our bodies and minds signals to act on this truth: fear is wisdom in the face of danger – it can immediately communicate what to approach and what to avoid; anger sees injustice and seeks to right wrongs; sadness gets us used to being without someone or something.

Primary emotions are simple, without drama, and intense. They have a quality of real contact; interpersonally and with truth. We are with *is* writ large. No constraining oughts get in the way. When we are in receipt of primary emotions from another person we feel compassion, but no obligation to respond; we are not being recruited into any loyalties or entanglements. Because primary emotions lead to a definite goal, they are not long-lasting. They take no detours, only appropriate action.

Secondary emotions are feelings that substitute for the original emotion *when the existence of the primary emotion is denied or not supported.* When our unacknowledged primary emotions turn into secondary ones, we stay stuck and caught up in them, losing any personal agency.

The function of these secondary feelings is to convince others that we cannot take action – the emotion becomes dramatic and exaggerated. Others present to the person with the emotion feel a need to help and rescue. Someone else has to take responsibility. When clung to, we must avoid looking at reality, as reality interferes with the inner images of change avoidance. Secondary emotions last longer and get worse, and you can make rather a fool of yourself. They prevent the courage for action, and impede the potential for contact and connection.

Whereas primary anger can cleanse a relationship to pass without scar, secondary anger becomes fury, bitterness, blame and an excuse for not acting. Sadly, I have been in the receipt of secondary anger from someone whose oughts could not entertain processing where his anger had come from and how I, innocently, was stoking it. Let's take guilt; whereas primary guilt leads to ameliorative action, secondary guilt turns helpful action into obsessive worry, which can last for years. And how about grief; whereas primary grief helps us face the loss of separation, secondary grief can become narcissistic regret, self-pity, or an attempt to garner pity from others. I can say that I could enter this zone from time to time, before my movement of the soul, my journey taken towards discovering my own *is*, thankfully kicked in.

Identifying the kind of emotion someone is operating from can be simple. As I have said earlier, if I am touched (I feel moved when someone is sad), I am in receipt of a primary emotion, and I can trust it. If I am bored or irritated by the emotion (I have an impulse to yawn or say, 'Get over it!'), unless I am totally devoid of empathy, then I am in receipt of a secondary feeling whose main task is to demonstrate their weakness and wish for me, or someone else, to do something about it.

Here's the point for this book: there is a magical reinforcing loop between primary emotion and acknowledging what is, leading to movement – *if* we are courageous enough to enter into the pure fullness of our emotion, free of our oughts (that could bat the feelings away) and explore its contours and purposes. A primary emotion, as Hillman writes, is the most 'alert form of attention': we travel through it and with it to reality.

If we want to learn how to be with what is, we need to learn how to honour the ultimate friendliness a primary emotion has for our lives, serving movement, and beware of any oughts that could suppress, twist or manipulate the emotion into a secondary one that has us staying exactly where we are.

A Story of Guilt, Grief and Joy – That Enabled Movement

I have chosen these three emotions – guilt, grief, and joy – as they seem to be key accompaniments on the pathway from *ought* to *is*, from our wiring to our reality. After briefly summarising these emotions' roles in serving movement towards truth and reality, I will conclude this chapter with a short story to illustrate how this can all come together.

Guilt: That Feeling of Worry or Unhappiness That You Have Done Something Wrong, Such as Causing Harm to Another Person

Guilt accompanies all courageous change, as we need to step beyond the innocence boundary of our conscience group and do something that will appear disloyal to this field of belonging or preceding events (change is always an implied criticism of what comes before). All movement is treachery towards the flock, and carrying this guilt can feel unbearable. Yet, unless we loosen this loyalty, we cannot step beyond our reality bubble or story and venture towards wider truths that serve movement to a different future. We can still hold deep empathy for 'our group', our past loyalty, but we need to bear the guilt that comes with the necessary un-belonging to prior allegiances.

Guilt can, therefore, be welcomed as a sign of our ability to travel independently, an indicator of our strength and maturity to loosen our bonds to our oughts.

Grief: The Normal Response to a Major Loss

Grief brings us into contact with the truth of the loss of what we must necessarily leave behind to allow something new to arrive; grief is the emotion that takes us from having something, to not having something. Loosening our loyalties to the oughts that secured our early belonging can be a very gut-wrenching, heart-wringing act, as these loyalties were conceived in love. The capacity to choose to head towards our highest potential self is, therefore, one of tolerating loss. Previous loyalties need to be cleanly and respectfully let go of, and grief is the natural way love honours what it will miss (I highly recommend *The Smell of Rain on Dust*[19] by Martin Prechtel, a precious book that shows how grief is, in fact, praise of life).

If we cannot grieve for what we lose in change, for what we must necessarily leave behind to travel from our oughts, then the grief will pass on to someone else and/or move into resentment and violence. Bow down and weep. Honour and bring visibility to those who will have to bear the price for any change to occur – if you are a change leader, it's not just your grief you need to take care of.

Joy: That Feeling of Great Pleasure or Happiness

'Joy is not made to be a crumb'. Another exquisite line by the poet Mary Oliver, from *Don't Hesitate*. Joy comes forth when we feel we are at one with everything; we are in a pure state of gratitude for the moment – not exhausting ourselves by wishing for experience to be anything other than it is. Joy gifts us the capacity to be with all that is, which is why joy, as an emotion, is a sign of our capacity to acknowledge that reality is all there is. Joy comes from relishing in reality; it's not about escapes, fantasies, or what might be magical and illusory (which is why C.S. Lewis became *surprised* by joy when he discovered it was something quite normal and readily available – even discovering God while travelling on the top of a double-decker bus[20]).

Joy is not a fizzy, frothy affair that tries to transport us from difficulty; indeed, joy can be the willing inclusion of pain, if it is real, a deep twin river running alongside grief, bringing us into communion with humanity and the world.

Joy is, therefore, a deep state of contentment when we are still and connected enough to have all the parts of us awake to be touched and permeated by all that comes our way. As joy often comes to us after hard work or intense change, this emotion is a welcome truth spirit that tells us we are learning to break free from our oughts and be at peace and ease with reality, becoming truthful with obstacles as well as resources. Joy is the ultimate achievement of the soul.

A Leadership Team Making a Big Transition, with Emotions as the Primary Resource

When change gets a little stuck, it could be a sign that the deeper, feelings-based undercurrents within the system, are not being attended to. What follows is a short story about how working with the systemic orders I wrote about in Chapter 4 – Time, Belonging, Place, and Exchange – through the portal of our emotions as truth messengers for the system's soul, can release stuckness and accelerate change.

I have mentioned above the leadership team I am working with that has taken a significant decision: to move out the key co-leader of the Managing Partner from an entity leadership position and replace that leader with a new co-leader, who, until this point, has been within the broader team of the company. The current co-leader and Managing Partner have been together growing the company for 10 years, and have become very close. The about-to-be co-leader has been with the company for around four years. This decision was made so that the company could grow to its next level of maturity and market impact, and that the current co-leader, at his stage of life, could move away from his entity responsibilities to enjoy a broader life (including non-work activities).

This transition is a significant change. This truth was perhaps underestimated by the leaders involved, as they approached the transition in quite a matter-of-fact, even 'pretend' way, dealing with the practicalities of new structural and employment arrangements and issuing ambiguous communications to the broader team. Despite the decision having been taken earlier in the year, nothing was quite landing in reality or moving ahead. As you can imagine, the wider team was anxious about this liminal state's lack of clarity and never-endingness.

In a small yet impactful way, I facilitated an (online) workshop with this leadership team to help release them from their prevarication and difficulty. All the leadership transition conversations within the trio had become extremely fraught and acrimonious, leaving each frustrated and stuck in judgements of the other. Here is a summary of what happened.

We Opened with Statements of Their Primary Emotions

After an opening tuning-in activity to get the team centred and present, to help them *lead with their insides*, I invited each of the three current leadership team members (the outgoing and incoming co-leader to the Managing Partner are together on the team in this transition state) to voice their predominant emotion(s). (Recall Hillman: 'Emotions are the most alert form of attention'.) What came out was hurt/sadness (a birthday had been overlooked), pain/embarrassment (I had no idea), and anxiety/fear (I might be leaving, but I don't know what I'm going to).

You can hear in these responses that the emotions came predominantly from the personal realm (I'm upset, I'm so sorry, it's been difficult for me). Yet, the team was also able to see that these emotions carried charge at the system level; they recognised that the grief and guilt they were experiencing about belonging needs not being met and attended to, and their anxiety over future place, were emotions also being felt within the wider firm. This insight brought a realisation of leadership responsibility: what they were feeling was not just about them – as leaders, they were also carrying the wider team, which meant that unless they, as the leadership team, could tune into and work with these truth messengers, they would not be able to shift how their organisation was feeling.

When personal emotions are placed and acknowledged within a system field, they lose their capacity to 'take over' the individual. By attending to them as primary emotions, we also voided the risk that they would become secondary, unhelpful feelings of bitterness, regret and vengeance between them (and, de facto, cast an unhelpful shadow onto their wider team).

Prouds and Sorrys Enabled a Release of Joy and Sadness

I next asked each of the three leadership team members to reflect on the last two months of their time together as a transition team and recall and relate to each other what they were most pleased about in how they were working through the change (prouds), and what they were most disappointed by in themselves (sorrys). This activity brought such a 'woosh' of deep reflection, openness and honesty that I, too, was *surprised by joy* at the maturity of disclosure.

Prouds included their growing capacity to discuss difficult topics together, hold space for their reactivity in a good way, become more vulnerable with each other, and loosen their attachment to fixed views. Sorrys included their sadness for when they had become reactive, overly entrenched, closed-minded, and ignoring each other's hurt and pain. In relating their stories of the sorrys, you could tangibly feel (even in an online setting) the healing power of truth-telling coursing through the team.

From this activity, they deepened even further their realisation that this transition, this 'handing the baton' from one co-leader to the next, was not an easy process for any of them *and* that this positional battle was getting played out due to a still lack of trust in, and compassion for, what each team member was going through – what was going to be lost, as well as gained. When I heard statements such as 'I will miss x …', I could sense that the soul of this leadership team was opening up for further work.

Heart to Hearts that Spoke to Time, Belonging, Place and Exchange

So, we next flowed through a series of paired conversations. While I directed the choreography and suggested sentences along the way, the three exquisitely 'went for it'. The soul of the field was in free flow – the Ordering Forces were being addressed, and their emotions released them on a truth journey from the big change decision being a pretence, to one of reality.

First, I invited the Managing Partner and his current co-leader to 'look at' each other – Hammarskjöld would say, 'dare to gaze'. During this activity, I invited the incoming co-leader to turn her video off and remain a silent witness to the conversation. After a silent, still moment, I asked the Managing Partner and his current co-leader to say sentences to each other to enable them to honour their ten phenomenal years of partnership and say goodbye to this time in their lives. Here is a flavour: 'We have walked many miles together', 'I'm going to miss it being x and me', 'I am moving from comfort to discomfort', 'I will miss the process of building the next phase', 'y (the incoming co-leader') will not let things slide, 'while I (the outgoing co-leader) might disagree with what you both decide, I will agree to it and be in support', 'I am sad, but I wish to move to my next life stage'.

Second, I set up the moment for the baton-passing experience between the current and the to-be co-leader (the Managing Partner now had his video off). Without batting an eye, the current co-leader (who had been showing a degree of resistance to this big decision, despite saying 'yes' earlier in the year) said, 'I entrust you (to-be co-leader) with the responsibility to hold what is unique about this firm, and to be creative to take it to the next level, and I am sure you can do that'. To which the incoming co-leader said, 'I will take forward that collaboration, this will not be autocratic, I will now soften the edges of this transition'.

Finally, I asked the outgoing co-leader to turn his video off, and the Managing Partner now had the chance to turn to his incoming co-leader. This time, without my prompting, the incoming co-leader spoke first: 'I have renewed empathy for what this transition is costing, and I now feel a tremendous responsibility to you to be the kind of partner like x (outgoing co-leader). I am new to this, I am both excited and nervous, but ten years from now, I'd like you to say the same kind of things about me'. The Managing Partner responded, 'You are bringing creativity and vitality, and I look forward to this. It is important to me for you to really respect what x and I have done. What you said touches me: I chose you and trust you'.

I hope that by reading these sentences, and listening to the earlier part of the story, you can feel the guilt, grief and joy running through this transition moment. From acknowledging their guilt in the previous activity (their sorrys), the Managing Partner also carried this emotion beautifully as he crossed the loyalty threshold from his erstwhile buddy to his new partner. In deciding to partner with his new co-lead, this leader had to tolerate a loss. This was painful. He also acknowledged that this leadership step up for him was going to take him beyond the level of leadership his father had reached, so he was also breaking a deep systemic loyalty there; to this moment, his oughts had wired him to not go beyond his father's achievements, which had kept him 'innocent' within his family realm but had proved a handbrake on his future leadership growth. But now, he was bravely bearing the guilt of disloyalty to achieve his and his, company's, highest potential in the world.

As to grief and joy, these two emotions are mysterious bedfellows. All three leaders needed to leave someone – and a part of themselves – behind, to effect the transition. Far from grief spilling into anger and the need to defend one's position 'against' the other, given the process we used enabled their grief to be made visible and witnessed (they said how powerful it was to have each taken turns to stand by with their video turned off silently), this allowed their sadness to seep respectfully into the contours surrounding and holding this team. No wonder they all reflected that they had been having difficulties making the leadership transition a reality.

And yet, by facing their grief and sadness, they discovered that 'the weight has lifted', and they were able to entertain the joy that would arrive as they travelled into their new futures. In debriefing the session, one of the team members said that 'compassion, grace, kindness and honesty' had arrived in the team. I could say (but I guess I would…) that they had encountered emotions held mysteriously within the sacred realm. But I will leave that one for you to ponder.

In the last chapter, we ventured through the workings of the soul as our conveyor belt towards truth and reality – being able to discover and be with what, fundamentally, is. In this chapter, we have looked at the vital role our emotions play in that process. To be able to fully be with 'what is', heading towards truth and accepting reality, requires a demanding level of skill to be with and alongside the rainbow of emotions that will arise from awareness.

I hope that, in whatever place you are reading this book and from whatever change leadership role you hold in your families, communities, institutions and societies, you now wish to, alongside me, 'fly the flag' for placing emotions more squarely and wisely into the world. They hold tremendous energy, and guide those scary, challenging, joyful, and welcoming moments of our lives, showing how we can all achieve the ease, equilibrium, and wisdom to be with *what is*.

8

The Journey Between Ought and Is – A Hothouse

While our journey to move from *ought* to *is* can be a life's work, this chapter offers you a series of guided application, or let's say, 'rapid transit' exercises, to hothouse this move. To assist you in this task, see Figure 8.1 – a 'SOAP', summary on a page, of the book's main messages.

Before you read on, cast your eye over this route map of our journey together and notice where your eyes most linger. What's that about? What is arresting you, and why might that be the case? When you take a second glance, what did you miss the first time? Register where you are most drawn, as that might determine how you wish to use this chapter.

On the left-hand side of the figure is the striving world of *ought*; a place where our inner instructional codes on how to be in the world, derived from various relational systems such as our families, communities and cultural ideologies, lead us to continually imagine, wish or bend reality to be other than it is. The value of our loyalty to these codes is that we secure our belonging to these groups, and that these groups will be the same tomorrow as they are today. While this function of ought has clear personal survival and collective continuity advantages, blind and unquestioned loyalty to oughts prevents us from seeing reality as it truly is, creates polarisation, breeds intolerance and sets us up for disappointment and disaffection. Ultimately, our fixed wiring and ideologies leave a stuck and divided world with little room for movement and change.

On the right-hand side of the figure is the world of *is*, a place where, free of our codes, we can be with and acknowledge what truly is the case, no matter how unsettling, uninvited, or personally challenging. This gift gives us the capacity to make an equal and unprejudiced space for everything to exist. We give all of experience our full-hearted and clear-eyed attention.

Figure 8.1   The Ought to Is journey

We have four resources to put into our rucksack for this journey from *ought* to *is*: how to read and move the dynamics of systems via the Ordering Forces of Belonging, Time, Place and Exchange, and change approaches that build attentional capability, frank speech and emergence; a personal checklist of leadership skills to make change far more effortless; the ballast of our soul – our character, calling and connector with wider fields and fate – that will ground us and be a torch in the darkness when we feel lost; and a way to read and regulate the messengers of emotions we will frequently feel on this journey, so that we stay on track.

The prize of reaching the world of *is* is that we will be more at ease with what comes our way in life. Free of ingrained loyalties, we can attain our highest potential self, and in the pools where we have influence in our lives, we will effect change and movement.

Ultimately, this journey rests on our twin capability to look with deep respect on the oughts that secured our belonging (they are not 'things to be got rid of') *and* to loosen our loyalties to these codes that run our lives (bearing the exquisite guilt and loneliness we are likely to feel in that move).

So Now It's Your Turn to Do Something ....

What follows are eight experiential steps to guide you through this transit journey from *ought* to *is*, based on each chapter of this book. As you take each step, I encourage you to refer to the reflection questions and activities I offered within each corresponding chapter as supplementary stimulus. The steps (marked out in Figure 8.1) are:

Step One: Preparation – grounding yourself in an intention, gathering your resources and choosing a particular case.

Step Two: Meeting My Oughts – an exercise to identify and acknowledge your oughts, see their costs and consequences and respectfully stand from them with greater distance to allow wider realities to come into sight.

Step Three: A Day in BED! – an activity (BED is an acronym ...) to help you step into pure phenomenological attention and acknowledge all of what is that comes your way.

Step Four: Restoring Ease to My System – a chance to take your case for which you wish movement – be that your team, organisation or community – and apply the lenses of the systemic Ordering Forces.

Step Five: Working on My Leadership – a guided embodied exercise for you to imagine yourself fully stepping into the skills required to effect movement and change.

Step Six: Firing Up My Soul – an activity for you to summon your essential character, calling and highest potential self in service of bringing movement to your case.

Step Seven: Recruiting My Emotions as a Resource – an exercise for you to travel from now to your desired future self, resourced by your emotions as truth messengers.

Step Eight: Consolidation – pulling together the main insights from the journey and offering you a chance to sit for a while in gratitude (and maybe a little celebration – joy is very welcome in this work).

Take each step every one to three days (to keep up the pace, yet also allow enough 'sink time' in between steps for consolidation of impact). The exercises take different formats, but all are designed for you to have an *embodied* experience – the most accurate route to truth and reality, and an approach whose impact will help you sustain the memory of the experience. The steps are designed as an integrated build, so I suggest you create a space and place to keep your notes always available. I will be asking you to write statements on various pieces of paper to chart your journey, and you can also make notes on the empty pages provided within this book.

Enjoy, and see you at the finale in Chapter 9.

Step One: Preparation – Getting Yourself Grounded

Naming My Longing: Why This Journey from *Ought* to *Is* Matters to Me

Reflect on these questions

⇒ What has most stirred within you, called out for your attention in this book?
⇒ How would you like your life to be different, and why does that matter to you?
⇒ What would your future life look like in its most joyous expression?

Put some words to this longing and write them down on a piece of paper. You will be using this piece of journalling throughout the journey as your *Attractor* energy.

Identifying a Particular Application

Now identify a specific case in mind – from your personal life or from within your workplace – where you dearly wish for more flow, movement and release from stuck patterns. A case where you feel that the stuck-ness is due to an inability of you/others to sufficiently and respectfully acknowledge the truth or reality of a situation. It might be a work team, your whole institution, family or other personal grouping, or a community movement you are associated with.

On a separate piece of paper

⇒ Can you draw an image or write up some words that capture the essence of the movement you long for in this situation?
⇒ When you think of, or imagine this future, what is beginning to emerge – capture your sensations, your feelings, your thinking, your willingness to really see.

How is it to bring this case to your heart and mind? Notice and register the impact as clues about how others in this situation might also be feeling and experiencing.

Gathering My Resources

Our journey from *ought* to *is*, is best achieved in community. Can you choose a buddy or close work colleague you'd like to take this journey with, maybe someone who has read this book alongside you? Choose them and agree together on how you wish to partner on this journey, connect, and commit over time.

Can you also select a daily, soul-nourishing practice in which you have intentional agency over your attention? It might be mindful meditation, a daily walk in nature or contemplating art. Set up your 'micro-monastery' – dedicated solo space, daily time and repeating rhythm – for this activity.

Step One: Preparation – Notes and Musings

Naming my longing for this journey.

Envisioning the movement needed in my case.

Gathering my resources.

Step Two: Meeting My Oughts – Identifying and Loosening My Loyalties

Identifying my oughts so that I can uncover the codes that run my life
Take four different pieces of paper and head each one separately: personal/familial, community/cultural/religious, professional, and political. On each piece of paper, write up, respectively and respectfully:

⇒ Personal/familial. The codes about how to be in the world that secured your belonging within your family realm; maybe transgenerational oughts from your ancestors, as well as those that kept you safe and innocent from within your early upbringing (for example, I have shared mine of pleasing and a loyalty to untetheredness).

⇒ Community/cultural/religious. Any oughts belonging to the wider contexts where you grew up and now identify with – your close-knit communities, national heritage, cultural groupings or any faith allegiances (as a Londoner I might have quite strong oughts about multiculturalism, for example).

⇒ Professional. Any oughts about how to be in the world that are affiliated with your work realm, trade or craft (doctors have strict medical oaths, but other work-related groupings have their oughts, including your hierarchical position – for example, management or staff?).

⇒ Political. Any political oughts that fiercely determine what you must, and must not, believe/think/say/do? (Right, left or centre? Liberalism or conservatism? All these affiliations can carry quite distinct oughts).

Loosening my loyalties so I can hold a wider space for movement
From your identified list of oughts, which 'shout the loudest' to you? Which of them *truly* demands your compliance? (The guilt factor goes up if you dare step beyond their boundary.)

⇒ Write no more than three of these oughts onto separate pieces of paper (they might all come from one of the four areas or a combination).

For each of these shortlisted oughts, can you identify their costs and consequences? What might they preclude you from being able to see and do in the world? What parts of the world might they shut you off to? Who, or what, do they make 'wrong'?

Return to two pieces of paper/cards from step one on which you wrote your longing and your case, and now:

⇒ place these two pieces of paper alongside those of your foremost oughts identified in this step – either on a space on the floor, or your tabletop. Fully 'inhabit' all these elements, separately, and register the inner state that comes to you as you flow through this activity. (You might wish to stand on the pieces of paper, or just place your hands on them.)

From this embodied experience, what have you registered about the impact your oughts might have on your longing for your life, and your case where you wish for movement? Have you noted any oughts you might need to gain distance from to travel towards your longing? To bring movement in your case, where might loosening your commitment to an ought release an unhelpful compulsion? Notice your willingness level to be 'disloyal' to your oughts. What might this loosening of loyalties bring you and cost you? Can you imagine bearing that price?

Finally, can you close this step by turning towards any ought you wish to have a less unquestioned attachment to, and in your mind's eye, say, 'thank you' to this ought, and 'now I must travel towards wider truths'?

Step Two: Meeting My Oughts – Notes and Musings

How was it to do any part of these activities? What got stirred up? Did you find yourself becoming indignant at any stage at the thought of loosening a loyalty towards a precious ought? Maybe a touch of guilt, or fear of becoming vilified or outcast from your belonging field?

What helped you step beyond that field of loyalty?

How might you describe this experience to your colleague or friend who is accompanying you on this journey?

Step Three: A Day in BED – An Activity to Practice Acknowledging All of What Is

Today is right-hemisphere brain activation day! How to direct your attention across the course of a day towards *concrete reality* uncluttered by your oughts? Hopefully, you are now more conscious of your oughts, which is a great starting point; when they inevitably pop up as you meet experience, they will no longer unwittingly cloud how you see reality.

Recall the wise words of Hammarskjöld, 'To have humility is to experience reality, not *in relation to ourselves*, but in its sacred independence. It is to see, judge, and act from the point of rest in ourselves'.

But how to try and spend a day in complete *is-ness*? Try spending it in BED (for sure a point of rest . . .). BED stands for bracketing, equalising and describing: a helpful acronym to keep you steering towards having impeccable phenomenological attention (unclouded by your categories, projections and ought-infused ways of distorting reality), experiencing reality as it is. So, alert yourself to how today you can:

- *Bracket.* Something will come your way, and you will have all kinds of personal responses and commentaries about the situation pop into your mind. Before you respond, put them to one side by imagining yourself putting ( ) around the words and feelings that you know are spurred by your oughts and judgements, to separate them from the actual context in front of you.
- *Equalise.* When you feel yourself biased towards something over another (might be a person you like better because they are from 'your tribe', or a view being expressed in a meeting that is on 'your side'), catch yourself doing this and instead intentionally give all that comes your way your generous and unprejudiced attention.
- *Describe.* In as accurate a way as possible, use only language and imagery that objectively reports the appearance, sound, smell, events, conversations, etc. that come your way today. When you find yourself tipping into explanations (using an a priori theory) or justifications or judgements about what you experience, desist!

Enjoy trying to be in this meta-witness position for a day – your task is to know reality and not to be 'right'. Reduce the temptation to quickly collapse into 'knowing what it is', relinquish your fabrications and become the clearest, most compassionate receiving eye you can be. Be that in a hotly debated meeting, an awkward conversation or taking in a strongly opinionated piece of writing/dialogue, get to the facts, keep bringing in more reality, and in so doing, register the impact your truth-pursuit stance has both on your inner state of being, and on the people and the situation around you (including your buddy).

Step Three: A Day in BED – Notes and Musings

How was it to do any of this activity? What felt easy, more difficult?

Where did you notice yourself slipping into *ought,* and how did you create the space within you to get out of that?

How have you learned to be, and what have you learned to do, that can help keep you heading towards reality and not your wiring?

Step Four: Restoring Ease to My System: Take Your Case and Apply the Lenses of the Systemic Ordering Forces

Having now identified and loosened yourself from some *oughts* and practised fully taking in *what is*, free of your codes and judgements – how can you now more clearly and spaciously see the actual dynamics of the situation in front of you? What might be being, yet hidden in the team, community or institution you wish change for?

Tuning into the System

In this step, we revisit the mini-audit from Chapter 4. Either refresh your memory or begin again; do you notice any of these symptoms within the system you have in mind?

Belonging	Some people feel more 'in' than others creating insecurity; there are split loyalties between this system and another, causing tension and feelings of guilt; something or someone seems to have been or is being excluded; strong identities are fiercely guarded; competing beliefs and ideologies are creating division and polarisation.
Time	A reluctance to face future realities; major events or people or upsets from the past are being ignored or disrespected; unclear or troubling founding energy; who came before and who came after (like length of service in a company, or sibling order in a family) is not made visible, recognised and appropriately 'weighted'; no one mentions present tensions.
Place	Unclear sense of role and place within the system and in relation to each other; sense of competence is draining away; people are taking up tasks that are not theirs to do; leadership feels faint and unstable; some people feel 'bigger' than they should be; little attendance to how this system fits within wider contexts.
Exchange	People feel they are putting in more than they are taking out; strong feelings of guilt and innocence, owing something or being owed; little gratitude and acknowledgement of contribution; over-giving creating weakness, dependency and even kickback among the receivers; benefits of this system's life are mentioned but never the costs, what it asks of you.

Moving the System

Contemplate this list of symptoms and identify the two to three realities that ring out as most true. If you are on this journey with a work colleague from the system whose case it is, do the audit separately and then compare notes. Notice the similarities and distinctions, and explore what that is telling you. Practice acknowledging and including all in the conversation.

How are these realities showing up in the life of the system you wish to change? How do they impact the system's members and how you all achieve your purpose? Both the troubling impacts, but also, what are these realities preserving? All these orders are, in some way, born out of love and loyalty.

Plan your next step – how might you bring this exploration to the system in your case, so that you are helping others to see themselves too? Just plan and take one intervention. For example:

- At a forthcoming team meeting, you could provide some input on these four orders, invite the team to select the order that feels most 'alive' for them right now, and encourage everyone to openly share what they chose and why (you could use the mini-audit itself).
- At a large community gathering, you write the main sentence describing each order on four separate flip charts (see Chapter 4), and invite people to walk to the flip chart that most resonates with their feelings about the current dynamics within the group. Invite frank conversation about where people walked and why. Ask for ideas about how to bring greater ease and flow to the situation.
- You take just one of the orders – did Belonging, Time, Place or Exchange feel most present for you? – and have a conversation with a member of this system who has some agency over attending to the group dynamics. Plan what you can do together to address what is most holding back ease and flow.

Remember the three aspects of approaching change from Chapter 4 that will most give you success in any next step you take:

- *Building attentional capability.* Help people value paying attention to how they pay attention and use right-hemisphere techniques in conversations, such as pictures and storytelling.
- *Encourage parrhesia.* Make it safe for people to speak up by being open, inviting and non-judgemental yourself.
- *Embrace emergence.* Clearly state your intention for your intervention, set a few ground rules (such as 'reality is always friendly'!), and then, with no fixed outcomes, see where the conversation takes you.

Step Four: Restoring Ease to My System – Notes and Musings

What did you say or do that seemed to bring the most aliveness, disclosure and strength to people and the system? What did you say or do that seemed to do the opposite, and what did you learn from this to adjust next time?

What was it like to uncover some of the more troubling and disturbing dynamics? What did you learn about yourself in how you handled that?

What are the two to three next steps you'd most like to take with your system to address the orders and bring positive movement to what you wish for? Write them up on separate pieces of paper.

Step Five: Working on My Leadership – An Embodied Exercise to Imagine Yourself Fully Stepping into the Skills Required to Effect Movement and Change

Consolidate Where You are in the Journey

Before you begin this step, note down what you have most learned about your change leadership skill so far, both areas of strength and where you feel you need greater capability. If you are working with a colleague, you could offer each other a conversation to discuss this together.

Now set up a little 'constellation' of the pieces of paper where you have written (either from the previous steps or do them afresh from your notes in this book):

⇒ your deepest longing for moving from *ought* to *is*
⇒ the movement you wish for in your case
⇒ the oughts that you wish to gain distance from
⇒ the two to three aspects of the Ordering Forces most requiring attention.

Place each of these pieces of paper on the ground in what feels like their 'right' place – with awareness and full attention. Where do you find yourself placing them in relation to each other? What elements seem closer to each other, and what are more distant? Experiment a bit until you feel you have a 'true' picture of your transit journey so far. Register how the final picture impacts you.

Identifying the Change Leadership Skill(s) I'd Most Like to Step into

Remind yourself of the eight skills within the Still Moving Change Leadership framework (see Figure 8.2, and for full descriptions, pages 118–137). Choose *one* Inner Capacity and *one* External Practice that you feel are the leadership skills most needed to bring movement to the system, and where you wish to develop more capability. For example, if your system is drenched in reactivity and feeling somewhat aimless, maybe you choose Curious and Intentional Responding with Attractor. If your system is split and fractured and nobody seems to be able to talk about the schisms, maybe you choose Acknowledge the Whole with Edge and Tension?

Write up the two leadership skills on two new pieces of paper and place them within the map where you feel they would be most impactful, bringing the most system strength. Now stand on/beside those pieces of paper and register your inner response (somatic data, feelings that arise) – what

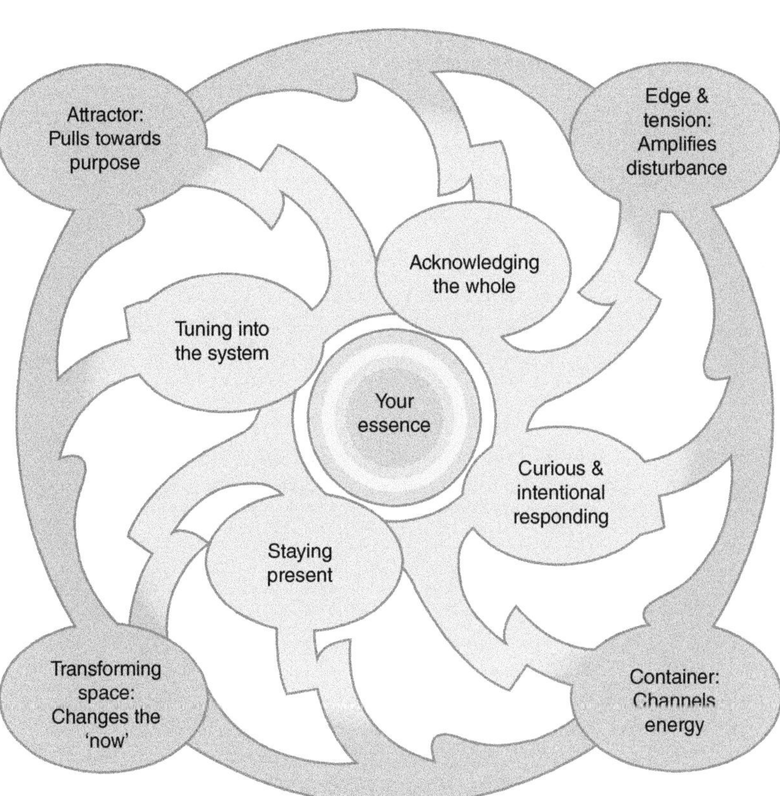

Figure 8.2   Still Moving Leading Change Skills Framework

clues might these inner responses be telling you about what to anticipate when you 'do this for real'?

Plan A Practice Field for Your Leadership Skill

Now identify a situation coming up in the coming days where you can try out both skills (such as a scheduled meeting or a forthcoming conversation). Using the full descriptions earlier in this book, plan out how you might approach this situation. Do stretch yourself in this practice field: recall in Chapter 5 what this kind of change leadership skill is likely to feel like – scary, humbling, revealing and liberating.

Go well with your practice!

Step Five: Working on My Leadership – Notes and Musings

In Particular, Debrief Your Practice

Reflect on what happened in this practice field (and share with your buddy if you are doing this transit journey 'a deux'). What did it feel like to practice the skill, what new mindsets and behaviours did it ask of you?

Did any practice require you to put aside a certain ought that you hold (I always have to put to one side my ought to please others when I bring Edge and Tension to a situation . . .)?

How did your practice help the situation release any stuck patterns, reveal truth and reality and move with greater flow?

Note down what you have most learned about personal leadership skills in change.

Step Six: Firing Up My Soul – An Activity for You to Summon Your Essential Character, Calling and Highest Potential Self in Service of Bringing Movement to Your Case

In Chapter 6, I broke the soul down into four elements: the unrepeatable person we are, our character, our essential self; our calling, 'for that I came'; our connector to wider soul fields; and our contact with fate ('my soul is a dark forest') - the power that is outside of ourselves and not in our hands.

Soul work is ought-releasing work. When we can uncover and fully accept our souls, loosening ourselves from any trapped loyalties, we begin acting from who we know we freely are. I gave you several exercises in Chapter 6 on all four soul elements, and I will draw from them here. If you took any notes in that chapter, bring them back to your awareness now.

I also gave you a soul-summoning exercise at the start of Chapter 6 – to look around you in your current surroundings and see with the eyes of your heart an object that deeply stirs you, giving you an inner riptide of longing, intimacy or a precious sadness. If you are in the same place now, can you move that object a little closer to you (or vice versa); if you are in different surroundings, repeat the activity. The object can be your soul guide in this step. You might like to put music on that stirs you, take a break or two during the exercises, walk outside, contemplate, or eat some nourishing food.

If you are physically with a buddy, or even online, this step would be great to do in reflection with a companion!

Firing up My Soul

My character, the unrepeatable person I am

⇒ What comes off you in sparks when people brush up against you? (Clue: this is not your personality factors, or what you say your values are, *but the distinct smell, shape, sight and experience of you.*)

⇒ What steps, significant people, events or landscapes were present at your birth, and among the ancestral forces that came before you, that have bequeathed you your essential character? What still mysteriously remains in your psyche?

⇒ Can you now put some salient, resonating words to your character? They should be words that 'make you tingle'.

My calling, my soul's natural authority

⇒ Spend some time pondering on the declaration, '... for that I came'. What words would precede that, for you? Maybe you could try and draw or paint it, consider the sound of it. Do whatever works for you and brings a soul-tingling sensation.

⇒ Looking to your future life, what may you be called towards? What is in your heart that you must do?

My connector with wider fields

⇒ When have you been in tune with the soul energy of a wider field – those moments when your soul danced under the night's stars, or upon the earth's beauty, or when some art, a piece of music, a paragraph in literature or a poem left you gasping?

⇒ In which landscapes or settings do you feel most alive, and can you 'touch the original church' within this soul system?

My contact with fate

⇒ Can you recall a moment of deep surrender when a persistent voice in you overrode an impulsive reaction to a new unsettling experience, and you instead trustingly let it all be? What was that voice?

⇒ Can you visualise your soul as a dark forest in which 'gods, strange gods', come forth now and then into your known self and then go back again? What is the 'bowing down' courageous move you can take to respect and submit to the workings of these gods in your life? Can you embody that move now?

Acting from My Soul

Now, return to the elements identified from your previous steps: your deep longing for this *ought* to *is* journey, your top listed oughts, the movement you dearly wish for in your chosen system, the Ordering Forces needs that the system has, and your leadership skill.

⇒ On a new piece of paper, write up the words 'soul, my highest potential self' and experiment with placing that soul element somewhere in the map you are creating where you feel this element brings strength, truth and movement.

Step onto or touch the piece of paper representing each element. On each, turn to look at your soul element to sense its impact on the field. Now that your soul energy is fully activated, you might wish to move some elements. Finish by stepping onto your soul and fully feeling its resourcing energy.

Step Six: Firing Up My Soul – Notes and Musings

As soon as we have a point of eternity in the soul, we have nothing more to do but to take care of it, for it will grow of itself like a seed. It is necessary to surround it with an armed guard, waiting in stillness.

Simone Weil, from Gravity and Grace.[1]

How was it to do this activity?

I wonder, what patiently waiting and attending 'armed guard' might you now surround your soul with? (This is not about becoming a 'defended' person, but Weil's invitation is for us to take our soul's growth seriously. Can we regularly stop, become still, and tune into our soul state to ensure we keep it free of any unhelpful oughts that could be impeding our relations with ourselves, others and the work we wish to do in the world?)

So, what will you now commit to doing to allow your soul's continued growth?

Step Seven: Recruiting My Emotions as a Resource – An Exercise for You to Travel from Now to Your Desired Future Self, with Your Emotions Fuelling the Movement

And so the chance to check in with our emotions, Hillman's 'most alert form of attention'. Can you now bring to full awareness all the experiences of the previous steps in this chapter and openly reflect on the following:

⇒ What primary emotions have you encountered on this transit journey (and maybe from the whole book to this point)? If you struggle to own the more 'difficult' ones, just notice that without judgement and with curiosity.

⇒ Can you describe, write down, and put full language to the emotion – how it felt, where you felt it in your body and the impulses that came (to do or not to do something) in response?

⇒ How did this emotion resource you, what truth did the emotion make you alive to?

⇒ If the emotion was troubling, how can you be with this emotion so that the feeling is supported and does not spill into becoming a 'secondary' emotion (e.g., fear does not become panic, anger does not become rage and grief does not become bitterness)?

A Time Walk from Now to Your Future in Its Most Joyous, Freest State

Please now write up on three separate pieces of paper, 'past self, 'present self' and 'future self' and mindfully place these three elements in a clear space on your floor: your *past*, how you came into and grew in this world; where you are in the *present,* with all your inherited oughts, codes that run your life and belonging needs; and where you wish to be at a *future* point, more able to stand free from these loyalties and attachments to take in wider realities in your life. (Note: I am not suggesting here that you give up all your current life, relations, work, etc., and head to a monastery! This is about an *inner* journey to break free of that pressure you feel to retain conformity to a set of beliefs about how to be, that could be seriously holding you back from fully meeting your life.)

Again, the following activity will be best done with a buddy, someone who can stand alongside you (either physically or online), guiding you through the following steps (so you don't have to look at the words in this book).

Now, slowly, either for real or in your imagination, walk this line from today to your future. As you do this guided activity, fully register all the emotions that come to you and let them freely flow, enabling movement. E•motion.

⇒ Start by *looking back* from the present to your past self and to all the people (either alive or now passed) and events that have made you and your life possible. Take each one of these elements in, deeply. Lingering on any faces and the memories you hold in your mind. Can you authentically say a 'thank you' to it all – even the events, people or episodes that felt difficult to bear at the time? Pause. Breathe.

⇒ As you gather yourself in the present, recall and face the *oughts* you identified in step two that secured you a loyalty ticket to your cherished belonging fields. Look at them with deep gratitude and respect – especially those that formed in early life: you would not have made it to adulthood without them. Smile and recall all they brought you, and all they cost you. Pause. Breathe.

⇒ Now, turn towards your future and see the longing there that awaits your arrival. What does it feel like to know that it is there waiting? As you prepare for the next step, fully feel the soul that you fired up in the previous activity being alongside you, willing you on, having your back. Pause. Breathe.

⇒ Now imagine or slowly walk, if you are using a physical space, away from your present state, your ought loyalties, and towards your future. Along the way, bring to mind the system you belong to where you wish for greater movement, and look on it with a clear and compassionate gaze. Also, take in the resource of the leadership skill you wish to step into more fully – imagine you are now *in* that skill, helping bring ease and flow to the system you long for movement within. Pause. Breathe.

⇒ And now, as Gabriel Conroy gazed out of the window in the final scene of the Dead, with his soul swooning softly, arrive at that place in the future where you have completed that inner journey to be free of your oughts and niggles that have kept you safe, yet exhausted in their relentless striving needs. What does it feel like, to stand there? That place where you can, from Safire Rose, 'let it all be', and where 'it is just that'.

Step Seven: Recruiting My Emotions as a Resource – Notes and Musings

Reflection

'Sit back down' and pause: what has been stirred up in you by this work?

What primary emotions did you experience, and what truths are they messengers for as you step away from this book and into a place to 'do this in the real world'?

How does my heart feel, now?

Step Eight: Consolidation

What main insights do you take from this guided journey from ought to is?

⇒ Both *what* you took from the journey, as well as *how* you completed it?
⇒ Could you imagine using any of the activities with the people in the system you wish change for?

What are you grateful for from this journey? To what and to whom would you like to say, 'thank you'?

Any little celebrations you'd like to now make happen? A 'pat yourself on the back' moment (take your favourite walk, cook your favourite meal, do a little dance, hug – even more than usual – your loved one).

9

Conclusion

> *Previously, Truth came from authority ... henceforth authority will come from truth.*
>
> Francis Bacon, Novum Organum (New Instrument), 1620

Four centuries on, Bacon's call for us to seek out reality from empirical ground truth, rather than tradition, authority or abstract reasoning, still resonates. And this book, *From Ought to Is*, likewise has invited us to loosen our blind allegiance to instructional codes about what has to be believed to be true, to discover the fullness of *what is the case*. While I have described how the 'authority' that governs truth is rooted in our neurobiology and systemic need to belong, the British philosopher's observation that we rail against truth and prefer our fixed views and lies was similarly grounded in a view that humankind seeks comfort in unquestioned attachments to a collective. To break free from the pack and dare seek data that might threaten such secure belonging, can feel like an existential threat.

And so, we loyally stay within our oughts, our wiring about how to be, think and act in the world that keeps us innocent within the affiliation groups we hold dear – familial, party political, cultural, professional, ideological, or faith-led.

In this book, I have shown how the prize of this loyalty to our oughts is personal survival and institutional continuity. As infants, such fealty guarantees us life within our familial and care settings. As we mature into adults, we join wider tribes, and it feels good, right and 'true' to uphold their values that we believe benefit society and our well-being. We derive our identity from these positions and narratives. We can meet others who 'think like us' and join our understanding of the world. This feels safe. The security of institutions like-wise rests on the loyalty of their members signing up to their ideals and codes.

Truth, however, is a field wider than our belonging and survival needs. Bacon's scientific method emphasised the importance of data gathering through systematic observation and conducting experiments to test hypotheses. We need to get down and dirty in the trenches (so says the former archaeology student).

I have put forward the case for us pursuing truth not as the correctness of a proposition – which can be so clouded by our oughts, but as the uncon-cealment of that which is being, yet hidden – which means the curious, patient and compassionate attending on the nature of reality to reveal itself. Julian of Norwich spent decades on such truth pursuit from one startling moment of awareness; can we likewise reclaim intentional attention over our minds to get as close to reality as humanly possible?

This call is critical in an era when so much of our attention is externally commandeered by advances in digital technology, the relentless addiction to social media that is dangerously skewed by inbuilt digital codes, and, at times, the deliberate falsification of reality by nefarious individuals, fac-tions, and interfering sovereign states.

The Price of Staying in Ought

And why is this more objective truth pursuit so needed? Why is the benefit of moving more closely to *what is the case* so much more advantageous than the comfort of staying stuck in our *oughts*, however well-meaning, morally justified and matched to what the world needs we imagine them to be?

In this book, I have set out the exacting price that our blind allegiance to oughts gives rise to in the world:

⇒ *Partial truths* – oughts can rob us of our intelligence, as we fail to see the whole terrain of a situation, dangerously adhering to just the parts of reality our oughts allow us to see (and so the UK's Post Office leaders in all 'innocence' punished their staff and not the faulty IT system);

⇒ *Polarisation* – our fixed allegiance to oughts will always make another part of the world, wrong, creating a divided and hardened ground (and so geopolitical conflicts and extremism to 'left' or to 'right' are on the rise, and the Israeli/Palestinian conflict still devastatingly rages on);

⇒ *Intolerance of others* – our fierce devotion to our oughts so takes hold that we at best ignore, and at worst, denigrate or do away with others, failing to create a respectful and collaborative 'we' in the world (and so the US Democrats lost the election and the majority of the US population by holding a monomaniacal Trump-denial delusion);

⇒ *Disaffection* – when the world inevitably does not always conform to our oughts, our sense about how things or we need to be, we hold our heads in our hands in disbelief, losing our agency for change as we fail to see that it is our ideology-striving and blind indignation, not 'the terrible world out there', that is causing us our distress (and so our culture wars and climate crisis despair continue).

If we do believe that truth is a powerful tool that ultimately leads to a clearer understanding of the world around us, bringing ease and movement, how come, notwithstanding the price of staying loyal to our oughts, we still fail to take that step from *ought* to *is*? Oughts can sabotage all our skills and conscious desires. Yet, it is desperately hard to leave them behind (my pleasing and perfection needs remain a threat to my capacity to lead in difficulty, despite all the leading change skills I know make a difference). What do we fear, and what might we lose?

In this conclusion, I offer some final thoughts as to why, if moving from our wiring to our reality is such an obvious journey to take, we still struggle to take that step, and what can we do to resource ourselves to give this passageway our best attempt? This is my parting shot at encouraging you to do so.

Why We Struggle to Take the Journey From *Ought* to *Is*, And Yet ...

I see four primary reasons that explain why the taking of this journey from *ought* to *is* remains so tricky: there is a lack of awareness and education about how we attend to the world; facilitating truth requires a challenging quality of presence; we fear the loss of what we most value; and ultimately, to practice non-attachment risks our very survival. All are obstacles, but all can be overcome – if we have the desire, belief and resources.

Lack of Awareness and Education About How We Attend to the World

Can any of us recall that moment when we were first helped to see how we see? Did we take any school classes in perception? Have we had teachers who patiently and skilfully held up the mirror to how the workings of our mind were influencing how we bring the world into being? No doubt, if we took science, literature, art or philosophy classes, we were taught about the processes through which we get to know the world – differentiating those with greater emphasis on deductive or inductive reasoning, imagination or objectivity, intuition or logical reason.

But did any of our epistemological education also show us how our attachments, preferences and loyalties fuel our perceiving? A psychology education, or taking a spell in psychotherapy, might have taught us how our deep habits and the instructional codes that underpin them are born out of love and hidden loyalties to our caregivers in early life, even trans-generational attachments. Our search to belong is the primal drive beneath all our striving and the choices we make about what we can and cannot see, what we are able to be alongside, and what we reject. Maybe if you have been introduced to the field of systemic perceiving, you have opened your eyes to the more out-of-awareness depths of reality that underlie our collective lenses and actions.

How we attend to the world affects the type of world that comes into being, and yet I doubt that many of us can say 'yes' to my questions above. So, what might a world look like that paid greater attention to creating awareness of, and education in, how we attend to the world? What teachers, observers and coaches might we need in our education systems, businesses, community movements, extended families and political institutions? What leadership development curricula could we create for business schools and in-house training functions that emphasise mindfulness, self-knowledge and impulse regulation, and the capacity to spot and work with the depths of systemic realities such as Belonging, Time, Place and Exchange that we explored in Chapter 4?

These are all massive tools that, when we engage with them, enable us to find order in the disorder, truth in the chaos and an inner centredness that gives us the courage to, as Hammarskjöld invites us, *dare gaze into les espaces infinis* of this world in very different ways. While a lack of education in how we pay attention is a reason we do not embark on the journey from *ought* to *is* (as we may not know the journey even exists), there are things we can do to rectify this.

It Takes a Challenging Quality of Presence to Be Able to Facilitate Truth

Even if we are aware of this journey and the bigger reality we could access if we took the step, prioritising truth over comfort is not for the fainthearted. Working with pure phenomenology, the reality that arises from directly lived experience and not that which is a priori constructed, sitting with the *is-ness* of what is being, not prodding a situation towards our *oughts*, can be a real threat to our personal beliefs and neuroses and other people's narratives and needs. Oh my goodness, how does truth prioritisation require one giant combine harvester of patience, compassion, courage and humility.

Do we have the presence to facilitate the pursuit and acknowledgement of truth? The patience to stay long enough in not-knowing, stretching out the *is* in is-ness, to keep on wishing to encounter more reality, so that the whole picture comes into sight (desisting any superego want to come in to say, 'I've got this and need to fix it'). Do we have the non-judgemental compassion to reach out to those people whom societal mores vilify, entertaining their views we might ordinarily find offensive or in fantasyland? Or, with our smug biases, do we exclude those with different oughts to our own, only to find that they then shout louder? Can we find the courage within to speak out an awkward truth that is being ignored, to invite in that disturbing voice that will challenge orthodoxy, so that reality can be fully faced and dealt with?

When humility is put alongside patience, compassion, and courage, we can accept all that is and look for wisdom in what we are aware of, whether it be more or less joyous. We will have a trustworthiness and deep friendliness that can adopt a meta stance – holding the widest possible space for realities to emerge – when we are not caught up in personal reactivity, narrow loyalties and a belief system that will close others down and narrow the field of perception.

This underlying disposition that the facilitation of truth asks of us is exceptionally demanding – far easier to let our oughts govern and protect us. But this disposition and presence are learnable. Recall the Still Moving Inner Capacities from Chapter 5 that can hone your quality of being, so that you can tune into and regulate your inner response to experience to enable truth and movement to flow around you. Can we make the qualities of present-moment noticing, curious responding, systemic perceiving and integrating all that comes our way a permanent state of how we show up in the world?

I believe so and have seen so. Just a minuscule shift in our being – such as a switch from irritation to curiosity – can allow a greater truth to emerge.

We Fear the Loss of What We Most Value

So, we might be aware of the *ought* to *is* journey, and feel we are learning the inner disposition required to take its path, but do we believe we are travelling to a destination we can sign up for?

I can find the statement, 'being with *what is* means the capacity to make an equal, non-hierarchical and unprejudiced space for everything to exist', a real challenge. Surely some views and beliefs are 'better' than others? Doesn't society evolve from being in a more brutal and primitive state, towards one of increasing goodness, advancement and sophistication? Isn't it an affront to humanity and human rights to have totalitarian despotic regimes, rather than open democratic ones? Who says conscientious objectors should move beyond their conscience and perform military service? Would it not be morally irresponsible to put the two figures of Hitler and

Mandela into the same space? Will we risk the trap of 'false equivalence' by putting everything on the same footing (can a sex offender in a position of power excuse him or herself by saying, 'Well, it was not only me that made advances; you should have seen how many of my underlings also made lewd comments to me!')?

Surely some oughts are more correct, justified and superior, and, in a sense, need to go into the 'is' category? Is the journey from *ought* to *is* just a trip towards one massive blob of acceptance, an escape to a world of relative facts devoid of any attached absolute value?

Yes, and well, no. Journeying towards *what is* does mean we retain those oughts that support seeing and truth encounters. But it also means we find the unflinching love within our hearts to recognise that no individual can help what they were born into. It does require us to journey into that field beyond right and wrong and dare put our conscience to one side, so that there is a chance to reconcile alternative truths and heal what has been broken. (When victims of even heinous crimes can somehow face the perpetrator, choosing acceptance and not revenge, it brings ease and strength to the system. I was recently sitting with someone who said that the father of her newborn child, who left them both just after their child's birth to go off with another woman, 'could not help who he fell in love with'; while desperately sad, this allowed her and the child to move on.)

Being with what is does not mean being void of feeling and morally neutral (we might as well find an AI large learning machine to facilitate groups in conflict, or teams and individuals who are frustratingly stuck). It does mean finding that deep disposition within ourselves that can befriend and stand alongside all elements of the impacted system in equal, unprejudiced measure. Putting everything in obviates the risk of partial truths. If we don't register the right starting point when we embark on intended change – allowing everything an equal place, seeing all the elements that impact a system, however disturbing – then we do not know what we are working with. We *do* need to make a fuss about that!

Not only that, but it also helps people see the costs and consequences of their choices and stance about what is true. That is a highly appropriate task. People's attachments to extreme ideologies and fixed views can soften when asked to face the consequences of their beliefs and actions, and respond to the question: 'How does my heart feel when I look at this situation, and can I bear the price?' That's tough stuff. Our response to that question can grant us inner ease with the hierarchies of values or fixed red lines we might have chosen: it enables leaders to stick to an unpopular decision that risks short-term pain, yet achieves a longer-term prize; it has enabled me to dedicate most of my life to the mission and ministry of helping leaders in all realms realise more effortless change, at the cost of a more stable and settled life in the personal realm.

So being with *what is,* is not a free-for-all or a complete surrender to fate. The search for objective reality *does* mean that some truths are (for a while) more valid than others, the desire for a good society *does* justify the creation of moral frameworks, and my conditioning *might* need me to make certain of my oughts absolute. The point I advocate is that if we value truth-seeking as an ongoing disposition, higher than truth-declaration as fixed correctness, then we need to be willing to have our propositions and hypotheses tested. To see our oughts for what they are, hold them in a more integrated way, carry our views on reality a little more lightly – not tempted to drown out the anomalies, and be able to dance with improvisation and a dynamic view of what is.

Learning to live well with the world as it is does not mean giving up, but turning that temptation we have to become angry, outraged and indignant towards a stance that is loving and open, which, paradoxically, through its radical inclusion, will move and change the world. Connecting with love enables ease and movement, whereas every act of will produces a kickback.

To Practice Non-attachment Risks Our Very Survival

So, we might be aware, skilled and signed up for the journey from *ought* to *is*, but what, ultimately, does the trip most ask of us?

I have conveyed throughout this book how existentially threatening it can feel to journey from our oughts to wider fields of reality, what is the case, as to give up our loyalties to our inner codes can feel like we are losing an orienteering function, points of reference, that bought us a survival ticket within our fields of belonging. This can feel extraordinarily uncomfortable and bring feelings of guilt and loneliness when we leave the centre of the flock. The threat of becoming vilified and an outcast from the tribe from which our beliefs originated can be at the top of what we fear most. And yet, what a wider field of ease and belonging awaits us.

Just this week, I was with a colleague, Nicole Brauckmann (also a super reviewer of this book), at a reunion event for a transformational leadership programme we ran together for over three years. It was an extraordinary evening in which the time-lapse felt insignificant. Nicole and I had not seen the leaders who had gathered for over a decade, yet it felt like we were 'back in the room' together on the programme. All the leaders who came to the reunion had moved on from their time within this organisation (because of the change, the company was also broken up and reconstituted). Yet, we all felt we still belonged within this wider field of a truth-contacting change leadership experience that had not been replicated in our careers since. I was struck by two seemingly contrasting explanations offered as to *why* this leadership experience had been such a transformative moment in time.

On the one hand, one leader talked of the extreme *discomfort* that the programme brought. We had designed an experience that replicated the challengingly disruptive external context these leaders would have to face to reinvent the entity. While not in the 'panic zone', we certainly took these leaders into uncomfortable territory – out of left hemisphere cognitive learning land and into a right hemisphere embodied set of experiences that took them to the very emotional and somatic core of themselves (simulations, constellations, mindfulness meditation, large group conversations where the risk to name awkward truths brought people to the edge of their seats).

To fully step into this more visceral phenomenological way of knowing the world (a necessary capacity for interpreting and responding to their rapidly changing marketplace), participants needed to loosen their attachments to their oughts that had secured their belonging as the most senior leaders in this stable institution. We invited them to trowel away their oughts on this programme, which had felt breathtakingly disturbing.

And yet, at the same time, one other leader at the reunion talked of how much more *at ease* he had felt on the programme. He said that the programme *'was what is'*. For the first time, he said that he could be 'my self' – his unique essence before the cloak of oughts (from his chosen profession and societal and cultural context) restricted how he could be, relate to others and make choices as to what to do in the world. He talked passionately at the reunion about how his peers had felt the same, and how that relational truth and soul-level, authentic contact, built the trust and the courage to go to the edge together in their company's transformation.

Both leaders were 'right' in that they each represented the twin peaks that make up the from *ought* to *is* journey experience: *yes,* it will feel scary and awkward and threatening to leave the comfort of one's oughts, and *yes,* this movement will bring an inner ease and freedom that has us all find our true selves, and a wider more real field within which to belong. Both will be on this journey. The discomfort is a bedfellow to the joy. Yet it need not be dramatic and damaging ... *that's the illusion we have in our heads that excuses us from taking the journey.* Remember Saffir Rose, 'In the space of letting go, she let it all be. A small smile came over her face. A light breeze blew through her. And the sun and the moon shone forevermore ...'.

Reaching What Is, What's on Offer

So, to summarise and conclude, what do we gain from taking the journey to live well with the world as it is, to learn to distance ourselves from our oughts, those stories we tell ourselves about how to be in the world that can be too small and too mean? What's to be immeasurably gained by standing back with our hearts open?

We will surely gain an inner ease and sense of peace in our lives. Just as Gabriel Conroy recaptured his soul in the thickly falling Dublin snow, we will discover Hammarskjöld's 'point of rest' in ourselves. While the hardest thing that consenting to the world as it is asks of us is that we are in a deep surrendering agreement with reality, the tension involved in resisting it is lifted. We will have the freedom to be in reality but not caught up in it, and with this lifting of entanglement and tension comes an expansion of relational and spiritual energy that restores what has been lost in ourselves. And goodness, what impact can that then bring to those around us.

We will become a more inspiring force in the families, communities, teams, organisations, nations and movements dear to us. The more we are in agreement with reality, the more that truth will be allowed to flow within these cherished systems, reuniting us and reviving community. However awkward it might initially feel to acknowledge what is, people will hold their heads up in attention, their hearts beat with relief, and their whole bodies relax when we invite in truth, not obfuscation, authentic speech, not wily witticism, unvarnished reality, not slippery deception. Movement requires truth.

If there is just one thing you can take from this book, when you are next with your team or any group of people you hold dear, write up on two separate pieces of paper, 'How we feel we ought to behave around here', and 'What is truly the case of our experience that we have been missing', and invite a brave and honest conversation around these two questions – giving an equal value and attention to both responses and seeing how they are interconnected.

Who knows, if more of us can grasp this *ought* to *is* invitation, what a difference we could make to the great injustices in the world, be that the more affluent nations damaging the poorer nations with our climate destruction, the power imbalances that lead to abuse and sexual and racial discrimination. When we can all see the world's reality accurately enough, we will navigate it in quite different ways; we will have the capacity to 'build a we' to face our most intractable collective challenges.

To close, I am reminded of the Mary Oliver line, 'May I be the tiniest nail in the house of the universe, tiny, but useful'. I do wish that this book, in its small way, has been of some help to you in your life and your workplace. They say that every book takes its writer on a journey. I have certainly been on one. Primarily, I feel I can now stand for something bigger than my loyalties and attachments to how I wish people and the world around me to be. *At the same time*, I feel I have shrunk a little to acknowledge that remaining in contact with the world is more important than being right.

While some bits of this book might not be 'right' in the purest sense, I hope I have remained in contact with you, the dear reader, throughout.

I wish you well on your journey from *ought* to *is* – bon voyage.

Notes

Chapter 1: Introduction

1 Hellinger, B. and ten Heovel, G. (1999). *Acknowledging What Is: Conversations with Bert Hellinger*. Phoenix, AZ: Zeig, Tucker & Co.

2 From Beisser, A. (1970). The Paradoxical Theory of Change. In Fagan, J. and Shepherd, I.L. Gestalt Therapy Now. New York: Harper & Row, 77–80.

3 Rowland, D. and Higgs, M. (2008). *Sustaining Change: Leadership That Works*. Chichester, West Sussex, UK: John Wiley & Sons.

4 Rowland, D. (2017). *Still Moving: How to Lead Mindful Change*. Chichester, West Sussex, UK: John Wiley & Sons.

5 Rowland, D. (2020). *Still Moving Field Guide: Change Vitality at Your Fingertips*. Chichester, West Sussex, UK: John Wiley & Sons.

6 McGilchrist, I. (2019). *The Master and his Emissary: the Divided Brain and the Making of the Western World*. New Haven, CT: Yale University Press.

Chapter 2: The Deep Power of Ought

1 McGilchrist, I. (2023). *The Matter with Things: Our Brains, Our Delusions, and the Unmaking of the World*. London, UK: Perspectiva Press.

2 Hellinger, B., Weber, G., and Beaumont, H. (1998). *Love's Hidden Symmetry: What Makes Love Work in Relationships*. Phoenix, AZ: Zeig Tucker & Theisen Inc.

3 Rowland, D., Brauckmann, N., and Thorley, M. (2022). How to get your team onboard with a major change. *Harvard Business Review*., blog, August 4th, 2022. https://hbr.org/2022/08/how-to-get-your-team-on-board-with-a-major-change

From Ought to Is: Catalysing Change and Movement in a Polarised World,
First Edition. Deborah Rowland.
© 2025 John Wiley & Sons Ltd. Published 2025 by John Wiley & Sons Ltd.

4 Lake, F. (1962). *Clinical Theology: A Theological and Psychiatric Basis to Clinical Pastoral Care.* London, UK: Darton, Longman & Todd.

5 Blok, S. (1978). *Lying.* New York, NY: Pantheon Books.

6 McCallum, I. (2008). *Ecological Intelligence: Rediscovering Ourselves in Nature.* Arvada, CO: Fulcrum Books.

7 McGilchrist, I. (2009). *The Master and his Emissary: The Divided Brain and the Making of the Western World.* New Haven, CT: Yale University Press, and (2023) *The Matter with Things: Our Brains, Our Delusions, and the Unmaking of the World.* London, UK: Perspectiva Press.

8 Barthel, M., Mitchell, A., and Holcomb, J. (2016). *Many Americans Believe Fake News Is Sowing Confusion.* Pew Research Centre.

9 Anderlini, J. (2024). Europe's growing polarization spells trouble. *Politico.*

10 Murray, M. and Marquez, A. (2023). Here's what's driving America's increasing political polarization. *NBC News.*

11 Falkenberg, M., et al. (2022). Growing polarization around climate change on social media. *Nature Climate Change.*

12 Glen Weyl, E., and Tang, A. and Community (2024). *Plurality: The Future of Collaborative Technology & Community.* Independently Published.

13 Solnit, R. (2017). *A Field Guide to Getting Lost.* Edinburgh, Scotland: Canongate Canons.

14 Lukianoff, G. and Haidt, J. (2018). *The Coddling of the American Mind: How Good Intentions and Bad Ideas Are Setting Up a Generation for Failure.* New York City, NY: Penguin Press.

15 Kaplan Mintz, K., et al. (2021). See or Be? Contact with nature and well-being during COVID-19 lockdown. *Journal of Environmental Psychology, 78,* 101714.

16 *The People and Nature Survey for England: Monthly Interim Indicators for May 2020.* Natural England.

Chapter 3: The Transformative Punch of Is

1 Oliver, M. (2019). *Upstream: Selected Essays.* New York, NY: Penguin Books.

2 Plato, *The Republic,* Book VII.

3 Proust, M. (1925), *Albertine disparue, The Sweet Cheat Gone,* ch.1. London UK: Chatto and Windus.

4 McGilchrist, I. (2023). *The Matter With Things: Our Brains, Our Delusions and the Unmaking of the World.* London, UK: Perspectiva Press.

5 Scharmer, O. and Pomeroy, E. (2024). Fourth person: The knowing of the field. *Journal of Awareness Based System Change, 4, 1,* 19–48.

6 Plato, *The Republic,* Book VII.

7 Kant, I. (2007) *The Critique of Pure Reason.* London, UK: Penguin Classics; Rev Ed edition.

8 Nagel, T. (1989). *The View from Nowhere*. Oxford, UK: Oxford University Press.

9 Foucault, M. (1983–1984). *The Courage of Truth: The Government of Self and Others II*; Lectures at the Collège de France. (2012) Picador; Reprint Edition.

10 McGilchrist, I. (2009). *The Master and his Emissary: The Divided Brain and the Making of the Western World*. New Haven, CT: Yale University Press.

11 Heidegger, M. (2013). *The Essence of Truth: On Plato's Cave Allegory and Theaetetus*. London, UK: Bloomsbury Academic.

12 Oliver, M. (2019). *Upstream: Selected Essays*. New York, NY: Penguin Books.

13 Saint Augustine, (408–410) 'Non intratur in veritatem nisi per caritatem' ('We do not enter into truth except through love') 'Contra Faustum', 32. 18.

14 Lorenzini, D. (2023). *The Force of Truth: Critique, Genealogy, and Truth-Telling in Michel Foucault*. Chicago, IL: University of Chicago Press.

15 Argyris, C. and Schon, D. (1992). *Theory in Practice: Increasing Personal Effectiveness*. Hoboken, NJ: Jossey-Bass.

16 Seneca, *Moral Letters to Lucilius*, Volume I, II, III.

17 Dickinson, E. (1929). *Further Poems of Emily Dickinson*. New York, NY: Little, Brown & Co.

18 Solzhenitsyn, A. (author), Whitney, T.P. (translator) (1972). *The Nobel Lecture on Literature*. New York, NY: HarperCollins.

19 Beisser, A. (1970) The paradoxical theory of change. In Fagan, J. and Shepherd, I.L. *Gestalt Therapy Now*. New York: Harper & Row, 77–80.

20 Resnick, B. (2020). Reality is constructed by your brain. Here's what that means, and why it matters. *Vox magazine*.

21 Brooks, M. (2023). The Purpose of Truth: How Our Brains Are Wired to Survive, Not See Reality. https://medium.com/@DrMikeBrooksTHL

22 Tomasic, M. (2022). The Five Stages of Grief: An Examination of the Kubler-Ross Model. https://www.healthcentral.com/condition/depression/stages-of-grief

23 Ganesh, N. (2023). Empty or full universe? *The Economic Times*.

24 Howell, E. (2017). *Humans Really Are Made of Stardust, and a New Study Proves It*. Space.com

Chapter 4: Systems and the Pursuit of Truth

1 Hammarskjöld, D. (1973). *Markings*. London, UK: Faber & Faber.

2 Hollander, A. (2023). 30 Lying Statistics & Facts: How Often Do People Lie? https://www.bridgecareaba.com/blog/how-often-do-people-lie (accessed 10th November 2024).

3 Hellinger, B. and ten Hövel, G. (1999). *Acknowledging What Is: Conversations With Bert Hellinger*. Phoenix, AZ: Zeig, Tucker & Co., Inc., 73.

4 Rowland, D. (2020). *Still Moving Field Guide: Change Vitality at Your Fingertips*. Chichester, West Sussex, UK: John Wiley & Sons, 77–94.

5 Rowland, D., Braukmann, N., and Thorley, M. (2022). How to Get Your Team on Board with a Major Change. https://hbr.org/2022/08/how-to-get-your-team-on-board-with-a-major-change.

6 Elias, N. (1939). *The Society of Individuals*. Dublin, Ireland: University College Dublin Press, 2010.

7 Writings of July 1918, quoted in Moore, W. (1994). *A Life of Erwin Schrödinger*. Cambridge, UK: Cambridge University Press.

8 Georgia State University (2016). Imagery an effective way to enhance memory, reduce false memories, study finds. ScienceDaily, 11 April 2016. https://www.sciencedaily.com/releases/2016/04/160411155240.htm (accessed 11th November 2024).

9 Julian of Norwich (1373). *Revelations of Divine Love*. Oxford, UK: Oxford University Press; 1st edition (14 May 2015).

10 Rowland, D., Brauckmann, N. and Thorley, M. (2023). The Most Successful Approaches to Leading Organizational Change. https://hbr.org/2023/04/the-most-successful-approaches-to-leading-organizational-change.

11 Rowland, D. (2020). *Still Moving Field Guide: Change Vitality at your Fingertips*. Chichester, West Sussex, UK: John Wiley & Sons Ltd, 62–66.

12 Owen, H. (2008). *Open Space Technology: A User's Guide*. Oakland, CA: Berrett-Koehler; 3rd edition.

13 Bohm, D. (2002). *The Undivided Universe*. Abingdon, Oxon, UK: Routledge; Reprint Edition (1995), 386.

Chapter 5: Leading Change From *Is*, the Personal Skills Required

1 Eliot, T.S. (1934). *Choruses from 'The Rock' VI*.

2 Rowland, D. (2017). *Still Moving: How to Lead Mindful Change*. Chichester, West Sussex, UK: John Wiley & Sons, 227–228.

3 Julian of Norwich (2015). *Revelations of Divine Love*. Oxford, UK: Oxford University Press; 1st edition.

4 McSpadden, K. (2015). You Now Have a Shorter Attention Span Than a Goldfish. *Time Magazine*, May 14th 2015.

5 In Julian's Revelations she noticed that she had seen no sin in her vision, and concluded from that that sin is no 'thing', we are inherently good as God's creation, yet when we sin the suffering it causes brings us closer to Him.

6 Zeitlin, M., Ghassemi, H., and Mansour, M. (1990). *Positive Deviance in Child Nutrition – With Emphasis on Psychosocial and Behavioural Aspects and Implications for Development.* Tokyo, Japan: The United Nations University.

7 Rowland, D. (2017). *Still Moving: How to Lead Mindful* Change. Chichester, West Sussex: UK: John Wiley & Sons, 125–126.

Chapter 6: The Journey of the Soul

1 Barry, D. (2014). Singular Collection, Multiple Mysteries. *The New York Times*, 26 June 2014. https://www.nytimes.com/2014/06/27/books/honoring-james-joyces-dubliners-published-100-years-ago.html (accessed 16th November 2024).

2 Joyce, J. (1914). *The Dubliners, The Dead.* London, UK; Penguin Books Ltd. Annotated edition first published 1992, 175–225.

3 Oatley, K., Djikic, M., and Mar, R. (2016). The inwardness of James Joyce's story, 'The Dead'. *Readings, 2,* 1.

4 Drawn from Dag Hammarskjöld, *Markings.*

5 Julian of Norwich (2015). *Revelations of Divine Love.* Oxford, UK; Oxford University Press; 1st edition, 97.

6 Teilhard de Chardin, P. (1959). *The Phenomenon of Man.* London, UK: William Collins.

7 Mullcr, M. (1897). *In Contributions To The Science of Mythology,* 1.

8 Porete, M. (1999). *The Mirror of Simple Souls.* Notre Dame, Indiana, US: University of Notre Dame.

9 Aristotle (1987). *De Anima.* London, UK; Penguin Classics.

10 Murphy, N. (2006). *Bodies and Souls, or Spirited Bodies?* Cambridge, UK: Cambridge University Press.

11 Hofstadter, D. (2007). *I am a Strange Loop.* New York, NY: Basic Books.

12 McGilchrist, I. (2023). *The Matter With Things: Our Brains, Our Delusions, and the Unmaking of the World.* London, UK: Perspectiva Press. Volume II.

13 Heraclitus fr xxxv [Diels 45, Marcovich 67] (trans IM^{c}G).

14 Strawson, G., et al. (2006). *Consciousness and Its Place in Nature: Does Physicalism Entail Panpsychism?* (ed. Anthony Freeman). *Journal for Consciousness Studies,* 13, 10–11. Imprint Academic, 285pp.

15 Huxley, J.S. (1942). The biologist looks at man. *Fortune,* 26, 6, 139–152.

16 Weil, S. (2002). *Gravity and Grace.* Abingdon, Oxon UK: Routledge Classics; 1st edition, 119.

17 Coehlo, P. (2014). *Manuscript Found in Accra.* Glasgow, Scotland: HarperCollins.

18 Pullman, P. (2012). *His Dark Materials.* London, UK: Scholastic.

19 Hillman, J. (1996). *The Soul's Code: In Search of Character and Calling.* NYC, NY: Ballantine Books.

20 Cottingham, J. (2020). *In Search of the Soul: A Philosophical Essay*. Princeton, NJ: Princeton University Press, 153.

21 Hammarskjöld, D. (1964). *Markings. Towards New Shores -? 1945–1949*. London, UK; Faber and Faber Limited, 8.

22 Lawrence, D.H. (1936). 'The real thing'. In E.D. McDonald (ed), *Phoenix: The Posthumous Papers of DH Lawrence*. Heinemann, 1961, 196–203.

23 McCallum, I. (2008). *Ecological Intelligence: Rediscovering Ourselves in Nature*. Lakewood, CO: Fulcrum Publishing.

24 F.W.J. Schelling. '*On the World Soul*', Translation and Introduction by Grant, Iain Hamilton. University of West England.

25 From Lawrence, D.H. (1923). *Studies in Classic American Literature*. NY, US: Thomas Seltzer, Inc.

26 Hammarskjöld, D. (1964). *Markings*. London, UK; Faber and Faber, 148.

27 Schlosser, R. (2011). Unconscious memory in organisations. *The Knowing Field*, June 2011, issue 18.

28 Handy, C. (1989). *The Age of Unreason*. London, UK: Randon House Business Books.

29 Julian of Norwich (2015). *Revelations of Divine Love*. Oxford, UK: Oxford University Press; 1st edition, 129.

Chapter 7: Emotions and Movement

1 Dewey, J. (1894). The theory of emotion: I: Emotional attitudes. *Psychological Review*, 1, 6, 553–569.

2 Lazarus, R.S., et al. (1986). Dynamics of a stressful encounter: cognitive appraisal, coping, and encounter outcomes. *Journal of Personality and Social Psychology*, 50, 5, 992–1003.

3 Schachter, S. and Singer, J. (1962). Cognitive, social, and physiological determinants of emotional state. *Psychological Review*, 69, 5, 379–399.

4 by Aristotle (Author), Robert C. Bartlett (Translator), Susan D. Collins (Translator) (2012). *Aristotle's Nicomachean Ethics*. Chicago, IL: University of Chicago Press.

5 Duff, A. S. (2023). Anger, hatred, and judgment in Aristotle's *Rhetoric*. *American Journal of Political Science*, September 2023.

6 McGilchrist, I. (2009). *The Master and His Emissary: The Divided Brain and the Making of the Western World*. New Haven, CT: Yale University Press, 184–186.

7 Darwin, C. (1872). *The Expression of the Emotions in Man and Animals*. New York, NY; D. Appleton & Company.

8 Ekman, P. (1972). Universals and cultural differences in facial expression of emotion. In J. Cole (Ed.), *Nebraska Symposium on Motivation*. Lincoln, Nebraska: University of Nebraska Press, 207–283.

9 Plutchik, R. (1962). *The Emotions: Facts, Theories, and a New Model*. New York, NY: Random House.

10 Janus, D. (Author) and Gastol, B. (Translator) (2021). *Systemic Constellations: Theory, Practice, and Applications*. Lanham, MD; Lexington Books.

11 Pert, C. (1997). *Molecules Of Emotion: Why You Feel The Way You Feel*. New York, NY: Scribner.

12 Nummenmaa, L., Glerean, E., Hari, R., and Hietanen, J. K. (2014). Bodily maps of emotions. *Proceedings of the National Academy of Sciences, 111*, 2, 646–651.

13 Zweig, S. (2011). *Twenty-Four Hours in the Life of a Woman*. London, UK: Pushkin Press.

14 Chödrön, P. (2002). *The Places That Scare You: A Guide to Fearlessness in Difficult Times*. Boulder, CO: Shambhala Classics.

15 Hillman, J. (1962). *Emotion: A Comprehensive Phenomenology of Theories and the Meanings for Therapy*. Evaston, IL: Northwestern University Press.

16 Weil, S. (2002). *Gravity and Grace*. Abingdon, Oxon UK: Routledge Classics; 1st edition (1952).

17 McLaren, K. (2023). *Language of Emotions; What Your Feelings are Trying to Tell You*. Louisville, Co: Sounds True Adult; 2nd edition.

18 Hellinger, B. and ten Heovel, G. (1999). *Acknowledging What Is: Conversations with Bert Hellinger*. Phoenix, AZ: Zeig, Tucker & Co, 86–95.

19 Prechtel, M. (2015). *The Smell of Rain on Dust: Grief and Praise*. Berkeley, CA: North Atlantic Books.

20 Lewis, C.S. (1956). *Surprised by Joy: The Shape of My Early Life*. Orlando, Fl: Harcourt Brace Jovanovich.

Chapter 8: The Journey Between Ought and Is – A Hothouse

1 Weil, S. (2002). *Gravity and Grace*. Abingdon, Oxon UK: Routledge Classics; 1st edition, 119.

Index

Page locators in **bold** indicate tables. Page locators in *italics* indicate figures.
This index uses letter-by-letter alphabetization.